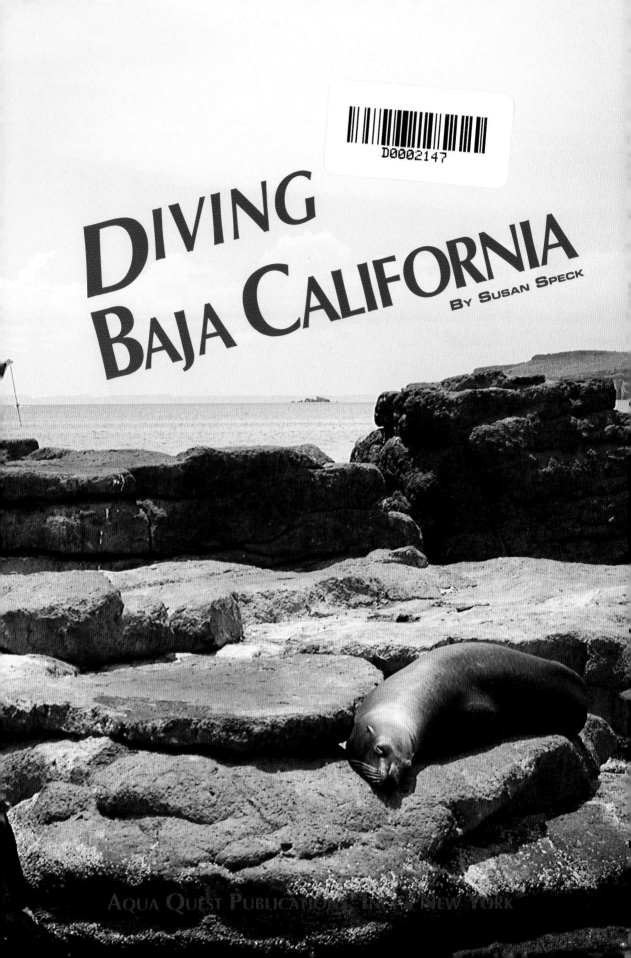

DIVING
BAJA CALIFORNIA

By Susan Speck

Aqua Quest Publications, Inc. • New York

D0002147

PUBLISHER'S NOTE

The Aqua Quest *Diving* series offers extensive information on dive sites as well as topside activities.

At the time of publication, the information contained in this book was determined to be as accurate and up-to-date as possible. The reader should bear in mind, however, that dive site terrain and landmarks change due to weather or construction. In addition, new dive shops, restaurants, hotels and stores can open and existing ones close. Telephone numbers are subject to change as are government regulations.

The publisher welcomes the reader's comments and assistance to help ensure the accuracy of future editions of this book.

Good diving and enjoy your stay!

Library of Congress Cataloging-in-Publication Data

Speck, Susan 1951-
    Diving Baja California / by Susan Speck.
        p.   cm. — (Aqua Quest diving series)
    Includes index.
    ISBN 1-881652-05-X : $18.95 (pbk.)
    1. Scuba diving—Mexico—Baja California (State)—
Guidebooks. 2. Baja California (Mexico : State)—
Guidebooks. I. Title. II. Series.
GV840.S78S626 1995
797.2'3—dc20
                        95-32601
                           CIP

Cover: A blenny finds safety inside a scallop shell on the Pacific side of Baja California.

Title page: Sea lions bask in the sun on Los Islotes Island while divers from the liveaboard *Don Jose* explore the underwater terrain.

Printed in Hong Kong
10 9 8 7 6 5 4 3 2 1

All photographs are by the author unless noted otherwise. Design by Richard Liu.

ACKNOWLEDGEMENTS

I would like to thank everyone who helped make this book possible: Bruce Williams and his skipjack boat *Morganna*; Bill Bolster and his Varga airplane *Baja Auk*; Dolphin Dive Center in Arcadia, CA; Gary Cotter and Baja Expeditions in San Diego, CA; *Solmar V*; Eric Ackerman and Sea Safaris in Manhattan Beach, CA; Patou Franger and Scuba Voyages in Corona, CA; Jordan Kimbriel and Arturo's Sport Fishing in Loreto; Jose Luis Sanchez; Roberto Davis; John Abel and Amigos del Mar in Cabo San Lucas; the Plaza Las Glorius Hotel in Cabo San Lucas; and the Loreto Inn at Loreto. And a very special thank you goes to those that really made this book possible—all the marine animals of Baja's surrounding waters.

DEDICATION

This book is dedicated to two very special people, my parents, Herb and Dee Williams, for their endless support and for giving me two basic philosophies to live by: respect all life for everything has its own purpose and reason, and never consider yourself an expert on anything, for an expert has no more to learn.

IN MEMORY OF MIKE MAHLSTEDT

A good friend to so many, Mike was one of the best divemasters and videographers the Sea of Cortez has ever known. As a longtime employee of Baja Expeditions, he lived by his motto: "Don't worry, be happy", and those around him were. Mike was lost at sea in May of 1994. Now encompassed by what he loved most—the Sea of Cortez—our physical world has incurred a great loss, but somewhere in another world, there has also been a great gain.

CONTENTS

FOREWORD

The great world dropped away very quickly. We lost the fear and fierceness and contagion of war and economic uncertainty. The matters of great importance we had left were not important. There must be an infective quality in these things. We had lost the virus, or it had been eaten by the anti-bodies of quiet.—John Steinbeck, <u>The Log From The Sea of Cortez.</u>

This parched, rugged and primitive peninsula stretches a thousand miles and consists of mountain landscapes with pine trees, immense valleys of cactus fields and vast areas of volcanic craters. Here you can experience sleeping under the eerie moonlit shadows of a 300-year-old 60-foot-high (18 m) cardon cactus, while your ears fill with the echoing sounds of wailing coyotes in the distance. And in springtime when bursts of rain showers stop suddenly and huge rainbows appear you can see the desert come alive with the pastel colors of wildflowers and thousands of monarch butterflies.

On the western shore is the mighty Pacific Ocean, portions of which are lined with kelp forests that host a wide array of marine life. Early spring months bring thousands of migrating gray whales to mate and give birth in the shallow lagoons.

On the eastern shore is the Sea of Cortez with its miles of empty sandy shoreline broken by an occasional seasonal fishing camp. Here uninhabited islands in every form jut up from the sea. They host several species of animals, and serve as nesting grounds for thousands of sea birds. Marine life is prolific in the Sea of Cortez with its submerged seamounts, walls, caves and reefs.

I have driven the length of Baja California, flown low above much of its coastline in a two-seater plane, lived on its waters for weeks at a time, and camped along its shorelines. In this book I have shared with you many of Baja's best known dive sites as well as some that are remote and rarely visited.

Through the years, I have witnessed the great toll that unregulated fishing and the use of gill nets and purse dredges have taken on the Sea of Cortez. This great body of water is an incredible and fragile ecosystem which needs to be nurtured, for when one part begins to vanish it is only a matter of time before the rest follows.

No matter how many times I visit this great peninsula and slowly sink beneath its surrounding waters, my fascination is renewed, and like John Steinbeck, my worldy cares disappear.

Susan Speck
Arcadia, California
August, 1995

CHAPTER I BAJA CALIFORNIA

THE PAST

Twenty million years ago, the Baja California peninsula was a land of palm jungles choked with ferns and lush primeval vegetation. It was home to the 23-ton, 50-foot-long (15 m) duckbill hadrosaur and other creatures that stalked through a steamy setting of erupting volcanoes and torrential rains. Huge upliftings and occasional collapses of the ocean floor gradually separated a land mass from the continent. Even today, the Baja peninsula creeps northwestward, along with a portion of California by the San Andreas fault, at an approximate rate of one inch per year.

The earliest evidence of human habitation is of the San Dieguito Indian culture dating back 9,000 years.

In pre-Hispanic times, nomadic Yumano Indian tribes lived along the Pacific coast of Baja, making their livelihoods by fishing and clamming. In 1535, the Spanish arrived under Hernan Cortes after reports of fabulous pearls to be found. They attempted to form a colony near La Paz but were eventually driven out due to few supplies and many hostile natives. In 1657, the first California mission, Nuestra Señora de Loreto, was founded in Loreto. This was the start of the Jesuit missionary period which lasted until 1767 and produced 20 missions.

From 1774 to 1834 eight more missions were established by the Dominican Order. In the early 1800's, Spanish land grants were given, and small farms and ranches were established. By mid century, the native Indian population had been decimated by European diseases and the Baja missions abandoned for points north.

In 1848, the Mexican-American war ended with a treaty which divided California between the countries. At the turn of the century Baja California enjoyed a boom when gold, silver, gypsum and copper were found, and Santa Rosalia became the largest copper mining and smelting operation in Mexico.

In 1952, northern Baja's population exceeded the 80,000 needed for statehood, and Baja California Norte was declared Mexico's 29th state. Before 1973, when the Transpeninsular Highway (Highway 1) was completed, the drive from Tijuana to La Paz took up to 10 days via rough dirt roads. The highway has greatly contributed to the modernization of one of Mexico's last frontiers. In less than a year following the completion of the highway, the population of southern Baja leaped past 80,000 and the territory became Mexico's 30th state, Baja California Sur.

THE PRESENT

You can easily throw away the key to the clock and forget the calendar in this land of little hurry or worry. The people are very friendly and simplicity is a way of life. This harsh land has produced a tough and adaptable people.

Today, Highway 1 winds serpentinely for 1,000 miles (1,613 km) from the U.S. border to Cabo San Lucas. It skirts by the cool waters of the Pacific Ocean on its western side; other stretches cut across arroyos, up mountains to an elevation of 3,200 feet (970 m) before plunging to desert jungles. Its mid-section overlooks the warm waters of the Sea of Cortez; south of La Paz it sweeps southeast

Two buzzards sit atop a cardon cactus which is found throughout much of Baja and can grow to over 60 feet (18 m) high. There are holes in the trunk of the cactus that are home to birds including small owls.

Without a licensed guide it is illegal to visit sites of Indian rock art, which can be found in Baja's mountains.

BAJA'S ROCK ART

Throughout the Sierras of Baja California far from Highway 1, the artistic heritage of a lost culture arcs across rock walls. These anonymous artists painted thousands of figures in hundreds of prehistoric mural sites, most of them concentrated in the central area. One of the more awesome paintings is in the Sierra de San Francisco area, and consists of a 500-foot (151 m) by 30-foot (9 m) mural with overlapping images of men, women, deer, bighorn sheep, rabbits and birds. In another area, a 12-foot (4 m) painting of a whale spreads across a rock overhang.

Harry Crosby, one of Mexico's leading rock art recorders, theorizes that the art illustrates ritual and symbolic aspects of shamanism. The shaman was the spiritual leader and often the artist in hunter-gatherer societies. The shaman served as conduit between everyday life and the spiritual world. Two aspects of shamanism that is frequently seen in the paintings are transformation and spirit travel.

It is against the law to visit any rock art site without a legal guide. Many guides can be contacted through the major hotels. Baja Expeditions (619-581-3311) offers pack trips, as does Garry McClintock (619-445-3946).

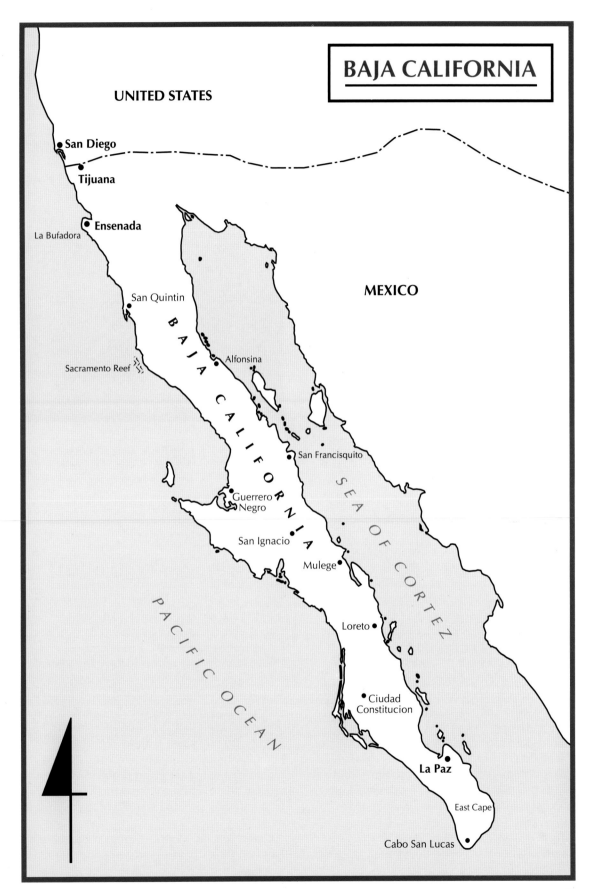

BAJA CALIFORNIA

UNITED STATES

● San Diego

● Tijuana

● Ensenada

La Bufadora

MEXICO

San Quintin

BAJA CALIFORNIA

Alfonsina

Sacramento Reef

San Francisquito

SEA OF CORTEZ

Guerrero
Negro

San Ignacio

Mulege

PACIFIC OCEAN

Loreto

Ciudad
Constitucion

La Paz

East Cape

Cabo San Lucas

past the Tropic of Cancer to Cabo San Lucas (Land's End), where the Sea of Cortez meets the Pacific Ocean.

The population of the entire peninsula is approximately 2.85 million, over 85 percent of which lives above the 28th parallel in Baja California Norte. Between the few major cities, small villages dot the peninsula.

Farming, fishing and tourism are Baja's main revenue earners. Fishing boats work both coasts, but the Sea of Cortez produces the largest catch. La Paz is the main fishing center. Tourism is concentrated in Tijuana, Ensenada, Mulege, Loreto, La Paz, East Cape and Cabo San Lucas.

USEFUL INFORMATION

Climate. The peninsula's isolated ecosystems range in climate from Mediterranean, to desert, to tropical. Two-thirds of Baja can be classified as pure desert, but even the driest areas receive some rain. In the interior of the Cape region's Sierra La Laguna, annual rainfall may reach 40 inches (103 cm). Along the Sea of Cortez, summer temperatures range from 90-110°F (32-43°C), with hot and sometimes humid nights. Temperatures cool off in spring and fall, dropping into the 50'sF (10-15°C) with some chilly winds.

Currency. The unit of exchange is the peso. Most places in Baja will take United States dollars as well as pesos. Paying with pesos, however, usually means a better deal as the vendor is prevented from determining the exchange rate. Banks offer the best exchange rate. The federal bank, Bancomer, has branches in every major city.

Dining. The major cities, Tijuana, Ensenada, Mulege, Loreto, La Paz and Cabo San Lucas, have a wide range of restaurants in all price ranges. In the small towns, one can always find clean restaurants with good basic food.

Electricity. The electricity is 110 volts, 60 cycles, the same as in the United States.

Entry Requirements. United States and Canadian citizens visiting Baja for less than 72 hours need only proof of citizenship—a birth certificate, voter registration card, certificate of naturalization or passport. If staying for longer than 72 hours, a tourist card is needed, which is available free of charge at any Mexican tourist office, on flights to Baja, or at the border in Mexican insurance offices.

Springtime in Baja is sensational as desert wild flowers like these at the base of the boojum tree are in full bloom.

Citizens from other countries may need visas in advance.

Getting There. Several major airlines fly into Baja, including Aero Mexico, Alaska, Mexicana and Aero California. Commercial airports are located at Loreto, La Paz, Los Cabos and Tijuana. Flights leave daily from Los Angeles, San Diego, San Francisco, Phoenix and some of Mexico's major cities.

Highway 1 begins at the U.S. border in Tijuana and continues to Cabo San Lucas. Highway 1 is a narrow, two-lane paved road. There are really only two simple rules to follow: Do not speed and do not drive at night. Many Mexican cars are poorly lit for night driving, but the main problem is that range cattle roam freely throughout much of Baja and they seek the warmth of the asphalt at night.

Green Angels. Motorists in need of a helping hand on Baja's paved roads will find that there is a fleet of specially-equipped green pickup

THE FASCINATING BOOJUM TREE

Baja is full of astounding cactus fields. Besides the 60-foot-high (18 m) cardon cactus, the cirios and ocotillos in particular take on a bizarre appearance because of the long "beards" of gray-green moss. The cirio, also known as the boojum tree, is a relative of the ocotillo. It grows in a 150-mile-wide (242 km) east-west corridor from just below El Rosario to north of Guerrero Negro. It is quite rare and survives in one of the harshest climates. It is an odd-looking tree with a long furry trunk, which has long, skinny twisted branches growing out in every direction. When the boojum is small, it is a round, stubby plant that slowly elongates as it extends up, looking a bit like a carrot that is growing upside-down.

After the winter rains tiny leaves appear, but they quickly die, only to leave barren, thorny stalks. In summer, bunches of small white flowers appear on the tips of the waving branches.

Botanists have identified over 100 species of cactus living in Baja and fully three quarters of these are found nowhere else. Baja's desert is an 800-mile-long (1,290 km) cactus garden that harbors cactuses ranging from 60 feet (18 m) high to barely an inch high.

Loosely regulated Mexican shrimp boats scrape the floor of the Sea of Cortez in search of shrimp. Unfortunately, many other species are caught in the nets.

DRIVING THROUGH BAJA

The Transpeninsular Highway (Highway 1), completed in 1973, is somewhat similar to driving on two-lane highways in some of the less populated areas of the American southwest. Two things to be aware of are that road conditions vary from one section of the road to another, and that some areas are quite remote so that accidents or errors of judgement can have serious ramifications. Skeletons of cars, vans and trucks that don't make it can be seen rusting among the ocotillo and cardon cactus along Baja's highways.

Most of the roads are kept in good repair though they tend to be narrow and lack hard shoulders, and curves are sometimes tighter than expected. The many *vados* (dips) into watercourses should be approached with caution. The *topes* (speed bumps), set up in many of Baja's towns, should always be taken seriously.

One of the most serious problems is the danger of a collision with the free-roaming cattle. It is not infrequent to go around a blind curve and find a few cows on the highway.

It is especially dangerous to drive at night since the cows will sleep on the highways, seeking warmth. Also, other vehicles will sometimes be driving without proper lights.

Gravel roads are normally in reasonable condition, but it depends largely on how long ago they were graded. Generally they can be expected to be stony, with occasional sharp inclines and stretches of washboard. For the real adventurer, there remain many miles of unpaved roads that will take you about as far from civilization as you would like to go.

A gray whale skeleton lies along the Pacific Coast.

The streets of Cabo San Lucas on the San Lucas Bay are lined with fine hotels, restaurants and craft stores.

trucks which patrol the main roads several times daily. Called *Angeles Verdes*, or Green Angels, it is their job to assist motorists in trouble.

Insurance. To be fully protected in Mexico, you must carry Mexican insurance on your car, trailer and boat or any other item you might be hauling. The insurance rates are based on the value of these and the length of stay. Insurance can be obtained at the Auto Club of California or at the border when crossing. More information and rate quotes are also available through the Baja Travel Club.

Language. Spanish is the national language. English is spoken occasionally in the tourist sections and larger hotels. The type of Spanish spoken in Mexico is referred to as Latin-American Spanish, in contrast to the Castilian Spanish spoken in Spain.

Shopping. In all of the major cities, there are gift, clothing and jewelry stores. Sterling silver is very popular.

Telephone. Telephones are found throughout the major cities and towns. The smaller villages usually do not have phones. To call Baja California from the United States, dial 011 + 52 + area code and number.

Time. Baja Norte (north) is part of the Pacific time zone along with the west coast of the United States, while Baja Sur (south) is in the mountain time zone.

Water. Hotels and restaurants serve only purified drinking water and ice. Tap water should not be consumed except in hotels where the water system is purified. Most grocery stores sell purified water.

Where To Stay. Accommodations in Baja run from free campgrounds to plush resort hotels. The small towns usually have a few simple motels, while the larger cities have a variety of hotels to choose from. The La Pinta Hotel chain is nice and has good food. If you are driving, they are located in Ensenada, San Quintin, Catavina, San Ignacio and Loreto. The El Morro Hotel is located in Guerrero Negro and Santa Rosalia. If you are flying into the major cities of La Paz or Cabo San Lucas, there are many more to choose from. For setting up hotel and diving packages, selected dive operators can be very helpful.

CHAPTER II DIVING

AREAS TO DIVE

There are many areas in both the Pacific and the Sea of Cortez which have dive sites frequented by divers. But there are still many more areas which are quite remote and have never been dived. This is one reason that makes diving these waters so alluring. In general, the diving may be divided into two categories: the Pacific Coast and the Sea of Cortez.

Pacific Coast. The entire coast of Baja's west side is fronted by the Pacific Ocean. Only here can one watch the great annual migration of the California gray whale, which come to mate and give birth in the calm, shallow lagoons found along Baja's Pacific coast.

These waters are also known for the largest mammal on earth, the 100-foot-long (30 m) blue whale, which is now making a slow comeback from near extinction.

Because of the currents caused by prevailing winds, an upwelling of offshore submarine canyons occurs, resulting in nutrient-laden waters and underwater forests of giant *macrocystis* kelp. These forests tower above brightly covered fields of strawberry anemones. The kelp canopies are home to a great variety of marine creatures. Colorful invertebrate life is extremely rich. Fishes, such as garibaldi, sheepshead, rockfish, lingcod, perch, and a few types of kelpfish and kelp bass, are commonly found in and among the branching kelp fronds on Baja's northwestern shores. Smaller species of bottom-dwelling sharks, such as horn, leopard and swell sharks, can be found lying on the sand patches around this rocky environment. The most common open-water pelagic sharks found here are the blue and the mako.

Several species of dolphins can be found in schools of hundreds frolicking along this rugged coastline, the most common being the Pacific white-sided and the bottlenose.

Because of the cold water currents that sweep through this area, water temperatures in the northwest will range from the low 50'sF (11-12°C) in the winter months to the low 60'sF (16-18°C) in the summer.

As one continues southward along the Pacific side, the water gets increasingly warmer. In and around the lagoons that dot Baja's central western coastline, water temperatures stay around mid-60'sF (18-19°C) to mid-70'sF (23-24°C) in the summer months.

Shellfish, mainly bay scallops, are in abundance along this mid-coastal region. Also one of the only known cold-water Pacific sea horses can be found around the grassy marsh areas of the lagoons.

Lying sprawled across the protruding rocks and islets, one can often spot the California sea lion. These great rock formations are also home to the brown pelican, sea gulls, grebes, sandpipers, cormorants, herons and further to the south, boobys.

Moving closer to the southwest end of Baja's peninsula, the water gets much warmer being in the low 60'sF (16-18°C) in the winter and high 70'sF (25-26°C) in the summer. As the ocean waters begin to mix with the Sea of Cortez, much of the sea life is also mixed. Divers can find tropicals from the Sea of Cortez along with some Pacific Ocean marine life.

The Sea of Cortez. The Sea of Cortez, which lies between the east side of Baja California and Mexico's mainland, has a truly amazing

Growing to over 100 feet (30 m) high, macrocystis *kelp forests line Baja's Pacific side. In central Baja's tide pools, it spreads over intertidal rocks, withstanding constant surge and crashing waves.*

assortment of marine life. Over 800 varieties of fish have been identified, and biologists believe there are around 3,000 species of marine animals altogether. This sea has acted as a giant "fish trap" that has collected marine species over many thousands of years from the nearby Pacific, the South Pacific and even the Caribbean (through a now-extinct water link between the two seas). Many of these have continued to evolve into species unique to the Sea of Cortez. About 90 percent of these species can be found close to the shores of the peninsula or outer islands. The 20-foot (6 m) tides create currents that aerate the water and stir up the nutrients which supports a food chain ranging from plankton to whales.

The water temperature ranges from 60°F-90°F (16-32°C), depending on the area and the time of year. The warm waters of the Sea of Cortez seem made for dolphins and whales. Twenty-five species of whales frequent Baja's sea, including the humpback, gray, sei, Bryde's, finback, minke, goosebeaked, sperm, dwarf sperm, false killer, killer and pilot. The dolphins mostly seen—sometimes in pods of thousands—are the Pacific white-sided, bottle-nosed, spotted, Risso's, spinner and striped. A rare dolphin, called the vaquita, is endemic to the northern part of the sea.

The Sea of Cortez is also well known for large pelagics, such as manta rays and giant whale sharks. Over 60 species of sharks have been identified though the scalloped hammerhead is the most talked about. If you're lucky, you can catch a glimpse of them over the seamounts and offshore pinnacles. These prehistoric-looking animals are known to school in the thousands.

The barren islands of Baja are as beautiful as the underwater world . These grandly sculptured land masses are home to a variety of rodents, rabbits, reptiles and thousands of birds, including the frigate, blue-footed booby, brown booby, masked booby, brown pelican, fisher eagle, cormorant, egret, grebe, heron, sandpiper and 10 species of gull.

Another local resident throughout the Sea of Cortez and the Pacific side of Baja is the furry California sea lion, found along island shorelines and protruding rocks.

Being one of the most prolific seas in the world, the Sea of Cortez continues to face one main problem: The illegal fishing by unlicensed boats. Gill nets and purse dredges have become the scourge of the area. Many foreign ships still use huge dredge nets to harvest marlin, swordfish, dorado and other elegant species which are reserved by Mexican regulations for sport fishing only. Dolphins, manta rays, sea lions, rays, sharks, eels and turtles all get caught in these slow-killing traps, not to mention the thousands of other so-called trash fish which are thrown back dead as there is no use for them.

BOAT DIVING

If you plan to drive down the coastline to dive in Baja, it is a good idea to bring your own boat. Of course, larger boats have more range, enabling you to reach the farther offshore islands, but small boats and inflatables are excellent for islands and reefs close to shore, and they are much easier to tow. You can also pay a local fisherman a relatively small fee to take you out in his panga (a wooden boat about 20 feet [6 m] long) to some of the islands and offshore dive areas. In the larger towns such as Mulege, Loreto, La Paz and Cabo San Lucas, there are charter dive boats available.

CONSERVATION

To take any game, you must have a Mexican fishing license. Inquire at the border or from Baja Travel Club.

CURRENTS

If you are exploring on your own, always watch for currents as they can pick up quickly, especially around the island points. Watch the moon cycles. The currents tend to be stronger on full and new moons. Both can also create currents which are normally not present.

EQUIPMENT

Most cities and small towns with dive shops rent equipment, but when it was last serviced can be a question. It is best to bring your own. Liveaboards provide tanks and weights.

NIGHT DIVING

Several hours after the sun goes down, the underwater world undergoes a remarkable transformation. A host of unusual creatures which are not seen in the daytime become very active at night. Also, many fish which are too shy to be approached in the daylight are found on the reef, or moving very slowly on the bottom. It is a great opportunity to get photographs of skittish fish. An amazing variety of invertebrates come out at night. The sandy bottom begins to come alive with the snake-like bodies of 3-foot-long (1 m) synapted cucumbers. Brightly colored anemones flower from of reef pockets. Moray eels are out feeding, and the brilliant red shrimps are everywhere. Octopuses come out to feed, and it is quite common to find sleeping turtles.

Shore Diving

There is some good diving along the shoreline, especially around the rocky points.

Snorkeling

Baja offers a lot of opportunity for snorkelers. Almost any beach with rocky outcroppings makes for good snorkeling. The shallow reefs are usually very prolific with tropical fishes.

Underwater Habitats

There are five main types of underwater habitats off Baja: reefs, seamounts, walls, kelp forests and sandy bottoms.

Reefs. Whether or not volcanically formed, every island has reef structures. Some of the reefs are made up of huge boulders where they are fitted together like a massive puzzle. Other boulders do a balancing act, forming caves, tunnels, giant overhangs and angular crevices. Local reef fishes inhabit all of the reefs, but in some locations you will find more of certain species. Among these are the colorful gray and yellow cortez angelfish, the brilliant blue-and-gold king angelfish, banded butterflyfish, wrasses, surgeonfishes, damselfishes, a variety of eels, tangs, hogfish, and grouper. It is not unusual to see large schools of butterflyfishes, triggerfishes and puffers. Most of the reefs gradually slope from quite shallow to deeper water. Around the offshore islets where reef crests break the surface, schools of jack, snapper, and yellowtail can be found, along with leather bass. On the leeward side of these outer islets,

beautiful fan-shaped gorgonian corals of bright orange, red and yellow cover the rocky terrain.

In the reef crevices and pockets, a variety of invertebrates can also be seen.

Seamounts. Seamounts are the tops of submerged mountains. They are usually deep dives, often starting around 50 feet (15 m). The tops of these mounts have the usual crevices and undercuts of most reef systems. Because of the deep-water upwelling around them, they have a great variety of marine life. Moray eels, turtles and a wide array of fishes including pompanos, roosterfish and Pacific amberjack thrive near the seamounts.

The outer walls of these peaks drop quickly to hundreds of feet. In the 80- to 120-foot (24-36 m) range is where divers are most likely to find large tuna, wahoo and schooling hammerhead sharks. On occasion, divers have seen swordfish, sailfish, manta rays and giant whale sharks hovering around these great peaks.

Walls. Many of the islands have walls that drop in steps to depths of over 100 feet (30 m). They usually have gorgonian gardens growing on their steep sides. As currents are usually stronger along walls, the corals open up to feed on the flowing nutrients. Black coral trees have been seen as shallow as 60 feet (18 m). The truly great walls are around the East Cape and Cabo San Lucas where the submarine canyon drops dramatically to thousands of feet. Walls are beautiful dives. Larger fish along with deep-water pelagics are more frequent in these areas.

Kelp Forests. Thriving only in the Pacific's cooler waters, beds of *macrocystis* kelp flourish from Canada down to wide portions of Baja's west coast. Marine animals seen on the Pacific side are much different from those of the Sea of Cortez. These giant underwater forests are home to sea lions; swell, horn and leopard sharks; and occasionally underwater, divers can see the California gray whale. Commonly seen are the bright-orange garibaldi, sheepshead, kelp bass, white sea bass, perch opaleye and blacksmith, along with a variety of rays. Some of the most beautifully colored invertebrates anywhere live in these kelp forests. Starfish, nudibranchs, anemones and shellfish abound here. Kelp grows in the 20- to 100-foot (6-30 m) range. Sunlight does not penetrate much deeper than

Elephant seals are often found lounging on the rocks of many islands off the Pacific Coast. These are on Cedros Island off central Baja.

The white-sided dolphin is commonly seen in the Pacific and the Sea of Cortez. They are a small species of dolphin with a pointy snout and are easily recognized by their white sides. They are often seen schooling in the thousands.

Rocky coves along Baja's pristine shorelines are good areas for snorkeling and shallow scuba diving.

100 feet (30 m), so photosynthesis ceases.

Sandy Bottoms. Sandy bottoms are found at the bases of all reefs. Large open sandy areas have their own unique inhabitants: beds of garden eels; flatfish including halibut, turbot, sand dabs and flounder, which camouflage themselves under a thin layer of sand; large stingrays, oversized bullseye puffers, and angel sharks which are commonly found lying on the bottom. Schools of goatfishes and mullet can be seen foraging on the bottom. Sandy areas start as shallow as a few feet in the intertidal zone to depths of hundreds of feet. At the shallow depths are shellfish, such as tiger paw scallops and chocolate clams. You will likely be amazed at how much you will see in this seemingly barren world.

VISIBILITY

The visibility varies with each location, but on calm days it can exceed 100 feet (30 m). The Sea of Cortez is generally clearer. At certain times on the Pacific side, large plankton blooms lower visibility. This can be a plus for whale watchers because plankton is what the whales feed on during migrations. Also, winter storms come from Hawaii and the north, hitting the Pacific Coast first.

Best visibility in both the Pacific and Sea of Cortez is in the late summer and fall, when storms on the Pacific side and tropical storms on the Cortez side have ceased.

WATER TEMPERATURE

The water temperature in the Sea of Cortez can range anywhere from 60°F (16°C) in the winter and early spring months to the mid-80's F (29-30°C) in the summer and fall months. The further south it is, the warmer the water. On the Pacific side of Baja, the water is always much cooler, rarely exceeding 70°F (21°C) except down by the tip of the peninsula.

WEATHER

Northern Baja weather is very much like southern California. In winter, cold fronts may move in with winds and rain. In the summer months, weather is more balmy. Southern Baja is subject to periodic tropical storms and hurricanes in June through October. *Chubascos* are rainy-season local winds with thunderstorms, prevalent from May to October and common along the entire coast.

Mexican fishermen know about weather, so if you are exploring Baja with your own boat, keep an eye on what they do. If they stay at anchor in a harbor instead of going out to fish, they probably feel that a storm is brewing. Ask their opinion, which if not scientific, is probably reliable.

The Sea of Cortez is known for its many days of flat, calm water. Diving is generally better in the mornings as occasional offshore winds can pick up in the afternoon.

The norris top snail or kelp snail found feeding on the kelp fronds can grow to over 3 inches (8 cm). Their bright orange shell matches their colorful "foot" used for locomotion.

CHAPTER III PACIFIC COAST

AT A GLANCE

Baja's northwest side attracts an estimated four million visitors annually, most of them North Americans. Tourism is one of the major industries, especially in the Ensenada area. Fishing is also a major industry and the other two major cities of San Quintin and Guerrero Negro are fishing towns. Many small villages dot the western coast where farmers raise grapes, olives, corn and wheat, along with cattle, sheep and goats.

The drive down this part of Baja is nothing less than sensational. The desert mountains and valleys of cactus fields, many endemic to Baja, appear endless. A stretch of several miles by the town of Catavina is piled with massive teetering boulders, and has been declared a park.

In the spring months, Indian tribes migrate from Mexico's mainland to Baja's Pacific shore to harvest thousands of bay scallops. The larger camps are set up on the sand flats outside of Guerrero Negro.

LA BUFADORA AND PUNTA BANDA

Approximately 16 miles (26 km) south of Ensenada, this rocky peninsula juts into the Pacific at the south end of the Todos Santos Bay. La Bufadora (meaning buffalo's snout) is famous for its Blowhole. During incoming tides, waves rush into an underground cavern and force the sea through a hole in the top, creating spumes as high as 100 feet (30 m). Because of the tremendous surges, you should not dive in this area. South of the Blowhole is Bahia Papalote, a bay and small residential community. The Punta Banda area is characterized by steep cliffs, blue water and offshore kelp beds.

GETTING THERE

From the United States border, the La Bufadora turnoff is 81 miles (131 km). From here it is another 13 miles (21 km) to the small community of La Bufadora. Following the signs to Ensenada will get you on the toll highway which has three toll stations. As you pass through the town of Maneadero the road forks, the right fork leading you to La Bufadora. The turnoff is marked by a sign.

WHERE TO STAY

There are several hotels to choose from in Ensenada, all varying in price and amenities. In La Bufadora there is a lodge available, but reservations must be made through Baja Dive Expeditions (Tel: 011-52-667-30220). There is also a small house owned by La Bufadora Divers. It is equipped with 16 bunk beds, a refrigerator and a stove, and can be rented by the night. It is great for small groups. Camping is permitted along the bay for a small fee.

LAUNCH RAMPS

A 13-foot-wide (4 m) ramp with good traction is located at La Jolla Beach Camp. It is recommended for boats up to 16 feet (5 m). The seawall offers limited protection from the wind and sea. Small boats can be launched at the La Bufadora town ramp. It is rocky and narrow, and even at high tide water does not reach the ramp.

The bright orange garibaldi lives throughout the kelp forests and along the reefs.

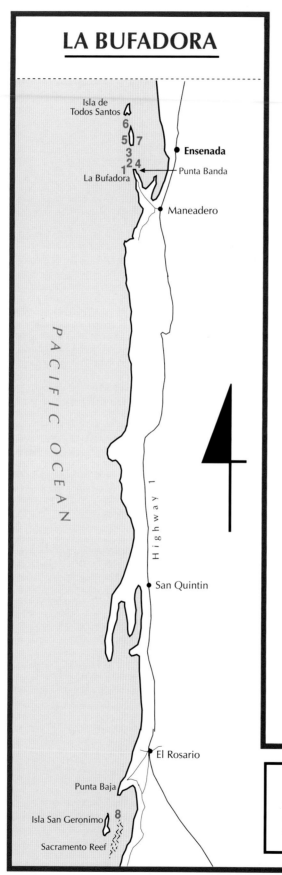

LA BUFADORA

Isla de Todos Santos

6
5 7
3
2 4
1

La Bufadora

Ensenada

Punta Banda

Maneadero

San Quintin

El Rosario

Punta Baja

Isla San Geronimo

Sacramento Reef

8

PACIFIC OCEAN

Highway 1

DIVING FACILITIES

La Bufadora Divers has a small dive shop with a compressor, tanks, weights and other rentals, along with panga boats to take divers out. There is also a dive operation through Baja Dive Expeditions located at the Baja Beach Resort, just before La Bufadora at the turnoff.

DIVING LA BUFADORA AND PUNTA BANDA

The Punta Banda area juts into the sea and catches a cold southward current from the north. These cooler waters occasionally bring in marine life typical of central and northern California. The bottom terrain consists of sandy areas that have large boulders, crevices and rock overhangs. Some areas are made up of thick kelp beds, while others have steep walls that can drop to over 100 feet (30 m). During the whale season, January through March, it is common to see gray whales swimming along the coast at the mouth of the bay. Sea lions are also frequently seen at La Bufadora. Water temperature is usually in the middle 50'sF (12-13ºC) to low 60'sF (16-17ºC), so at least a 1/4-inch suit (6 mm) is needed.

1. LA BUFADORA COVE (S)

DEPTH:	10-70 FEET (3-21 M)
LEVEL:	NOVICE TO EXPERIENCED
ACCESS:	SHORE

This cove provides easy access to the bay itself where a kelp bed is located. Scattered rocky reefs jut up to large boulders which protrude from the sandy bottom. The kelp reef, where kelp holdfasts fasten to the rocks forming an

1. La Bufadora Cove
2. Arch and Wall
3. The Pinnacles
4. Punta Banda Point
5. West Island
6. Middle Ground
7. East Island
8. Sacramento Reef

underwater forest, harbors quite an array of marine life. Multicolored sea urchins and bat stars creep along the bottom, while kelp bass, blacksmith, lingcod, sheepshead and kelpfish find refuge in the kelp fronds. Sheepshead are hermaphroditic—all are born female, but some later become males (with large red heads), only if more males are needed by the species. The cove is good for snorkeling as well as scuba diving. When it is calm, this is also an excellent spot for a night dive. Visibility is usually better in the fall months.

2. ARCH AND WALL

DEPTH:	20-100 FEET	
	(6-30 M)	
LEVEL:	INTERMEDIATE TO	
	EXPERIENCED	
ACCESS:	SHORE	

The most common entry to this popular site is from the cliffs on the north side of the bay. This area is easily identified by several large rocks that stick out of the water. After a careful climb down the cliff, the water entry is fairly simple. On calm days, one can jump off the rocky area and be in 10-15 feet (3-5 m) of water. Avoid diving on rough days as the surge can push you into the rocks. The underwater arch and wall area is an easy 100- to 200-yard (91-182 m) surface swim away. Descending on the northern edge of the rocks and working along the edge around to the west side of the rocks, you will pass by the underwater arch and end up on a steep wall that drops down to 100 feet (30 m). The top part of the wall levels off in some areas to 30 feet (9 m). There is an abundance of marine life throughout the ledges and overhangs. This area is a haven for invertebrate life, and divers can find a variety of shellfish, sea stars, nudibranchs, sea fans and anemones at this site. It's a good area for macro photography. Gamefish, such as bass, perch and sheepshead, are also prevalent along the wall.

Spanish shawl nudibranchs, along with an array of invertebrate life, are found throughout the La Bufadora area. Here the nudibranchs are eating bryozoans which make their colonies on kelp blades.

3. THE PINNACLES

DEPTH:	30-100+ FEET
	(9-30+ M)
LEVEL:	INTERMEDIATE TO
	EXPERIENCED
ACCESS:	BOAT

By boat about a half-hour run north of the bay are three large protruding rocks. The pinnacles are a beautiful place to dive and a photographer's paradise. Jagged formations and deep undercuts make up the steep walls of the pinnacle. Every square-inch of the wall is alive with some type of life. Including a variety of nudibranchs, shellfish, starfish, giant green anemones, gobys and blennys, these animals seem to be piled on top of each other. Large sheepshead, opaleye, rockfish and lingcod can be found all around the pinnacles. The bottom drops to over 100 feet (30+ m). It is a good idea to make your dive to at least 50 feet (15 m) as these open-ocean rocks are subject to weather and there is usually quite a

Gray whales will sometimes nuzzle divers and roll over to have their stomachs rubbed.

surge in the shallower depths. With the surge, it can be difficult to fix yourself in one position if using a camera. The deeper you go, the calmer it becomes. Deep lacerated pockets, about 10 feet (3 m) in length, cut into the wall. Moray eels and some lobster can be found here. Purple coral is also found growing along the walls.

4. PUNTA BANDA POINT

DEPTH:	60-100+ FEET
	(18-30+ M)
LEVEL:	INTERMEDIATE TO
	EXPERIENCED
ACCESS:	BOAT

The point at the very tip of the La Bufadora peninsula can be an exciting dive. At times, though, there can be heavy surge. Groups of large rocks project over a rock and sand reef which extends seaward towards Todos Santos Island. The outermost group of rocks has deep walls with many caves and grottos. This area

THE GRAY WHALES OF BAJA

Each year, from January through April, an estimated 17,000 Pacific gray whales mate and give birth in Baja's Pacific Coast lagoons and some areas of the Sea of Cortez. Their yearly migration from Alaska's food-rich Bering Sea is one of the longest on record for any mammal. Once spring arrives, the grays will head back north. Cruising at 4-5 knots, they parallel the coastline for an estimated 5,000 miles (8,065 km) each way, feeding on plankton, krill, pelagic red crabs, eelgrass and kelp.

Gray whales get to be 40-50 feet (12-15 m) long and weigh 30-40 tons (27-36 mt). At birth, calves measure nearly 15 feet (5 m) and weigh almost a ton (1.1 mt). Their growth is rapid, sustained by a thick milk that contains nearly 55 percent fat. Known for their high intelligence, these animals gained their description as "gentle giants" by their tender demeanor among other whales and in their encounters with humans.

During mating, their slow courtship of playing and touching often involves two males and one female, and lasts several hours. Their gestation period is believed to be between 12-13 months.

In the 15-foot (5 m) shallows, there is almost constant physical contact between mothers and calves. The baby calf swims at its mother's side, watching and repeating all her actions. When the mother stops to rest, however, the playful baby will cross back and forth over the mother's tail and head, pull itself onto her back, bump into her side and tease her until she plays.

These whales are quite gentle around humans and often enjoy having their heads and stomachs scratched. It is an amazing experience to have one of these magnificent creatures nuzzling and nosing against you, slowly turning over to have her stomach rubbed. After decades of slaughter, the gray whale has made a remarkable comeback, and in January 1993 it was taken off the endangered list. The lagoons are now official sanctuaries, and no boats are permitted in certain lagoons.

is incredibly colorful with groups of invertebrates and larger game fish, such as bass, corvina and rockfish. Because of the occasionally heavy surge, you will want to make your dive to at least 60 feet (18 m) to get beneath the wave action.

TODOS SANTOS ISLAND

Approximately three miles (4.8 km) from the point are two large rocky masses of land encircled by kelp beds. This is the island of Todos Santos. The two land masses are known as the West and East Islands, and are approximately 300 yards (273 m) apart.

Kelpfish can often be found hiding amongst the kelp fronds.

5. WEST ISLAND

DEPTH:	10-100 FEET (3-30 M)
LEVEL:	INTERMEDIATE TO EXPERIENCED
ACCESS:	BOAT

West Island has the best potential for diving because of its larger kelp beds and detached rock formations. The north side, called Brucitos, has a sloping wall to about 100 feet (30 m). Because of its exposure to the prevailing winds, it can get very rough with surge here. Early morning is the best time to dive, and once again, keeping your dives a little deeper, around 50 feet (15 m), helps to stay beneath the surge.

Marine life seen here include rockfish, sculpin, yellowtail, sheepshead and opaleye, along with leopard and horn sharks. Larger game fish are also abundant on the north side. The kelp beds provide a sanctuary for many marine animals. Several species of kelpfish, looking very similar to the kelp fronds, are extremely well camouflaged. Not too many lobster are left here, but they can be found along with abalone.

6. MIDDLE GROUND (S)

DEPTH:	10-50 FEET (3-15 M)
LEVEL:	NOVICE TO EXPERIENCED
ACCESS:	BOAT

The middle area between the islands is quite shallow. The terrain is made up of rocks and eel grass. Lobster can sometimes be found hiding in the grass. This is a good area for snorkeling as it is relatively shallow. Small schools of perch and opaleye move around this area. The eel grass is used as a nursery for many fishes where the fry can find protection within the thick greenery.

7. EAST ISLAND (S)

DEPTH:	15-100 FEET (5-30 M)
LEVEL:	NOVICE TO EXPERIENCED
ACCESS:	BOAT

The southeast tip of the island has rock pinnacles and kelp beds off its point. The sloping terrain of rocky ledges and kelp fronds in calm waters offer excellent opportunities for photographing both invertebrates and fish life.

The maximum life span of a kelp frond is approximately six months. Encrusting bryozoans have evolved a rapid life cycle that matches that of their host. The bryozoans settle on the kelp as microscopic larvae that soon become visible as tiny white specks. Within a few days, they can reproduce. Within three weeks, the colonies enlarge and form a layer of lacy white crust. They are then prey for nudibranchs.

The bright coloration of some nudibranchs, such as the purple and orange Spanish shawl, makes them stand out against the kelp. But at the same time, conspicuous coloration warns other animals that the nudibranch is not a very tasty meal.

This is also a good spot for snorkelers. Shellfish can be found in 10 feet (3 m) of water.

SACRAMENTO REEF

Sacramento Reef is hard to get to. An inflatable from Punta San Antonio, which can be reached through very rough dirt roads, is your best bet. The reef is considered dangerous to boaters because of its unseen shallow depths. Many a sailboat has found its resting ground here.

A small cove at Punta Baja further north, where lightweight boats and inflatables can be launched from the beach on calm days, is accessible by a rough dirt road from El Rosario. Larger boats can be launched at Ensenada or San Quintin, many miles north. The reef can be located by breakers approximately 5 miles (8 km) out from Punta San Antonio.

Caution. If you decide to take your small boat out to Sacramento Reef, plan to do it with the company of another boat as there is no coast guard patrolling the waters.

8. SACRAMENTO REEF

DEPTH:	10-100+ FEET (3-30+ M)
LEVEL:	EXPERIENCED
ACCESS:	BOAT

This shallow, rocky reef measures over 2 miles (3.2 km) in length and is a shipwreck graveyard. Years of wave action have scattered wreckage in all directions, camouflaging it within the rocks and kelp. From these shallows, the reef drops off rapidly to over 100 feet (30+ m). This area is noted for its abundance of large fish, including white and black sea bass, sheepshead, rockfish, kelp bass and very large spiny lobster. Conditions can get rough here, but in calm weather Sacramento Reef, along with San Geronimo Island 1-1/2 miles (1 km) northwest of the reef, are well worth the trip as both are almost virgin dive sites.

Appearing like a little space alien, the sand crab burrows beneath the sand.

GUERRERO NEGRO LAGOON

The town of Guerrero Negro (Black Warrior) sits on the edge of a lagoon. It was named after a Hawaiian whaling vessel that was so overloaded with whale oil in 1858 that it couldn't leave the lagoon under its own power. It sank while being towed out to sea. The town is now known for the local saltworks southwest of town, that produces around six million tons of salt a year. This huge system of diked ponds takes in seawater from the lagoon and impounds it while the sun turns it into thick layers of salt. It is then transported to Cedros Island and eventually shipped to mainland Mexico, the United States, Canada and Japan.

In these back lagoons and estuaries is some interesting diving. To get there follow the road through the town of Guerrero Negro. It will then veer to the left. At the salt factory next to the Bancomer Bank, turn right. Follow the road out to the lighthouse.

The bright blue dots of this free-swimming scallop are his eyes. These mollusks are filter-feeders and are usually found where there is a slight current.

9. GUERRERO NEGRO LAGOON

DEPTH:	3- 50 FEET
	(1-15 M)
LEVEL:	NOVICE TO
	EXPERIENCED
ACCESS:	SHORE

At the end where the lighthouse is, it is usually quite windy especially in the afternoons, but the lagoon has no currents so the wind chop is only on the surface. On the north side of the lagoon, the depth starts at 3 feet (1 m) with a very gradual decline. The bottom is covered with a short type of eel grass. Scattered between the green blades are myriad bay scallops which live on the sand. Also throughout this area are clumps of rocks and debris which make terrific homes for octopus.

Even though the visibility is only about 10-15 feet (3-5 m), the lagoon offers some interesting sights that you would not see elsewhere. There are gold- and blue-striped nudibranchs which can be found on the grass blades. The only sea horse that lives in the cool Pacific waters is found uniquely in this area, hiding in the swaying fingers of the eel grass. The little pike blennys seem to pretend that they are grass blades, lying vertically between them.

California spiny lobsters make their homes under ledges and inside cubbyholes.

Blue sharks thrive mainly in open water, but on occasion divers are lucky enough to spot one seaward of the reef area.

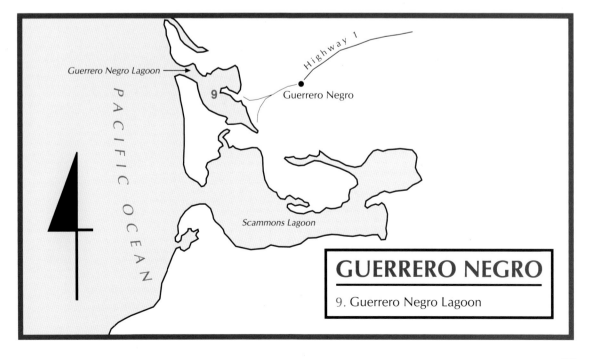

PACIFIC OCEAN

Highway 1

Guerrero Negro Lagoon

9

Guerrero Negro

Scammons Lagoon

GUERRERO NEGRO

9. Guerrero Negro Lagoon

CHAPTER **IV** ALFONSINA

AT A GLANCE

For many years, this area on the Sea of Cortez has been a community of small fishing villages, but vacation homes are now being built by Americans along the shoreline. Most of the vacationing people fly here by small private plane, as there are only small dirt runways. If you fly in to Alfonsina, be sure to check the tide charts since much of the runway is underwater at high tide.

GETTING THERE

If you are driving, this area is for the real adventurer. There is a very rough 45-mile (73 km) dirt road leading from San Felipe to the north. Four-wheel-drive is recommended. There is another road just south of Catavina and north of Chapala off Highway 1. It is approximately 40 miles (65 km) on a somewhat better dirt road where four-wheel-drive is not an absolute necessity.

More travel information can be obtained at the La Pinta Hotel in Catavina.

WHERE TO STAY

There is the cantina in Alfonsina that serves food and rents rooms. Down the hallway are restrooms and rustic showers. If you plan to camp, the coastline is open. It is a good idea to bring as much food and ice as you expect to need.

DIVING

There are no diving facilities, but local fishermen are usually willing to take divers out in their pangas for a small fee. Small boats can be easily launched from the sandy shoreline.

10. BAHIA SAN LUIS GONZAGA (S)

DEPTH:	10-40 FEET
	(3-12 M)
LEVEL:	NOVICE TO
	EXPERIENCED
ACCESS:	SHORE

The shoreline around the large bay is scattered with rocky outcroppings which are good for snorkeling. Off the point just to the north, the rocky terrain stairsteps down to a sandy bottom in about 40 feet (12 m) of water. Spiny oysters, along with several species of invertebrates, such as sea stars, urchins and anemones, can be found clinging to the rocky substrate. Local reef fish, such as boxfish, filefish, black durgon, convict tangs and parrotfishes are seen along the outer edges of the rocks. Throughout the bay, sea lions occasionally frolic in the shallows. The late spring and early summer months sometimes bring in giant whale sharks. They have been known to hang around the shallow bays for days at a time, allowing divers to snorkel with them.

Large gorgonian sea fans line the insides of many of the rock walls. The walls are a good place to search for invertebrates.

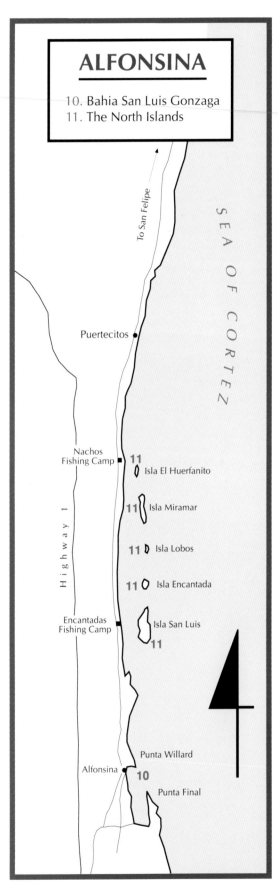

ALFONSINA

To San Felipe

SEA OF CORTEZ

Puertecitos •

Nachos
Fishing Camp ■ **11**
Isla El Huerfanito

11 Isla Miramar

Highway 1

11 Isla Lobos

11 Isla Encantada

Encantadas
Fishing Camp
Isla San Luis

11

Punta Willard

Alfonsina • **10**

Punta Final

11. THE NORTH ISLANDS

DEPTH:	15-100+ FEET
	(5-30+ M)
LEVEL:	INTERMEDIATE TO
	EXPERIENCED
ACCESS:	BOAT

There are four islands a couple of miles offshore and about 10 miles (16 km) north of Alfonsina that are accessible by boat. Because of the great tidal changes in the Sea of Cortez, these islands do not have the same underwater visibility as further south. Visibility is about 20-30 feet (6-9 m). In the shallow water surrounding these islands are detached rocks which are interesting to explore. The depth starts at about 15 feet (5 m), but the jagged walls drop quickly into water over 100 feet (30+ m) deep. Small reef fish, along with grouper, cabrilla and snapper, are plentiful. The largest of the islands is Isla San Luis. Three more, further north are Isla Encantada, Isla Lobos and Isla Miramar. The entire chain runs about 12 miles (19 km).

The thornback ray is easily identified by its three rows of spines. They are usually spotted on sandy bottoms.

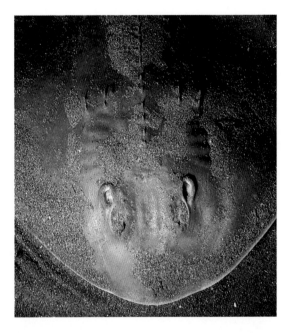

This desolate island, so typical of the Sea of Cortez, is in the small island chain between Puertecitos and Alfonsina.

BAJA'S MOUNTAINS

The mountain range west of San Felipe is called the Sierra San Pedro Martir. It is nearly 75 miles (121 km) in length and contrasts greatly with its surrounding regions. On the east it drops 6,000 feet (1,818 m) to the Sea of Cortez. This is the dry side of the Sierras where there are a number of rocky, palm-dotted canyons with small streams. These were once used by the nomadic Indians of the region who hunted deer, bighorn sheep and rabbits.

The 8,000-foot (2,424 m) plateau which makes up the central portion of the San Pedro Martir is less forested and contains an array of wildlife that live near streams winding through alpine meadows. There is a species of trout in these streams which is believed to live nowhere else. A small village called San Telmo lies 5 miles (8 km) east of the highway and is on the way to the Meling Ranch—a cattle ranch that accommodates about 12 guests. The entire range is dominated by Picacho del Diablo, a 10,126-foot (3,069 m) mountain, which has become popular with mountain climbers. Each winter the high plateaus of both the Martir and Sierra Juarez to the north are covered with snow.

To the northwest at the 9,200-foot (2,788 m) level of the Sierra San Pedro Martir, the government has built an observatory. It offers a spectacular view of the desert and the Sea of Cortez. To get there off-road vehicles are recommended.

CHAPTER V BAHIA DE LOS ANGELES

At a Glance

Bahia de Los Angeles is probably one of the most picturesque bays in Baja. The coastline is made up of miles of white sandy beaches, while the bay is studded with islands and islets. In times past, the bay was a productive turtle fishing region, but over-harvesting has greatly decreased their population.

The town really hasn't grown much since the pre-Transpeninsular Highway days and telephones are still non-existent. There is a small park, behind which is a museum with gold- and silver-mining exhibits, shells, fossils, whale skeletons and a few Indian artifacts. The toy-like locomotive in front of the museum was once used on the San Juan Mine railway, 11 miles (18 km) south of the bay.

A few miles north along the beach is a lighthouse which provides a nice lookout at the end of the point. There are usually shark skeletons around the point as this seems to be a cleaning ground for local fishermen. Thousands of small fiddler crabs make their homes in sand holes along the miles of beautiful yet desolate beach. A few miles north of town, beside the airstrip, is a building which is a small turtle farm.

Getting There

No major airlines fly into Bahia de Los Angeles, however, there is an airstrip for small private planes. From Highway 1, there is a 41-mile (66 km) paved road from Parador Punta Prieta that leads to the bay. There is a Pemex gasoline station on the south end of town, across from the Casa Diaz Motel.

Where To Stay

There are a few motels in town. The **Las Hamacas** in the center of town is clean, has three rooms and a restaurant with good food

and good prices. The **Villa Vitta** is also in the center of town, and usually has moderate prices that fluctuate. The **Casa Diaz**, located at the south end of town, has large, colorful rooms and moderate food. There are RV hookups available here as well. **Guillermo's** is located on the water. The rooms are very nice and the restaurant has good food. There are *palapas*—palm-roofed huts with open sides—on the beach. They also have a clean mini-mart with a gift shop.

Camping

You can camp almost anywhere along the coastline for free. Just north of town near the paved airstrip is the rustic **Brisa Marina**, a trailer park on the water with its own generator. On the beach, three miles (4.8 km) south of town, is **Camp Gecko** where there are small cabins and campsites, along with toilets and shower facilities available for a small fee. To get there take the road to San Francisquito and turn left at the freeway sign.

Launch Ramps

The **Villa Vitta ramp** is 12 feet (3.6 m) wide and made of concrete so it can be used whether it is high or low tide. In addition, there is a rock jetty that breaks up waves kicked up by the afternoon winds. Check at the Villa Vitta Motel before launching.

The **Casa Diaz ramp** is also concrete, 14 feet (4.2 m) wide and has a small breakwater. Check at the Casa Diaz office before launching.

Sergeant majors can be seen on almost every reef and are usually swimming in small schools.

DIVING FACILITIES

Small dive operations seem to open for short periods before closing up, so you must supply all of your own equipment. Ask at the motels for fishing boats that will take you out for a fee.

DIVING

The offshore region surrounding the town of Bahia de Los Angeles includes numerous islands and reefs which are easily reached by boat. This area contains a number of great dive sites. Early morning dives are recommended as afternoon winds can really pick up in the bay area.

The water temperatures are cooler here— from 65°F (18°C) in winter to 75°F (27°C) in summer—than in other areas in the Sea of Cortez because of the currents from the deep submarine canyons which are constantly being forced to the surface by the extreme tidal ranges in this area. Tidal currents reach their maximum during full and new moons. The moon phases and strong afternoon winds should be considered when planning a dive. Most currents lose their strength during times of the half-moon phase. For drift dives you can take advantage of the stronger currents as long as there is a reliable person following in a boat.

Year-round fish, such as grouper and bass, reach tremendous sizes around the outer offshore islands. The big channel between the largest island of Isla Angel De La Guardia and the closer islands is alive with sea lions, manta rays, migrating whales and schooling dolphins.

More prevalent at certain times of the year are the yellowtail, sierra mackerel, snapper and halibut.

12. PUNTA LA GRINGA (S)

DEPTH:	6-10 FEET
	(2-3 M)
LEVEL:	NOVICE
ACCESS:	SHORE

Punta La Gringa is the point just north of the

Bay of Los Angeles and is a good snorkeling area for finding shellfish, flatfish and a variety of tropicals. The point is also a good place to camp.

The Bay of Los Angeles itself is a massive field of white sand. In shallow water, divers and snorkelers can find chocolate clams, tiger paw scallops and bay scallops. Stingrays and flatfish can always be found on the sandy bottom as can angel sharks and large bullseye pufferfish. The host of other critters also thriving in this granular environment include sea stars, sea pens, burrowing anemones and the spotted snake eel. The latter's head can be seen sticking out of the sand; when fearful, he will sink back into the sand, his hole caving in and then vanishing.

13. ISLA CORONADO

DEPTH:	15-90+ FEET
	(5-27+ M)
LEVEL:	NOVICE TO
	EXPERIENCED
ACCESS:	BOAT

This island, also called Isla Smith, measures four miles (6.5 km) in length. There are sandy beaches toward the middle of both sides of the island.

East Side (13A). The east side of the island is typical of the Sea of Cortez. Large boulders teeter on each other, spilling onto a colorful reef. There are detached rocks from the middle of the island to the southern tip. The reef area starts at about 15 feet (5 m) dropping gradually to over 90 feet (27 m). This rocky terrain has crevices and small chimneys which give way to flickering sunlight. Deeper crevices harbor soldierfish, glasseyes, and cardinalfish which spend most of their lives in the darker corners of the reef.

The mauve-colored flower urchin with its tiny pedal-like appendages ripple slowly along the flat areas, picking up pieces of shells to wear. Other colorful invertebrates, such as crown of thorns, pencil urchins and feather duster worms, live throughout the reef structure. There are also an abundance of reef fishes, such as guinea puffers, cortez chubs,

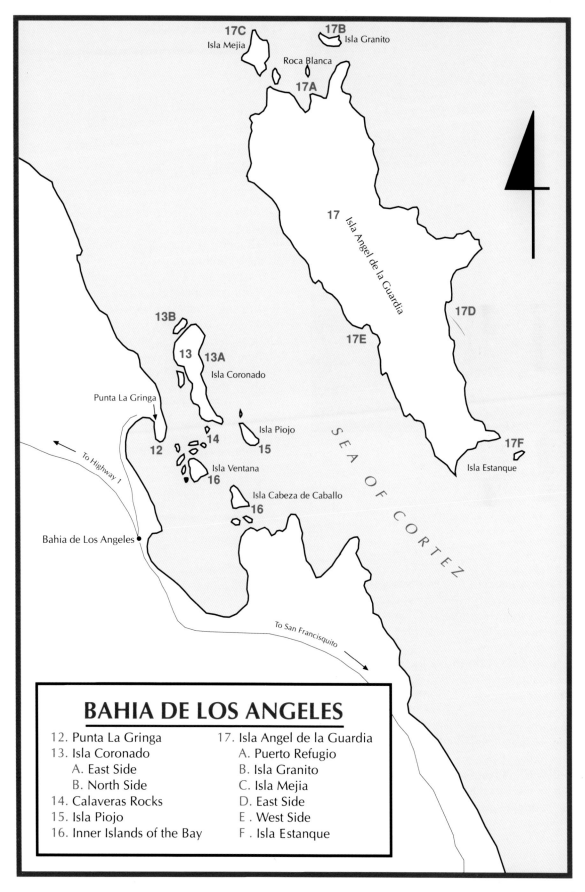

17C
Isla Mejia

17B
Isla Granito

Roca Blanca

17A

17 Isla Angel de la Guardia

13B

13 13A
Isla Coronado

Punta La Gringa

17D

17E

17F
Isla Estanque

To Highway 1

12

14

Isla Piojo

15

Isla Ventana
16

Isla Cabeza de Caballo
16

Bahia de Los Angeles

S E A   O F   C O R T E Z

To San Francisquito

BAHIA DE LOS ANGELES

12. Punta La Gringa
13. Isla Coronado
    A. East Side
    B. North Side
14. Calaveras Rocks
15. Isla Piojo
16. Inner Islands of the Bay

17. Isla Angel de la Guardia
    A. Puerto Refugio
    B. Isla Granito
    C. Isla Mejia
    D. East Side
    E . West Side
    F . Isla Estanque

The guinea puffer is a black fish with white polka dots. When caught, they swell up to almost twice their size and their little faces almost disappear, giving them a cartoon-like appearance.

14. CALAVERAS ROCKS

DEPTH:	30-40 FEET
	(9-12 M)
LEVEL:	NOVICE TO
	EXPERIENCED
ACCESS:	BOAT

Located a half mile (.8 km) off the south end of Isla Coronado is Calaveras Rocks. The locals call it Sea Lion Rock. The depths close to these protruding rocks average between 30 and 40 feet (9-12 m) with a gradual slope. Colorful gorgonian soft corals are sprinkled throughout. There is a large sea lion colony which lives on this big rock formation. Underwater, these big-eyed clowns are nothing more than super curious. They speed up, stopping inches from your mask, blow bubbles, then dart away. At certain times of the year the large bulls can become aggressive, particularly when new pups have arrived. They will give a noisy underwater warning, at which time it is best to respect their request and keep your distance.

15. ISLA PIOJO (S)

DEPTH:	30-40 FEET
	(9-12 M)
LEVEL:	NOVICE TO
	EXPERIENCED
ACCESS:	BOAT

Isla Piojo lies just southeast of Coronado Island. There are large rocks scattered around the island's points. The bottom terrain is sandy with huge boulders, which makes for good snorkeling and shallow diving. A cabbage-like algae plant grows throughout the bay and among the rocks, attracting many invertebrates which feed on it. Nudibranchs decorated with frills of green, navy, yellow, orange, purple, black and white can be found needling their way through the undergrowth.

At certain times, massive schools of small bait fishes will cloud up the water, bringing in

rock croakers, blue and gold snapper, and soapfish. Soapfish live in small caves and crevices in the daytime, but come out at night to feed. If touched, a soapy film is secreted from their bodies.

North Side (13B) (S). At the north end of Isla Coronado, there is a small islet called Isla Coronadito which is separated from the island by a deep, narrow channel. The islet is characterized by its sharp drop-offs. Currents can get quite strong in the channel, which in turn brings in larger fish such as grouper, yellowtail and jacks. On the north and west side of the islet the water is about 20 feet (6 m) gradually sloping to deeper water. This is a good spot for snorkeling as well as scuba diving. Large rocks dominate the terrain. Reef fishes and invertebrates, along with shellfish, are scattered throughout the rocky fissures.

The blackbar soldierfish, usually pinkish red in color is found under long, deep ledges, and in small caves and grottos.

There are many small caves and chimneys around the reefs to swim through. Tiny bait fish often cluster around the openings. Inside, fishes such as squirrelfishes, soldierfishes and bigeyes can be found.

The gulf star has very distinctive robust arms covered with bright red spines. These sea stars are found from the Gulf of California to Peru. The white blotches on this sea star are actually bryozoans which live on the star.

Small boats and inflatables are excellent for most areas in the Sea of Cortez.

larger reef fishes which make their homes in the nooks and crannies. Roosterfish, jacks and corvina can all be found here. The best diving is in the morning before the afternoon winds kick up.

16. INNER ISLANDS OF THE BAY (S)

DEPTH:	15-60+ FEET
	(5-18+ M)
LEVEL:	NOVICE TO
	EXPERIENCED
ACCESS:	BOAT

Most of the small islands dotting the inner bay, such as **Isla Ventana** and **Isla Cabeza De**

Caballo, are good areas for snorkeling and shallow scuba diving. In the shallow waters along their shores are rocky boulders and smaller river rocks. The bottom slopes gradually to deeper depths. There is an abundance of shellfish including the large pen scallop that can reach up to over one foot (31 cm) in length. It buries itself where just the upper portion protrudes above the sand. Reef fishes are more sporadic. Schools of jacks and yellowtail are more often seen from December through June, while October through April bring in more roosterfish and snapper. Tropicals such as Cortez angelfish, surgeonfishes, barberfish, gobies, blennies and wrasses are seen among the rocks year round.

Local fishermen frequent these islands often, so lobster and larger game fish are relatively scarce.

Isla Angel de la Guardia

The island of Angel de la Guardia, the largest of the offshore islands, sits 20 miles (32 km) out from Bahia de Los Angeles. The north end of the island is actually 40 miles (65 km) from the bay. The island's 4,000-foot-high (1,212 m) mountains and 42-mile (68 km) length make it a prominent landmark. It is home to coyotes, mice, rats, sea birds and lizards. Good camping is found at both the north and south end of the island.

17. ISLA ANGEL DE LA GUARDIA

DEPTH:	20-100+ FEET (6-30+ M)
LEVEL:	INTERMEDIATE TO EXPERIENCED
ACCESS:	BOAT

At the north end of the island is **Puerto Refugio (17A)**, which has good anchorage from weather. Its almost surrealistic pinnacles of white and black rocks, jutting from the water's surface form a majestic backdrop. The isolated reefs that start in about 30 feet (9 m) of water and slope gradually provide outstanding diving. Tropical fishes, such as schooling yellowtail, triggerfishes, grouper, pargo and grunts frequent this entire area, along with a menagerie of small reef fishes. During night dives, divers often see the four types of lobster which live in the Sea of Cortez: the blue spiny lobster, the socorro lobster, the California spiny lobster and the slipper lobster. All are very tasty.

Approximately one half mile (.8 km) offshore from Puerto Refugio is a large rock pinnacle surrounded by a rock-covered 40-foot-deep (12 m) ledge. Further out a series of sheer walls stairstep quickly to a sand bottom at around 90 feet (27 m). A great variety of marine life can be found at this area.

Beyond the pinnacle is **Isla Granito (17B)**, a small narrow islet. A few hundred yards off its northwest end is a large reef that begins in 40 feet (12 m) and drops to 70 feet (21 m). Here the bottom is sandy with scattered rocks. Vegetation, sponges, white gorgonians and stinging hydroids cover the hard substrate. Large parrotfishes, cortez angelfish, cabrilla, hawkfish and cortez chubs are only a few of the local residents. This entire area is known for its abundance of large game fish.

On the west side of Puerto Refugio is **Isla Mejia (17C)**, a small island with jagged cliffs. The north end of this islet is excellent for macro photography when the sea is calm, usually in the morning. Tiny hermit crabs, feeding barnacles, anemones, nudibranchs and spiral worms are just a few of the little inhabitants. Some exposed rocks, along with submerged boulders, make up a reef which extends for over half a mile (.8 km). There are many excellent dive spots around these rocks.

On both the **east (17D)** and **west side (17E)** of Angel de la Guardia, there are small coves with beaches, many harboring sunbathing sea lions. Rocky clusters mark excellent dive spots. These two sides plunge rapidly to deep water, and currents can be very strong during certain times of the month so caution should be observed.

The southern tip of the island is the closest anchorage from the Bay of Los Angeles. Here there is a long reef which is connected to an islet, **Isla Estanque (17F)**, which lies off the southeast end of La Guardia. Several groups of detached rocks along its shoreline are also good for snorkeling. The depth starts at 40 feet (12 m) and drops quickly to hundreds of feet. The east side of Estanque has a steep wall. The many overhangs, nooks and crannies in this area are great to explore. There is a wide variety of fish along with a good selection of shellfish, including spiny oysters and bay scallops. On the sandy bottom, chocolate clams can be found just beneath a thin layer of sand. Look close—you may see a halibut. In deeper water, divers are more likely to see manta rays, tuna and sharks, nurse and whitetips in particular.

The channel between the Bahia de Los Angeles and Angel de la Guardia is frequented by a variety of dolphins and whales, including the California gray, finback, minke, humpback, blue, sperm, pygmy sperm, pilot and orca. The gigantic finback whale, which reaches a length of 70 feet (21 m) is usually found here in the summer months and is the most commonly seen.

CHAPTER VI   BAHIA SAN FRANCISQUITO

AT A GLANCE

Bahia San Francisquito is a well protected bay located 83 miles (134 km) by land and 50 miles (81 km) by sea south of Bahia de Los Angeles. It has very limited gasoline and supplies. Some provisions can be bought at the small ranch community of El Barrill, just south of San Francisquito Bay, but it is still best to pack in everything that you will need.

GETTING THERE

In Bahia de Los Angeles, between the main street and the small museum, is the only road which goes south to San Francisquito. The road passes through the Sierra San Borja, where there are several important ancient Indian petroglyph sites. You can inquire at local ranches for trail guides. The rough dirt road can take up to 3-1/2 hours to drive. It is best to have a four-wheel-drive vehicle. There is also a small dirt airstrip for private planes.

WHERE TO STAY

San Francisquito is equipped with about ten cabanas, each having two cots with blankets. There are restroom and shower facilities, and very simple meals are served. Ice is a rare commodity here, so bring in as much as you will need. Bringing your own food is also a good idea. The desolate coastline is open for camping.

DIVE FACILITIES

At the small dining building, there are some scuba tanks for rent, a compressor, and a couple of pangas can take divers out.

DIVING

There is a long chain of offshore islands which

extends north from San Francisquito to within about 10 miles (16 km) south of the island of Angel de la Guardia. The water between these islands and the shore, known as the Canal de Salsipuedes, can get heavy tidal currents so exercise caution when planning your dive.

18. PUNTA MUJERES AND PUNTA SAN GABRIEL (S)

DEPTH:	6-10 FEET
	(2-3 M)
LEVEL:	NOVICE
ACCESS:	SHORE

There are two points that can be dived from the shore of the bay itself, one to the north, Punta Mujeres, and one to the south, Punta San Gabriel. Both are great for shallow scuba dives and snorkeling. Small schools of mobulas, which are a small type of manta ray, can be found around the rocky points, slowly gliding like alien aircraft over the bottom. Angelfishes, surgeonfishes and butterflyfishes thrive around the rocky outcroppings. Large boulders litter the bottom as it slopes seaward to open sand where a variety of flatfishes, including halibut, dig themselves in. Rays and angel sharks are often found in water shallows, 6-10 feet (2-3 m) deep. Around the tips of the points are usually currents, but if you stay just inside of the points, the water is normally calm. You can drive over to either of

A male Mexican hogfish is best identified by the fleshy lump on its head. A school of king angelfish surrounds him.

The female Mexican hogfish is usually red in color with two dark lines down her body. The juveniles also have the dark lines.

the points, or you can hike there, which is about a half mile (.8 km) either way. There is an easy entry from the shore with rarely any surf to speak of, and the beaches are desolate and serene.

19. ISLA SAN LORENZO

DEPTH:	50-100+ FEET
	(15-30+ M)
LEVEL:	EXPERIENCED
ACCESS:	BOAT

The island of Lorenzo is the largest of the chain, over 10 miles (16 km) in length. It is also the closest to the bay of San Francisquito. Because of the tidal currents which push up deep nitrogen-rich water, the water around the island is usually cool. Most diving along the submerged cliffs start at about 50-60 feet (15-18 m). Diving is excellent when the sea is calm and the turbidity is down. The depth drops very quickly, plummeting to hundreds of feet.

This is the place to see large fish. In the winter and spring months there are white sea bass, giant sea bass, whitefish, sheepshead, goldspotted bass and schools of yellowtail. The summer months bring in groupers, yellowfin tuna, dorado and giant squid. The ledges and deep ravines are home to pargo, snapper and cabrilla.

Caution. The island can get some very strong currents, so this area is recommended for experienced divers only.

SAN FRANCISQUITO

18. Punta Mujeres and Punta San Gabriel
19. Isla San Lorenzo

Punta de Las Animas

Isla Partida

Isla Raza

Isla Salsipuedes

Isla Las Animas

Isla San Lorenzo
19

Punta Mujeres
18

San Francisquito 18
Punta San Gabriel

SEA OF CORTEZ

Along the shallow reef walls barberfish can be seen eating the algae on the rocks and corals.

Barberfish can often be found schooling between shallow reefs.

CHAPTER VII MULEGE

AT A GLANCE

The town of Mulege, with a population of 6,000, sits nestled in a lush tropical setting. Palm trees line the Rio Santa Rosalia, an estuarial river that meanders lazily through the valley, finally to swing around and meet the waters of the Sea of Cortez. The abundance of water made this a desirable mission location in the early 1700's. Date, fig, banana, olive and orange production comprises most of the local livelihood, along with fishing and tourism. The local facilities, including a dive shop, laundromat, auto mechanics, markets, restaurants, hotels and campgrounds, have made it a favorite stop for travelers. Weather conditions along the coast from Mulege to Loreto are typically subtropical. Annual rainfall is about 4 inches (10 cm). The winters are cool, the summers hot and humid.

The **Sierra de Guadalupe** contains the largest number of known prehistoric cave paintings in Baja. Several of the hotels in Mulege can arrange excursions to the more accessible sites.

GETTING THERE

Following Highway 1 will take you into Mulege. An airstrip for private aircraft is located 2-1/2 miles (4 km) east of town, next to the Hotel Serenidad.

WHERE TO STAY

Mulege has a number of hotels in and just outside of town. In town, the **Hotel Las Casitas** is popular. It has modest accommodations, and a restaurant and bar. Just east of Las Casitas is **Hotel Rosita**, which has budget apartments with kitchenettes. Others include the **Hotel Baja Hacienda** with clean rooms, and the **Hotel Vista Hermosa**, which has a

river view, and a restaurant and bar. East of town is Mulege's largest hotel, the **Hotel Serenidad**, which has a restaurant, bar and pool. The turnoff is 2.1 miles (3.4 km) south of the Mulege bridge on Highway 1. Restaurants are scattered throughout the town. The **Los Equipales** serves good Mexican specialties. The **Las Casitas** across the street from the dive shop, and the **La Palma** are also good.

CAMPING

Probably the nicest camp area is the **Orchard Huerta Saucedo** east of town on the river about a half mile (.8 km) off of Highway 1. There are tent sites and full hookups. Also along the river in the same area are **Jorge's**, **Pancho's**, **Rio Oasis** and **Villa Maria Isabel**, all well-kept spots. There is a Pemex station in Mulege and one 15 minutes south of town.

LAUNCH RAMPS

All of the ramps are located on the river, so be sure to check the tides when launching and returning as the river can get very shallow in spots.

At **Villa Maria Isabel RV Park**, 1.4 miles (2-1/4 km) south of the Rio Santa Rosalia bridge, is a 12-foot-wide (3.6 m) ramp composed of a concrete and rock mix.

Lighthouse ramp is along the north bank of the river towards the lighthouse 2.5 miles (4 km) and is made of hard-packed sand and small rocks. The slope is adequate to handle most boats.

The **Orchard ramp** surface is rough concrete and 12 feet (3.6 m) wide and is located .7

Octopuses can usually be found hiding between rocks or sleeping in debris. This one is nestled in a broken beer bottle.

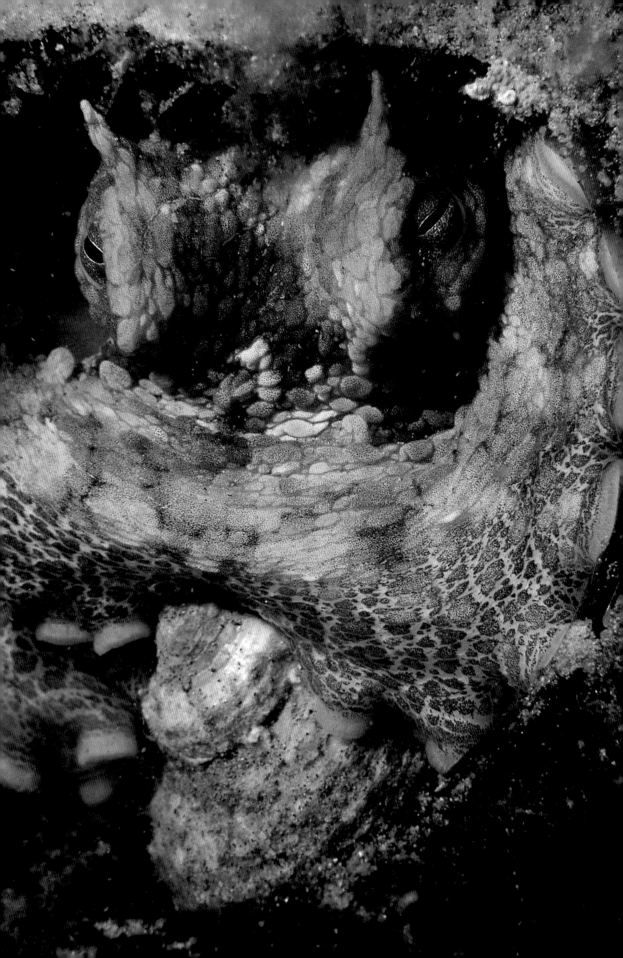

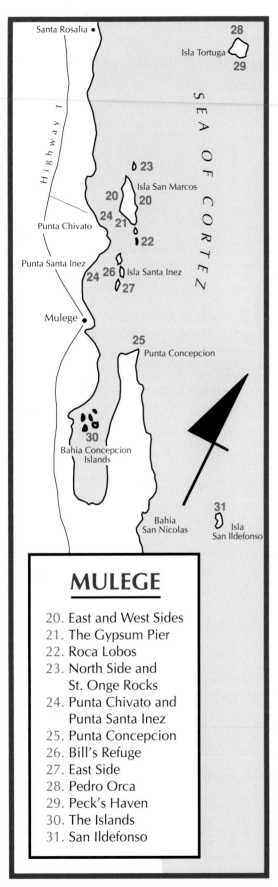

MULEGE

miles (1.1 km) past the Rio Santa Rosalia bridge on Highway 1. Go left at the RV park sign. This ramp is not usable, nor is the river navigable at low tide. Check in at the park office before launching.

Oasis Rio Baja ramp is 1.2 miles (1.9 km) past the Rio Santa Rosalia bridge. Made of large flat rocks set in concrete, the 14-foot-wide (4.2 m) ramp has good traction.

The **Hotel Serenidad ramp** is 9 feet (2.7 m) wide and made of rough concrete. Stay to port side when launching as there is a hole at the bottom of the ramp. It is located .5 miles (.8 km) on the south side of the Rio Santa Rosalia after the turnoff from Highway 1, which is 2.1 miles (3.4 km) south of the Mulege bridge.

PUNTA CHIVATO

Punta Chivato is part of the surrounding area of Mulege. South of the town of Santa Rosalia and north of the town of Mulege on Highway 1, there is a dirt road turnoff going to Punta Chivato. The road is a 13-mile (21 km) sandy, rocky washboard. At the end of the road will be the very nice **Hotel Punta Chivato** which overlooks the Sea of Cortez. The rooms are large and clean, and there is a restaurant, bar and pool. There is also an airstrip for small planes.

There are no diving facilities here, but if you are equipped with your own gear, pangas are available for rent. Approximately one-half mile (.8 km) south of the hotel along the coastline is some of the best fossil hunting in Baja. Look along the cliffs—they're loaded! Also, shell collecting is excellent along the empty beaches.

If you have your own boat, there is a 17-foot-wide (5.2 m) rock-concrete launch ramp at the hotel. The ramp can handle most boats.

Punta Chivato is much closer than Mulege for diving San Marcos Island and the Santa Inez Islands.

Camping is available a mile (1.6 km) north of the hotel on a white sandy beach. There are outhouses and running water nearby.

DIVING FACILITIES

Mulege Divers is a full-service dive shop, equipped with scuba equipment, boats and a compressor. Located in Mulege at Madero #45 (on the main street near the church), they

Baja's coastline is dotted with seasonal fishing camps. Many areas are so remote that the fishermen live here throughout a season, while boats come to collect their catch.

THE CHURCH OF SANTA ROSALIA

The church of Santa Rosalia has an interesting story. Just exactly how it got there is still a mystery. Alexandre Eiffel, who also designed the Eiffel Tower in Paris, designed a pre-fabricated church in the late 1800's which consisted of large pieces of sheet metal. The pieces were used as ballast on ships, and could then be removed and assembled. The church was to be displayed at the World Columbian Exposition at Chicago in 1893. Whether it ever made it there is not confirmed. In any case, it ended up in Santa Rosalia. It was the first building to go up in Santa Rosalia which at the time was a tent city.

Today, the small church is in the middle of town and is used regularly for services.

usually do half-day trips to the Santa Inez Islands or to Pt. Concepcion.

DIVING

The diving areas surrounding Mulege consist of the northernmost **Isla Tortuga**, well out to sea from Santa Rosalia; **Isla San Marcos** off Punta Chivato; **Isla Santa Inez**, a small group of three islands a few miles further south; islands in the **Bahia de Concepcion** and **Punta Concepcion**; and **San Ildefonso Island** over 25 miles (40 km) to the south. Most of the area has low-lying reefs made up of angular boulders and rock formations. There are large populations of reef fishes, rays, invertebrates, shellfish, and along the outer rocky points, sea lions. Like many of Baja's offshore islands, they appear to be lonely, desolate outposts, yet the underwater landscape and marine life are in sharp contrast to the land above water.

ISLA SAN MARCOS

Isla San Marcos, 5-1/2 miles (9 km) long and 2 miles (3.2 km) wide, lies 5 miles (8 km) north of Hotel Punta Chivato and a mile (1.6 km) offshore.

20. EAST AND WEST SIDES

DEPTH:	20-60+ FEET
	(6-18+ M)
LEVEL:	NOVICE TO
	EXPERIENCED
ACCESS:	BOAT

The underwater terrain on the east and west sides of the island is similar in appearance. They are dominated by big scattered boulders and rocky outcroppings. Beginning in about 20 feet (6 m) of water, the boulders spill down a gradual slope into deeper water.

Divers will encounter small drop-offs, ledges and deep cavities. Reef fishes are in abundance on both sides. Large, odd-looking bumphead parrotfish and bright green-and-orange azure parrotfish can be found among the boulders' passageways.

Crevices and holes are home to the green moray eel, along with striped zebra morays and jewel morays dressed in chains of light gold spots ringed by dark brown halos. Black durgons cruise the reef with convict tangs and damselfishes. The multi-colored giant hawkfish which grows to over 18 inches (46 cm) hover beneath the craggy edges, using its mottled coloration as camouflage.

Invertebrates seem to glide effortlessly over the hard substrate. Red gulf and chocolate chip sea stars feed on algae growth while spiny oysters latch tightly onto coral branches. The entire perimeter of the island is a good area for fish photography.

21. THE GYPSUM PIER

DEPTH:	10-40 FEET
	(3-12 M)
LEVEL:	NOVICE TO
	EXPERIENCED
ACCESS:	BOAT

There is a small community on San Marcos Island which runs the gypsum-mining operation. The pier where the gypsum is loaded into boats is located on the southwest side of the island, and is 290 feet (88 m) long. The huge, dark pilings frame an incredible underwater setting. Literally thousands of fishes find refuge in this shadowy artificial forest. Schools of cortez chubs, zebra perch, sergeant majors, jacks and cortez angelfish are so thick, they actually block out almost all sunlight.

Incredible Night Dive. Night diving on this pier is equally incredible. There is not one inch on the pilings that is not moving with life. Brightly hued anemones are opened up, clusters of golden coral cups are flared out to feed and a variety of purple, gold, blue, white and yellow nudibranchs are everywhere.

The bottom at 40 feet (12 m) is covered with broken pilings and hunks of metal where creatures have found refuge. Octopuses, morays, slipper lobster and an array of invertebrates make their homes here. The large 6-inch (15 cm) pink warty sea slug can be found at night under the blanket of pilings. This pier is an excellent spot for close-up and macro photography.

The San Marcos pier is located on the southwest side of Isla San Marcos. The small community that lives on the island mines gypsum. When no boats are loading gypsum, this 290-foot-long (88 m) pier is a good spot to dive.

These red epizoanthids are usually covered with sand or mud. They are often found on rocky reefs and rubble substrates, encrusting gorgonian stalks or covering rock surfaces. Here they are growing over the shell of an oyster. Opening at night to feed, they make colorful subjects for photographers.

22. ROCA LOBOS (S)

DEPTH:	18-50 FEET (6-15 M)
LEVEL:	NOVICE TO EXPERIENCED
ACCESS:	BOAT

Roca Lobos is a rock a few hundred yards off the southern tip of Isla San Marcos that rises 20 feet (6 m) above the sea. The reef and shoals here are very wide, and in some places as shallow as 6 feet (2 m) in spots. There is plenty of fish life among the jagged reef formations. Shellfish such as tiger paw scallops and chocolate clams are quite prominent. A local man told us that he had found pewter plates here in the 1950's while free-diving.

Caution. Boats need to be very careful when approaching this area because of the many shallow rocks.

23. NORTH SIDE AND ST. ONGE ROCKS

DEPTH:	30-80 FEET
	(9-24 M)
LEVEL:	INTERMEDIATE TO
	EXPERIENCED
ACCESS:	BOAT

The north end of Isla San Marcos offers good diving and snorkeling. Prominent rocky points with numerous detached rock formations characterize the shoreline. Depths start at about 30 feet (9 m), dropping to between 60 and 80 feet (18-24 m) close to the points. On the northeast side, a group of rocks known as St. Onge Rocks sit clustered together. Sea lions fill the air with their barking, while in swift silence their brethren barrel underwater around the reef. The rocks are filled with gorgonians and sea fans. Grouper, pargo and cabrilla hang out on these offshore rock groupings along with a wide variety of reef fishes.

Caution. Currents can become strong in between these rocks. If the surface water shows a rippling pattern, it is best to choose another dive site.

Shore Points

24. PUNTA CHIVATO AND PUNTA SANTA INEZ (S)

DEPTH:	5-50 FEET
	(2-15 M)
LEVEL:	NOVICE TO
	EXPERIENCED
ACCESS:	SHORE

Approximately 10 miles (16 km) north of Mulege are two points jutting from Baja's mainland. One is Punta Santa Inez, and the other is Punta Chivato which is one mile (1.6 km) to the north. Punta Chivato lies directly in front of the Hotel Punta Chivato. Depths here range from 6 to 20 feet (2-6 m), and the

bottom is a rock jungle abundant with shellfish and small reef fishes. This is a good area for snorkeling.

Punta Santa Inez can be reached by boat or by dirt road from the Hotel Punta Chivato. The underwater reef system here extends several hundred yards directly offshore. The reef is surrounded by a sandy bottom where depths start at about 10 feet (3 m) gradually descending to 50 feet (15 m). Colorful gardens of hard corals, sponges and sea fans dot the reef. Schools of tangs and sergeant majors glide over the maze of rocks while parrotfishes, puffers and triggerfishes are seen solo. Little fish such as the yellow- and red-striped rainbow wrasse, the checkerboard-patterned longnose hawkfish and the largemouth blenny swim slowly along the tops of rocks, then scurry away in a frantic dash. In the sandy patches, one can find sand anemones, crown of thorns starfish, and huge, two-foot (62 cm) brown sea cucumbers. During the day the many lobster are often betrayed by their antennae protruding from under ledges.

25. PUNTA CONCEPCION (S)

DEPTH:	20-60 FEET
	(6-18 M)
LEVEL:	NOVICE TO
	EXPERIENCED
ACCESS:	BOAT

Punta Concepcion, the east side of the mouth of Bahia Concepcion, is about a 45-minute boat ride from Mulege. The visibility on the point rarely exceeds 50 feet (15 m). There are few currents here. The waters surrounding the point are about 20 feet (6 m) deep, where piles of huge boulders have formed a wall which drops to a sand bottom at 60 feet (18 m).

Large balloonfish swim along the edge of the boulders. The sandy area is cobbled with smaller rocks. Spotted tiger snake eels slither over the granulated floor, living in small round holes in the sand which they enter tail first. Larger green morays hide under boulders while fields of garden eels poke their tiny heads above the sandy bottom, quick to

The spotted sharpnose pufferfish rarely exceeds 3 inches (8 cm). These solitary individuals are found near crevices, caves and under ledges in shallow waters.

withdraw as you approach. Triggerfishes can be found wedged in narrow crevices. Between the boulders in patchy sand spots are holes which are home to the peacock mantis shrimp. Up to 12 inches (31 cm) long, these colorful little crustaceans are very inquisitive and are interesting to observe. They will peek out from their holes, their eyes moving 360° intently watching you. They come out at night, feeding on shrimp and snails. Be careful as they have sharp razor-like appendages.

Other areas outside the Bay of Concepcion offer fine beaches, coves and natural harbors ideal for camping and beachcombing. Many rocks and reefs extend seaward from several prominent points and await exploration.

SANTA INEZ ISLANDS

The Santa Inez Islands are a series of three small low-lying islands that are 7 miles (11 km) northeast of Mulege. The southernmost island is the largest, approximately 1 mile (1.6 km) in length. The other two are somewhat smaller and are separated by shallow patches of submerged rocks.

26. BILL'S REFUGE (S)

DEPTH:	10-70 FEET
	(3-21 M)
LEVEL:	NOVICE TO
	EXPERIENCED
ACCESS:	BOAT

The leeward or western side of these islands, also known as Bill's Refuge, is comprised of a series of sandy alleyways with rocky edges sloping gradually to a depth of 50 feet (15 m) where the bottom levels out to a sandy floor at about 70 feet (21 m). This is a good area to look for flatfish and halibut. This granular environment is also home to the horse conch. This common species is the largest native gastropod. Up to 18 inches (46 cm) long, this conch (mollusk) has a tan shell. The body of the animal is brilliant red with blue spots. Good for macro photography, divers can find a variety of olive snails, nudibranchs and murexes.

57

27. EAST SIDE (S)

DEPTH:	15-70+ FEET
	(5-21+ M)
LEVEL:	NOVICE TO
	EXPERIENCED
ACCESS:	BOAT

The seaward eastern side drops off gradually to a depth of over 70 feet (21 m) near shore. This side lacks protection from prevailing winds, but sea life is more abundant. The rocky crevices are home to grouper, king angelfish, cornetfish and a wide variety of wrasses and damselfishes. In the sandy alleyways it is not uncommon to find bullseye stingrays and angel sharks.

The visibility fluctuates, but in the fall months the water is clearest. Since there are so many shallow spots around these islands, it is an excellent area for snorkeling as well as scuba diving. The Mexican hogfish, a cousin to the California sheepshead, can be identified by the large hump on the head of the male, and two dark stripes on the pink-and-yellow body of the female. Up to 2-1/2 feet (77 cm) long, they are found on the shallow reefs.

ISLA TORTUGA

Tortuga Island is a long way out—about 35 miles (56 km) northeast of Mulege and 22 miles (36 km) northeast of Punta Chivato. It is a relatively small island with some small coves. It is not the place you want to be during bad weather. The visibility usually averages between 75 and 100 feet (23-30 m).

28. PEDRO ORCA

DEPTH:	40-100+ FEET
	(12-30+ M)
LEVEL:	INTERMEDIATE TO
	EXPERIENCED
ACCESS:	BOAT

The northeast end of the island, known as Pedro Orca, has some of the best diving. Here there are layered stairsteps of rock and sand. A layer of rock descends for 25 feet (8 m), then a margin of sand, then another stairstep, repeating itself as it plunges into the depths. Amidst the massive boulders, hundreds of leopard grouper can be seen, many weighing over 50 pounds (23 kg). Other fish usually seen here include the panama graysby, spotted cabrilla, red-eyed mutton hamlet, leather bass and a variety of large parrotfishes. Socorro lobster are also usually plentiful.

29. PECK'S HAVEN

DEPTH:	35-100 FEET
	(11-30 M)
LEVEL:	INTERMEDIATE TO
	EXPERIENCED
ACCESS:	BOAT

On the south end of the island, known as Peck's Haven, a high sheer cliff drops to the water level, but underwater it is very rocky and not quite as sheer. Car-sized boulders sit delicately balanced upon each other. These monolithic formations create a maze of holes like catacombs. Large moray eels protrude agape from their lairs. Most of the angelfishes and other reef fishes are much larger here than in other areas. The tiger paw scallops, also called lion paw, which live in the sand areas average 5-8 inches (13-21 cm) inches across. They are harvested in enormous quantities by commercial divers. Whitetip sharks are sometimes seen off the south end as are lone hammerheads.

Two red hermit crabs venture out of their shell at night to search the reef for bits of food. During the day they usually hide in their shells on the sand or wedge themselves between rocks.

Nudibranchs and sea slugs are found throughout Baja's waters, although in certain areas they are in greater abundance. Pier pilings and jetties are excellent areas to find them. This sea tiger is an impressive predator. Carnivorous on other nudibranchs (including its own species), the sea tiger swallows its prey whole, using large, hook-like radular teeth to pull the prey inside its mouth.

BAY OF CONCEPCION

The Bay of Concepcion (Bahia Concepcion) runs north and south, and is over 22 miles (36 km) in length. Open to the north and sheltered on the east, the bay has a string of sandy beaches along its west side. **Playa Santispac** has restrooms, showers and large umbrella-like huts with palm-thatched roofs and open sides for camping. Following the unpaved road which parallels the highway provides access to other beaches and campsites.

30. THE ISLANDS (S)

DEPTH:	10-60+ FEET
	(3-18+ M)
LEVEL:	NOVICE TO
	EXPERIENCED
ACCESS:	BOAT

There are half a dozen or so small islands in the bay. A couple of them lie within swimming distance from shore, but most are only accessible by boat. Winds can kick up in the afternoons so it's best to plan your dives in the morning.

The water around the islands is relatively shallow, ranging from 10 to 50 feet (13-15 m), and is good for snorkeling. In some areas the bottom only slopes gradually eventually reaching a maximum depth of 120 feet (36 m).

The bay is noted for its abundance of pink-and-black murex shells. Also to be found are colorful sponges, anemones, sea stars, nudibranchs and reef fishes. Shellfish include rock scallops, pen shells, spiny oysters and other mollusks which thrive along the sandy bottom. The visibility is usually fairly limited in the bay, but more than adequate to enjoy these sights.

The flower urchin has the appearance of being covered with flowers or bows. They are commonly found with little pieces of shells attached to their bodies. This is thought to be a way of camouflaging themselves to look like part of the reef.

ISLA SAN ILDEFONSO

31. ISLA SAN ILDEFONSO

DEPTH:	30-100+ FEET
	(9-30+ M)
LEVEL:	EXPERIENCED
ACCESS:	BOAT

The island of San Ildefonso is located between Mulege and Loreto, approximately 25 miles (40 km) south of Punta Concepcion by sea, and 9 miles (15 km) offshore from San Nicolas Bay. This low-lying island, 1-1/2 miles (2.4 km) long and barren, is surrounded by a steep and rocky shoreline. The jagged lava cliffs are inhabited by a menagerie of bird life.

There is a large reef 150 yards (136 m) off the southwest point. Big rock formations and steep pinnacles frame the island, dropping to depths of over 100 feet (30 m). The rock walls are lined with fissures to explore. On the west side of the island is a large sea lion colony which always makes for a wonderful dive. On the north end there is a cluster of offshore rocks. The latter can yield great photographs.

The radiant colors of the moorish idols, rainbow wrasses, butterflyfishes, juvenile angelfishes and the redtail triggerfish which is seldom-seen this far north, create a world of color. Larger fishes such as grouper, snapper, bonito and jacks are likely to be seen here. The island of San Ildefonso is still largely unexplored by scuba divers.

Caution. Heavy currents can pick up around this entire area.

CHAPTER VIII LORETO

AT A GLANCE

This town of 10,000 was once the first European settlement in the Californias and served as the capital for 132 years for a territory that extended as far north as San Francisco. After a hurricane in 1829, Loreto all but vanished for three-quarters of a century. Since the completion of Highway 1, Loreto is being discovered by vacationers, sport fishermen and divers who are drawn to the quiet beauty of this serene area. It is part of the 17-mile (27 km) coast that includes Nopolo and Puerto de Loreto (formerly Puerto Escondido).

With a panoramic view of incredible angular, jutting mountain peaks of the Sierra Giganta mountain range which surrounds the area, Loreto and its adjoining communities lay nestled along this island-studded, aqua-blue coastline.

GETTING THERE

There are non-stop daily flights from Los Angeles, Tijuana and La Paz on Aero California.

WHERE TO STAY

There are several good hotels along the waterfront in Loreto. The **Hotel Oasis**, which has nice large rooms with board, the **Hotel Mision de Loreto**, and the **Hotel Pinta** all have clean rooms with views. They also have a restaurant, bar and pool.

Away from the waterfront is the **Hotel Salvatierra**. It is less expensive and has clean rooms with showers, but little else in the way of amenities. The **Plaza Loreto Hotel** is downtown, and has nice new rooms, a restaurant and an outdoor bar. Also in town is a very good restaurant called **Cesar's**.

Nopolo is 4 miles (6.5 km) south of Loreto. The only hotel there is the **Loreto Inn** (formerly the Stouffer Presidente). It has all the amenities of an international hotel and sits on well-kept, palm-shaded grounds overlooking the Sea of Cortez. There is a beautiful golf course beside it.

Puerto de Loreto (formerly Puerto Escondido) is 15 miles (24 km) south of Loreto. It overlooks a beautiful bay with a marina. Presently there is only the **Tripui Motel** which has nice but small rooms.

CAMPING

One mile (1.6 km) south of Loreto via Calle Madero is the **Loremar RV Park**. It has full hookups, tent sites, showers, laundry service and large umbrella-like thatched-roof huts with open sides along the water. In the same area is **Las Palmas RV Park** with similar accommodations. North of Juncalito toward Nopolo, there is camping on the beach for free. At the **Tripui Motel** there is a trailer park with hookups, showers and a store.

LAUNCH RAMPS

From the town of Loreto, turn left on the Malecon; go .3 miles (.5 km) to get to the **Malecon ramp**. The 28-foot-wide (8.5 m) ramp is concrete, and has good traction.

Las Palmas RV Park has a 16-foot-wide (4.8 m) ramp with a concrete rock surface. In town stay to the right of the traffic circle, pass the gas station, and continue .6 miles (1 km).

Colonial cup corals can usually be found on the undersides of ledges and overhangs. In the daytime they are closed, but at night the reef can appear like a golden wall when they open to feed.

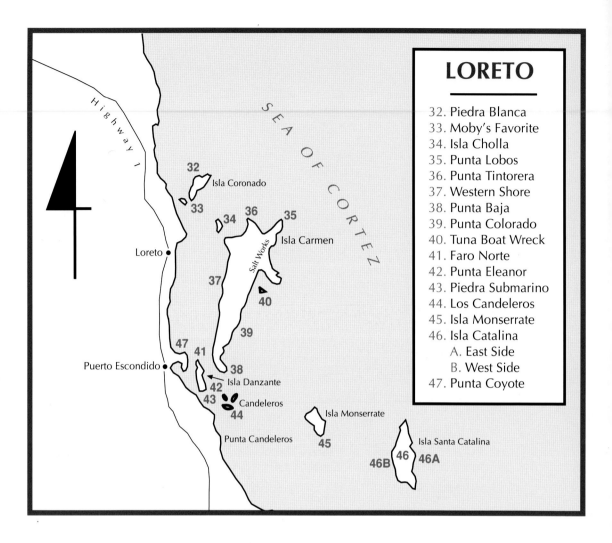

LORETO

32. Piedra Blanca
33. Moby's Favorite
34. Isla Cholla
35. Punta Lobos
36. Punta Tintorera
37. Western Shore
38. Punta Baja
39. Punta Colorado
40. Tuna Boat Wreck
41. Faro Norte
42. Punta Eleanor
43. Piedra Submarino
44. Los Candeleros
45. Isla Monserrate
46. Isla Catalina
   A. East Side
   B. West Side
47. Punta Coyote

Turn right on the dirt road with the RV sign and go .7 miles (1.1 km).

Marina de Puerto Loreto is located in Puerto de Loreto (formerly Puerto Escondido). Fifteen miles (24 km) south of Loreto, turn left at the sign for **Tripui RV Park**. Go 1.4 miles (2.3 km) and turn into the dirt parking lot. The ramp is 33 feet wide (10 m), made of concrete and has good traction.

DIVING FACILITIES

Arturo's Sports Fishing Fleet is located on Hidalgo Blvd. in downtown Loreto. It is a full-service diving operation with some rental equipment, a compressor and a fleet of 22 panga boats. There is also a small fishing store in the town of Loreto on Miguel Hidalgo Street named **Deportes Blazer**. They also rent tanks and weights, and have a compressor.

A dive operation also works out of the Loreto Inn, 4 miles (6.5 km) south of Loreto, in Napolo.

DIVING

The diving area around Loreto comprises five islands: **Isla Coronado**, 1-1/2 miles (2.4 km) offshore, 6 miles (10 km) north of Loreto; **Isla Carmen**, 8 miles (13 km) east of Loreto; **Isla Danzante**, approximately 14 miles (23 km) south of Loreto and a few miles offshore from Puerto de Loreto (formerly Puerto Escondido); and farther offshore are **Isla Monserrate** and **Isla Catalina**. The islands have quite a diversity of diving including shallow rocky bottoms, walls with deep canyons, a wreck site, and reef systems. All are teeming with colorful marine life. There are many pristine white sand beaches where one can relax and have a picnic.

Water clarity ranges from 50 to 100 feet (15-

Scorpionfish are so well camouflaged that they are often mistaken for part of the reef. They usually will not move unless disturbed. Their dorsal spines can inflict painful wounds that often become infected.

30 m). The late summer and fall months bring in warmer water, around 80°F (27°C). Besides the local species of tropical fishes, some seasonal game fish frequent these waters, the most common being jacks, yellowtail, roosterfish and snapper. In the fall months the large humboldt squid pass through the channel between Isla Carmen and Isla Danzante as they migrate to shallower waters to lay their eggs and mate.

ISLA CORONADO

The island of Coronado has some incredible-looking formations. Huge volcanic rocks cover the island, many of which have been formed into majestic pillars and steeples.

32. PIEDRA BLANCA

DEPTH:	35-100+ FEET
	(11-30+ M)
LEVEL:	INTERMEDIATE TO
	EXPERIENCED
ACCESS:	BOAT

The north end, known as Piedra Blanca or White Rock, is a great dive spot. The current can get quite strong here so the pangas follow divers as they drift along the reef.

Depths begin at 35 feet (11 m) where

massive boulders appear to have toppled like dominoes down the declining wall. The underwater terrain is as exquisitely sculptured as the formations on the island itself.

At 60 feet (18 m) a steep drop-off starts, continuing down into the depths. This wall is fractured with deep slices and wide fissures, along with drooping overhangs. Purple gorgonian sea fans sporadically dot the wall. Clumps of black coral bushes can be seen as shallow as 60 feet (18 m), but grow more profusely in deeper water where at 150 feet (45 m) the bottom is covered. Rock scallops are scattered in clumps across the ledges along with a variety of invertebrates. Schools of triggerfishes are plentiful at this end, as are the big bumphead parrotfish. Divers can find pufferfish hovering within rocky channels, or resting on the sandy channel bottoms.

This entire drift dive offers a great variety of marine life and unusual-looking terrain. Expect to see schooling tuna and yellowtail.

33. MOBY'S FAVORITE (S)

DEPTH:	20-80 FEET
	(6-24 M)
LEVEL:	NOVICE TO
	EXPERIENCED
ACCESS:	BOAT

At the south end of Coronado Island is a site sometimes referred to as Moby's Favorite. It is made up of a sandy bottom dotted with rocky outcroppings. A jumble of good-sized boulders create a refuge for fish and moray eels. There is usually a slight current, so the pangas follow the divers. Southwest of the point, a reef extends out to where monolithic rocks overlap each other down a gradual slope. There are small grottos throughout the rocks which

A hermit crab forages around the reef at night.

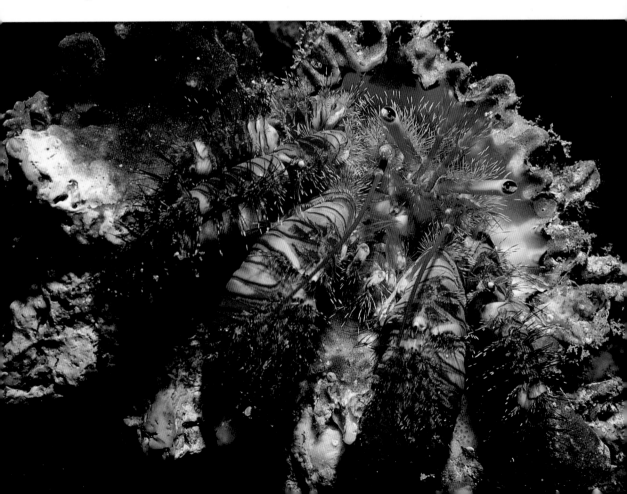

These reddish, bicolor parrotfish are found throughout the reefs of the Sea of Cortez. At night, they can be seen sleeping under ledges.

harbor octopuses, lobster and reef fishes such as Mexican hogfish, hawkfish, damselfishes and angelfishes.

On the east side near the south end is a nice cove for snorkeling and swimming. The shallow sandy bottom is a great spot to collect chocolate clams which can be found just under the sand.

ISLA CHOLLA

This small islet is south of Isla Coronado just off the northeast part of Isla Carmen.

34. ISLA CHOLLA (S)

DEPTH:	15-60+ FEET
	(5-18+ M)
LEVEL:	NOVICE TO
	EXPERIENCED
ACCESS:	BOAT

Depths are quite shallow, then drop to 60 feet (18 m) where a sloping rock and sand bottom meander down into deeper water. Diving around this small islet is excellent. There is a great diversity of marine life. Colorful tropicals inhabit the area.

ISLA CARMEN

Isla Carmen is one of the largest islands in the Sea of Cortez. It is over 18 miles (29 km) in length and once had a large salt mining operation. It sits 8 miles (13 km) east of Loreto, and is surrounded by protected bays and coves. There are some very good diving areas around the points. The island is characterized by steep rocky bluffs with a number of large detached rocks around the points.

35. PUNTA LOBOS

DEPTH:	20-60 FEET
	(6-18 M)
LEVEL:	NOVICE TO
	EXPERIENCED
ACCESS:	BOAT

At the far north tip of the island is Punta Lobos which has good diving whether the winds are coming from the southeast or northwest. When it is too rough on one side of the point, you can often dive the other side, although there can be some surge. The depth begins at 20 feet (6 m), works its way down to an intermediate slope to 60 feet (18 m), then gradually moves deeper.

This entire area is excellent for seeing large grouper, bass and parrotfishes. It is sometimes difficult to see the mottled scorpionfish that lie very still around the rocks, but sudden movement quickly jolts their instincts to move. They are great subjects for photographers because they are easy to approach, but because of their poisonous spines they should not be approached too closely. Some people call this spot moray city because divers can see moray eels in and around all the grottos and fissures. You can find a little hard coral at 40 to 50 feet (12-15 m).

36. PUNTA TINTORERA (S)

DEPTH:	15-60+ FEET (5-18+ M)
LEVEL:	NOVICE TO EXPERIENCED
ACCESS:	BOAT

Punta Tintorera is located on the northwest side of Isla Carmen. Starting at 15 feet (5 m), gigantic boulders make up the shallow reef while smaller rocks are nestled on the bottom at depths beyond 60 feet (18 m). Throughout this rocky reef are chiseled passageways of sand and coralline algae. Along the tops of and in cavities cut in the rocks, look for patches of purple. Swimming back and forth over them will be a sergeant major. The purple patches are eggs. Oddly enough, it is the male fish that guards the nest from predators. Goatfishes and triggerfishes are seen in abundance. Moray eels ranging from 6 inches (15 cm) to 6 feet (2 m) can be spotted moving about beneath the protruding shelves.

On the sandy bottom there will be what looks like little craters in the sand. These are the nests of triggerfishes where they fan out a hole with their fins, then lay eggs. At certain times they perform quite a dance ritual over these craters.

37. WESTERN SHORE

DEPTH:	15-100 FEET (5-30 M)
LEVEL:	NOVICE
ACCESS:	BOAT

If you continue to the south by boat down Carmen's shoreline, you will come to some fantastic lava cliffs. Caves have been carved into the cliffs by eons of wind and water action. Sun-dappled reflections from the water flicker and dance on the cave walls. The massive cliffs continue down underwater almost vertically to about 100 feet (30 m). The walls are sprinkled with red and purple gorgonians, as well as yellow and brown sea fans. Grouper, pargo and scrawled filefish, along with an array of other marine critters, can be found around the sculpted crevices. Diving conditions are almost always good due to protection from southerly winds.

38. PUNTA BAJA (S)

DEPTH:	15-50 FEET (5-15 M)
LEVEL:	NOVICE TO EXPERIENCED
ACCESS:	BOAT

This site is located at the southern tip of Isla Carmen. The average depth is 30 feet (19 m), and the sea floor stays shallow for a distance from shore. The granite rocks are filled with cracks and cubby holes. The water is usually quite clear as there is not much sediment, and it is filled with a diverse variety of marine life. Don't overlook the seemingly barren sand bottom. Particularly interesting to watch is the Pacific razorfish, a little wrasse about 10 inches (26 cm) long. When approached, it will actually dart head first into the sand, totally disappearing from sight. Several species of flatfish, including halibut, linger in the sand mounds along with stingrays. Invertebrates such as flower urchins, sand anemones and the feathery sea pen are common here.

Caution. Currents can pick up and sweep around the point, so exercise caution.

A school of barberfish have discovered a triggerfish nest with eggs. Here at 100 feet (30 m), they are swarming the nest which looks like a small crater in the sand, and eating the eggs.

The abandoned town of Bahia Salina is on the east side of Carmen Island. This is where the salt mine used to be and a large salt pond is beyond the bay. It is believed that fishermen from seasonal camps may still come here to worship in the tiny chapel that remains intact.

Inside the 120-foot-long (36 m) wreck at Bahia Salina lives a moray eel. This artificial habitat is a haven for a variety of fishes.

39. PUNTA COLORADO (S)

DEPTH:	35-60+ FEET
	(11-18+ M)
LEVEL:	NOVICE TO
	EXPERIENCED
ACCESS:	BOAT

This point is on the east side towards the south end of Isla Carmen. At an average depth of 35 feet (11 m) is a reef system which runs parallel to the shoreline. Of volcanic origin, the reef is full of short crevices. Lobster can be found in the rock cavities along with a variety of other reef dwellers. This shallow area is also an excellent spot for snorkeling.

40. TUNA BOAT WRECK

DEPTH:	35 FEET
	(11 M)
LEVEL:	INTERMEDIATE TO
	EXPERIENCED
ACCESS:	BOAT

On the east side of Isla Carmen is a large bay named Bahia Salina. This is where the salt-making operation used to be, and you can still see the large salt pond beyond the bay. In 1985, the small town of Bahia Salina was abandoned when salt-making ceased to be profitable. But it has the appearances of having been abandoned abruptly. A couple of stray dogs roam the ruins. Doors squeak open and close, then slam in the wind. The schoolhouse has worm-eaten books toppled across dusty desks, and old beds sit with stuffings exposed. Salt carts are silent on their tracks beside a rusty beached shipwreck. But most fascinating is that the little church is still intact. From the gold-leaf madonna still set behind glass to the nativity set standing on a table, it is almost as if the little church is just waiting for its congregation to come back. The bell over the church is now quiet, but when you walk through this unique setting, your head rings out the theme song to "The Good, The Bad and The Ugly."

As interesting as the abandoned town is, the highlight for divers lies about a half mile (.8 km) outside the bay. Here the remains of a 120-foot (36 m) Mexican fishing boat, once part of the Ensenada tuna fleet, poke above the water. The ship went down in 1981 when a butane tank blew up, and the ship caught fire and sank. She now lies in 35 feet (11 m) of water on her port side. The stability of the wreck is questionable, so be wary of penetrating it.

For photography, however, this wreck is sensational. Sunlight streaks through the openings of the wreckage, exposing parts inside. Thousands of fish linger about its skeletal frame. Schools of barracuda, angelfishes, snapper, trumpetfish, grunts and jacks move through the sunlight like glittery sheets. The visibility is only about 30 feet (9 m) as the wreckage sits on a silty sand bottom which gets kicked up by currents and surge. There are parts of the wreck that even have some small black coral growing on it. The glass windows are still intact, but radio gear and other wreckage lie strewn across the sandy floor.

ISLA DANZANTE

This small island is located off the southwest side of Isla Carmen, 2-1/2 miles (4 km) offshore of Puerto Escondido. The shore on the north end of the island is characterized by steep rocky points.

41. FARO NORTE

DEPTH:	15-100+ FEET
	(5-30+ M)
LEVEL:	NOVICE TO
	EXPERIENCED
ACCESS:	BOAT

Faro Norte is located on the northeast side of Isla Danzante. The underwater terrain is a series of short walls that eventually drop to over 100 feet (30 m). There are deep canyons and crevices lined with hard and soft corals, and below the 50-foot (15 m) depth are a lot of black coral. The short walls start as shallow as 15 feet (5 m), and are made up of heavy block-like boulders which make wonderful homes for marine life. Local reef fishes can be found throughout the area and octopuses are seen quite often here.

42. PUNTA ELEANOR (S)

DEPTH:	15-60+ FEET
	(5-18+ M)
LEVEL:	NOVICE TO
	EXPERIENCED
ACCESS:	BOAT

Punta Eleanor is located on the east side towards the middle of Isla Danzante. There are a number of places on this point to dive. Shallow diving around 20 feet (6 m) is interesting as there is a good variety of reef fishes swimming throughout the rocky terrain. The white sandy areas seem to attract an ample number of parrotfishes. There is usually a current here, so this is often a drift dive at around 60 feet (18 m) while the pangas follow. The reef which extends off the southeastern point shoots to deeper depths with sheer vertical walls. Use a dive light even in the daytime to really bring out the colors, especially of marine life hidden back in the deep crevices.

43. PIEDRA SUBMARINO (S)

DEPTH:	15-100 FEET
	(5-30 M)
LEVEL:	NOVICE TO
	EXPERIENCED
ACCESS:	BOAT

From a distance Piedra Submarino (Submarine Rock) looks like a submarine. Located off the south tip of Isla Danzante, this monolithic structure is made up of short walls with intervening crevices running back into the

rocks. The shallow slope begins on a reef in 15 feet (5 m) of water and extends southwards towards Candeleros. The west side of this giant rock formation drops off quickly. The surrounding area is great for exploring, as the ledges and undercuts provide a habitat for colorful murex snails. Sea stars, such as the purple star and the yellow-spotted star, are also found here as are octopuses, rock scallops and an occasional lobster.

44. LOS CANDELEROS

DEPTH:	40-80+ FEET
	(12-24 M)
LEVEL:	INTERMEDIATE TO
	EXPERIENCED
ACCESS:	BOAT

Los Candeleros (The Candlesticks) is named for three large rock pinnacles which lie between the south tip of Isla Danzante and Punta Candeleros on Baja's mainland. Sitting several hundred yards from each other, these pinnacles are visible from Puerto Loreto (formerly Puerto Escondido). They look like gigantic granite steeples, rising from the depths. The peak on the north side is called **Islotes Colorado** and is so loaded with sea stars that the water has the odor of iodine, a chemical they release. The second pinnacle is called **Islotes Tijeras**, referring to the scissor tail of the prehistoric-looking frigate bird. This area is part of their nesting grounds. The third pinnacle is known as **Islotes Pardo**, referring to its dark color and plunging depths.

The shallower areas around the pinnacles are made up of short walls and clumps of rocks. Numerous submerged large boulders lie close to the shore while larger jutting boulders loom upwards from the depths. Marine life is prolific around these submarine cathedrals. The drop-offs and drooping ledges are also quite dramatic and make for excellent photographs.

The middle pinnacle is connected to a smaller rock formation off the northwest side by a shallow channel. This spot is good for snorkeling. Large game fishes, including grouper and yellowtail, are common around the pinnacles especially in deeper water. The Candeleros are really recommended for those with deep-water experience.

45. ISLA MONSERRATE

DEPTH:	20-100+ FEET (6-30+ M)
LEVEL:	NOVICE TO EXPERIENCED
ACCESS:	BOAT

The island of Monserrate is located 8 miles (13 km) from Baja's nearest mainland point. The island is a low-lying volcanic land mass that appears barren. It is 4 miles (6.5 km) long and 2 miles (3.2 km) wide. Around the shoreline the depths are shallow, but drop quickly to deeper water. The southeast side forms a series of finger-like reefs. Sandy, narrow channels intrude throughout the reef fingers. Marine life around Monserrate is typical of that found throughout the Loreto area. This island along with Isla Catalina is quite remote and rarely dived. They are great areas for those coming to Baja with their own long-range boat. But for those that arrive boat-less, trips to these outer islands can be arranged through the dive shop in Nopolo or Arturo's in town.

46. ISLA CATALINA

DEPTH:	20-100+ FEET (6-30+ M)
LEVEL:	NOVICE TO EXPERIENCED
ACCESS:	BOAT

Isla Catalina is very remote, lying 12 miles (19 km) southeast of Isla Monserrate. It is 8 miles (13 km) long and 2 miles (3.3 km) wide.

The **East Side (46A)** of the island is made up of a series of sheer angular cliffs which continue underwater. This is a great area for seeing larger fishes, turtles and occasional single manta rays which linger in the depths.

But be sure to watch for currents as they can pick up.

The **West Side (46B)** is radically different in appearance. Here, there are more protected coves and beaches nestled in the rocky shoreline. The points which encompass the coves are excellent sites for diving, with depths as shallow as 20 feet (6 m). Inside the crevices found on the rock canopies, divers will discover scallops and lobster, large populations of reef fishes, invertebrates and rays, along with schooling mobulas and occasional nurse sharks.

47. PUNTA COYOTE (S)

DEPTH:	15-60+ FEET (5-18+ M)
LEVEL:	NOVICE TO EXPERIENCED
ACCESS:	BOAT

From Bahia de Loreto off the mainland, divers can have a panga drop them off at Punta Coyote. This point is located northward and outside of the bay. With large rocks and boulders that have tumbled down a gentle slope, the diving is not spectacular, but it is good. Gorgonians and sea fans are sprinkled over the reef below 60 feet (18 m). Angelfishes, pufferfish, butterflyfishes and myriad tiny fast-swimming wrasses and damselfishes inhabit the area. This is also a good location for night diving because of its easy accessibility by boat. Darkness brings out the huge, hairy hermit crabs, lobster, free-swimming morays, long-legged arrow crabs and nudibranchs. Brilliantly colored golden cup corals and anemones open to feed.

CHAPTER **IX** LA PAZ

AT A GLANCE

La Paz (The Peace) now lives up to its name after being one of the most violent towns on the peninsula in previous centuries. This was the site of the first Spanish attempt to settle what at that time was believed to be an island called Santa Cruz. The captain of the expedition, Diego Becerra, was murdered by his crew in 1533. Shortly after, the new leader, Fortun Jimenez and twenty-two of his soldiers were killed by the Indians. Spain's most infamous conquistador, Hernan Cortez, himself, led a group of soldiers and colonists to La Paz. Eventually this group returned to the mainland because of the difficulty of resupply.

The first permanent colony was formed in 1811. In 1829 following the big hurricane that damaged Loreto, La Paz was named the capital of the Southern Territory of California.

The prime lure of La Paz were the rich pearl oyster beds. In the 18th century, many of the finest pearls of the royal treasury in Spain came from La Paz. Pearling continued until the 1940's when a mysterious disease destroyed the oyster beds in the Sea of Cortez. The 1950's brought sports fishermen from the United States, and La Paz acquired the reputation of being one of the billfishing capitals of the world. It was commonly visited by North American literati and Hollywood celebrities, and after the completion of Highway 1 the city became a tourist destination for mainland Mexicans. Statehood was bestowed on the Territory of Baja California Sur in 1974 and La Paz, which has over 100,000 residents, was made its capital.

One place worth visiting is the **Museum of Anthropology**, where three floors of exhibits cover the cape region's anthropology from prehistoric to modern times. On display are fossils, minerals, Indian artifacts and maps of rock-painting sites throughout central and southern Baja.

There are restaurants for all tastes and budgets in La Paz, many located along the main waterfront street. The seafood is especially good as are the Mexican-style dishes. There is also a **Carlos'n Charlie's** that has great food.

GETTING THERE

Two international carriers that fly into La Paz are Aero Mexico and Aero California. If coming to La Paz by vehicle, just continue south on Highway 1.

WHERE TO STAY

There are several good hotels to choose from. The **Los Arcos Hotel** is equipped with all the amenities including a television, pool, restaurant and bar. The **Hotel La Posada** is also very nice. Its cottages with fireplaces definitely bring out the cultural atmosphere with a Spanish decor. The **Hotel Perla** is a nice hotel, a little lower-priced, but is air conditioned and has a pool and restaurant. There are several other hotels in town to choose from. They include the **Cabanas de Los Arcos**, the **Club El Moro**, the **Hotel Gran Baja**, and the **La Concha Beach Resort**, all in the medium price range. Lower-priced rooms can be found at the **Hospedaje Mareli**, the **Hotel Acuario's Mar de Cortes**, the **Hotel Gardenias**, and the **Hotel Miramar**.

Sea lions love to frolic and play. They zip around divers, pulling at their snorkels and fins. Occasionally, they just float on the surface, basking in the sun.

CAMPING

There is beach camping north of the Pichilingue ferry terminal at **Playa Pichilingue, Puerto Balandra, Puerto El Tecolote**, and **Puerto El Coyote**. There is no fresh water and all supplies must be brought from La Paz. There are also trailer parks on the west side of town off Highway 1.

LAUNCH RAMPS

When approaching La Paz from the north, you will see a large white dove statue. Keep to the left and you will come to the tourism office on your right. The **Fidepaz ramp** is to the left. The concrete ramp is 30 feet (9 m) wide and has good traction. It is located at the far west end of the La Paz channel down the bay.

To get to the **Marina de La Paz ramp**, go three miles (4.8 km) past the dove statue. Turn left one block before the second stop light and proceed to Marina La Paz. This ramp is 14 feet (4.2 m) wide and also of good concrete.

The two concrete **Pichilingue ramps** are 12 feet (3.6 m) wide. To get there go 10.9 miles (17.6 km) past the Hotel Los Arcos. One-half mile (.8 km) past the ferry terminal turn off the highway and follow the dirt road another half mile (.8 km).

DIVING FACILITIES

A full-service dive shop in downtown La Paz is **Baja Buceo y Servicio** which also has boats for one day charter dives.

Some rentals and a compressor for air fills can be found at **Deportiva La Paz**. They also have boats for one day charters.

Some of the best diving in the Sea of Cortez is off La Paz on the far outer islands and pinnacles which can only be reached by liveaboard boats. Unlimited day dives along with night dives are included on most liveaboards as are tanks, weights, meals and sleeping cabins. **Baja Expeditions** is equipped with two boats: the 80-foot (24 m) *Don Jose*, which comfortably holds 16 divers; and the 72-foot (22 m) schooner, *Copper Sky*, which takes eight divers comfortably. The boats are based out of La Paz, but the bookings go through San Diego. Their itineraries include Isla Los Islotes, El Bajo Seamount, Isla Las Animas, Isla San Diego and the wreck of the *Salvatierra*.

Baja Expeditions also offers one day trips to Isla Los Islotes and the El Bajo Seamounts.

DIVING

The area around La Paz consists of a series of islands, islets and seamounts. None of the islands are really inhabited full time, but there are Mexican fish camps which dot the shorelines of some of the larger islands.

Typically, the undersea terrain is characterized by mammoth pieces of broken granite, jumbled rocks and boulders which form unique-looking structures and winding grottos. Many of the huge reef systems are honeycombed with arches, tunnels and caves. There are steep walls that plummet to sand bottoms and mountain peaks that jut from the sea floor to within 60 feet (18 m) of the surface. There is an exciting mixture of deep-water pelagics along with inshore reef animals.

Water temperatures during the winter and early spring months are in the 65-75°F(18-24°C) range. During the early summer and fall months, temperatures reach a warmer 80-85°F (27-29°C). This period is considered the rainy season, but is also the best time for diving. Occasional hurricanes and tropical storms called *chubascos* can occur usually from June to October.

48. ISLA ESPIRITU SANTO AND ISLA PARTIDA (S)

DEPTH:	20-100+ FEET
	(6-30+ M)
LEVEL:	NOVICE TO
	EXPERIENCED
ACCESS:	BOAT

These islands are located 18 miles (29 km) north of La Paz and together they are about 15 miles (24 km) in length, with Isla Espiritu Santo being much larger. Isla Partida sits just north of Espiritu Santo, and in one small section they are only about 15 feet (5 m) apart.

There are numerous wind-protected coves which line the more protected west sides of both these islands. The rocky reefs around the

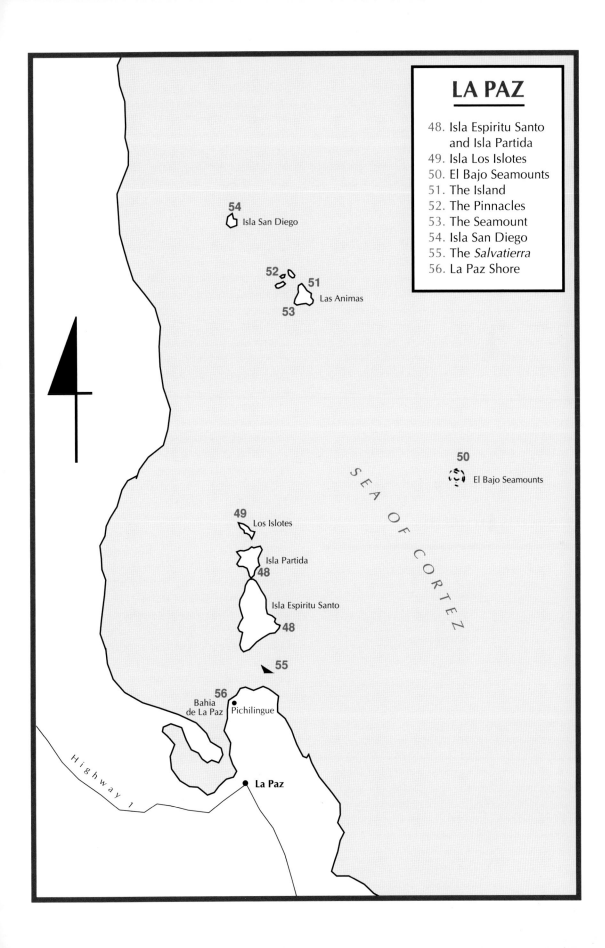

LA PAZ

54
Isla San Diego

52
51
Las Animas
53

50
El Bajo Seamounts

SEA OF CORTEZ

49
Los Islotes

Isla Partida
48

Isla Espiritu Santo
48

55

56
Bahia
de La Paz Pichilingue

Highway 1

La Paz

coves appear barren, but a close inspection will reveal quite a variety of marine life. Snorkeling is good around the west side because of its shallow depths of around 20 feet (6 m).

The best diving areas are located along the north end of Isla Partida and east side of both islands, but they are more affected by weather. The rocky points along the east side have a greater variety of marine life and the drop-offs are deeper. The most eastern point of Espiritu Santo is **Punta Lobos**, which is a rocky bluff that drops quickly to deep water. Around the point, depths of 80 feet (24 m) can be easily reached. A 600-foot (182 m) submarine trench lies about a half mile (.8 km) offshore. The rich nutrients from the deep-water currents provide a constant source of food, which explains the large abundance of marine life. There are over 20 types of commonly-seen, brightly-colored sea stars. The chocolate-chip star looks almost edible. The brilliant pink smooth star and the red cushion star really stand out. Large aggregations of the cushion star are reported in the summer months.

Tropicals such as cornetfish, triggerfishes, parrotfishes, hogfish and grouper are plentiful around the point, so photography is excellent.

49. ISLA LOS ISLOTES (S)

DEPTH:	25-50 FEET
	(8-15 M)
LEVEL:	NOVICE TO
	EXPERIENCED
ACCESS:	BOAT

Located just north of Isla Partida is the small islet of Los Islotes. It is rugged in appearance with awesome-looking angular formations. A tour around the island is a must. California sea lions lie strewn across the sun-dappled rocks, soaking in the warmth. The adolescent sea lions mouth each other in playfulness and courtship. They jump off the rocks, gliding effortlessly through the water.

Underwater these furry marine dogs are the clowns of the sea. The lively antics of these big, brown glassy-eyed goofs is overwhelming. Allowing divers to get very close, they will

somersault and blow bubbles in your face, only to quickly zip away. Inquisitively, they will gently pull at snorkels and fins. During mating season, the big bulls can become aggressive when they are protecting their harems. They will come at divers head-on, occasionally baring teeth and bellowing a loud bark. For an instant, your vision might be full of bubbles. Remember, like all warnings these should be respected so you should back off. Easily recognized, these big males are much larger than the females and have a big bump on their heads. Females choose their mate partially on the quality of the shoreline that the male is defending. The males are greatly out-numbered by their harems of females.

At about 25 feet (8 m) there are beautiful undercuts, small caves and grottos. An ecosystem of colorful soft gorgonians and golden cup corals hang in clusters from the grotto ceilings. This islet seems to rate highly in its great diversity of sea stars, each having a kaleidoscope of colors. There are usually large schools of blue-and-gold king angelfish, yellow surgeonfish, and a large variety of other tropicals especially around the east end.

Usually seen in the shallows around 20 to 25 feet (6-8 m) deep are massive glittering balls consisting of thousands of anchovies. They move along the reef like great waves of glitter. Once in a while the perfect photo opportunity appears when this glittery ball opens up to let a sea lion through.

On the east side of the islet is a huge archway which extends underwater to a depth of 30 feet (9 m). It is an overwhelming area of beauty, as schools of fish and lone sea lions silhouette themselves under this big arch beneath the sun's rays above.

Great Night Dive. This arch tunnel also creates a passageway to get to the other side of the islet, which is equally nice especially for a night dive. The side walls are lined with golden cup corals that are open and feeding, guided by their nocturnal time clocks. Guinea

The chiseled features of Los Islotes make it easily recognizable. Known as the island of the sea lions, here they bask in the sun on the adjoining rocks.

A passageway cuts through Los Islotes and is the best way for divers to visit both sides of the island on the same dive.

79

Coral hawkfish, which are about 3 inches (8 cm) in length, are one of the common small reef fishes.

puffers are found sleeping in crevices along with parrotfishes. Many of the parrotfishes wrap themselves up in a cocoon of mucus which helps protect them from predators by masking their scent. They are easily approached for photos, but be careful—you don't want to wake them. In the morning hours, they eat their way out of this mucus wrapping, abandoning it on the reef. Nudibranchs, anemones, octopus and resting turtles can be found here at night. This island is also an excellent area for snorkeling.

50. EL BAJO SEAMOUNTS

DEPTH:	60-100+ FEET
	(15-30+ M)
LEVEL:	EXPERIENCED
ACCESS:	BOAT

Located east of Isla Espiritu Santo is a group of three submerged pinnacles known as the

seamounts. The tops of these mountain peaks begin at around 50 to 60 feet (15-18 m) below the water's surface, dropping to well over 100 feet (30 m). Manta rays were once abundant here, but due to overfishing they are less readily seen. Still, occasionally they are sighted gliding over the seamounts. Because of the upwelling water from the surrounding depths, this area is a prime location for large pelagic animals.

The middle seamount is the most abundant with life, and also begins in the shallowest depth—60 feet (18 m). There is one small area that begins at 50 feet (15 m), then the rest of the plateau area is between 70 and 80 feet (21-24 m). At the edge of the plateau is the wall which drops to over l00 feet (30+ m). The top of the mount is alive with clumps of coralline algae where hundreds of flower urchins live. At certain times of the year when the current picks up, they come out marching across the rocks releasing sperm and eggs in the current. Once this sex-march is over they rebury themselves in the algae.

The middle mount is also called Moray

Condos because of the great abundance of moray eels. In almost every crevice, a green head will be sticking out. The morays are found doubled and tripled up, many with a large family all living in the same hole. An occasional green sea turtle, along with curtains of fish, surround the seamount's edges. Seen here often are schools of scissortail damselfish, king angelfish and barberfish. In the sandy patches are what appear to resemble small craters where triggerfishes have laid their eggs. Many times, great bunches of barberfish will have the little crater surrounded, swarming in to feed on the eggs.

In the deeper water below 80 feet (24 m) while cruising the perimeter of the seamount, divers frequently see the schooling hammerhead sharks that are almost always present. They are found at different depths depending on the time of year, usually in deep open-water pinnacles throughout the Sea of Cortez. Because of the surrounding upwelling, these prehistoric-looking creatures feed on the pelagic fishes that also are part of this food chain. Other large fishes that are exciting to watch can be found over the seamount and around the deeper ledges, and include tuna, jacks and grouper.

Between dives, try snorkeling over the seamount. Schools of pompano can be seen swimming just under the surface. Tiny 4-inch (10 cm) combed jellyfish drift through the water like some type of little alien as rainbow colors pulsate through their glassy bodies. They are beautiful to watch and make good subjects for photographers. But a few of the most exciting fishes that can occasionally be spotted while snorkeling here are the sleek billfish including marlin, sailfish and swordfish. The exquisite sailfish will open his iridescent blue-spotted sail when he spots you

Arrow crabs are easily spotted at night as they forage for food on the reef. In the daytime, they are found under ledges and overhangs where sunlight is scarce.

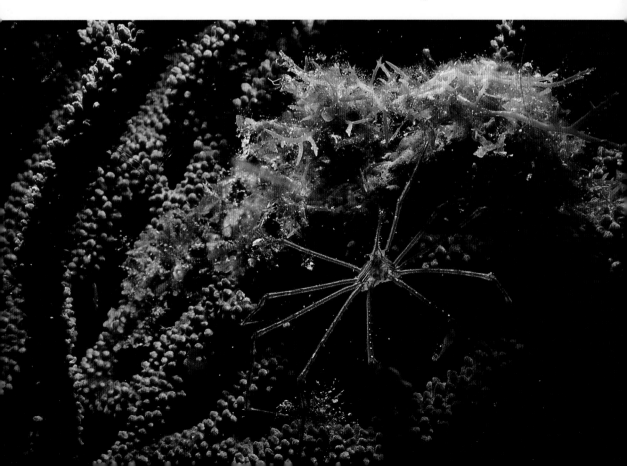

BLUE WATER DIVING

By swimming out into blue water from deep-water pinnacles or seamounts, divers can often see large pelagic animals that are rarely seen on the shallow reefs, such as tuna, swordfish, marlin, sailfish, hammerhead sharks, schools of large jacks, barracuda and jellyfishes. The best way to blue water dive is to have the panga driver follow your bubbles in case the current picks up. Diving the blue water at about 60 feet (18 m) can give divers that "Alice in Wonderland" feeling which can be disorienting. Remember, your buddy is a good reference point and bubbles always float up. Be sure to keep an eye on your depth gauge as it is easy to drop deeper than you plan.

The balloonfish is most easily recognized by the dark bar over the forehead that extends down past the eye, and the long spines on their bodies. They are usually found solo in shallow sandy areas and around rock crevices, but will school in certain areas.

and then fold it down as he realizes that there is no danger. The billfish are very inquisitive and graceful, and it is a magical experience to meet them underwater.

Isla Las Animas

According to local legend, "spirits" have been seen walking on Las Animas, known as the island of the spirits. There is certainly something spiritual about this island because of its phenomenal beauty, and it has three excellent dive spots: the island itself, the pinnacles and the seamount. Las Animas is one of the most exciting and colorful dive spots in the Sea of Cortez.

51. THE ISLAND

DEPTH:	20-100+ FEET
	(6-30+ M)
LEVEL:	INTERMEDIATE TO
	EXPERIENCED
ACCESS:	BOAT

Divers can stay as shallow as about 20 feet (6 m), but the slanting wall drops to over 100 feet (30+ m). Sandy horizontal channels cut into the wall, leading divers to coral-covered overhangs, deep rock cavities and flat, sandy plateaus. Reef fishes and invertebrates are dense in the many crevices. There are usually a number of turtles on the reef structure surrounding the island.

On the northeast side of the island at 80 feet (24 m), there is a large opening to a cave which extends far back into the wall. The walls and ceiling of the cave are filled with golden cup corals, and sometimes turtles are seen here catching a nap on the cave floor. Taking a dive light along to check out the walls of the cave is a good idea, as many fish and invertebrates display incredible colors.

Caution. No cave should ever be deeply penetrated without proper equipment and training. At 60 feet (18 m) on the northwest side of the island is a shallower cave which does not extend back very far. This cave is interesting to explore as a variety of nocturnal creatures can be found, such as lobster, squirrelfish and shrimp.

52. THE PINNACLES

DEPTH:	40-120+ FEET
	(12-36+ M)
LEVEL:	INTERMEDIATE TO
	EXPERIENCED
ACCESS:	BOAT

On the northwest side of the island are three pinnacles which protrude above the surface. The dive starts at about 40 feet (12 m) and drops to over 120 feet (36+ m). On sunny days, rays penetrate between the massive boulders and jagged reef formations. Schools of small scissortail damselfish swim through these sun-dappled areas in swirls of thousands. The scissortail damselfish is characterized by its forked tail and white spot below the soft dorsal fin. They grow to only about 5 inches (13 m), but are found in large numbers around reefs to depths of about 250 feet (76 m).

The walls of the pinnacles slope down in big sculptured steps to deep water. The steps form undercuts, ledges, and a variety of small tunnels large enough for divers to swim through. The tunnels are fringed with purple and orange sea fans. A large variety of fishes are found around the entire perimeter. Some of them are the moorish idol and the beautiful redtail triggerfish whose tail is lined with a brilliant blue border. The latter is also easily recognized by the blue streaks across its golden-colored head. Other fishes seen around the pinnacles are large grouper including the rarely-seen golden grouper, leather bass, cabrilla and Pacific amberjack.

On the outer edges of the pinnacles, it is common to spot cruising hammerhead sharks as well as large pelagics, such as tuna and several species of jacks. By swimming out a distance from the pinnacles at about a depth of 50 to 60 feet (15-18 m), divers commonly encounter massive schools of the big-eyed crevalle jacks. The average size of the jacks is about 50 pounds (23 kg) and they can be so thick that they are layered in the hundreds. At certain times of the year, they are seen in pairs swimming one atop the other. During this courting ritual the male will turn black, and when the mating is over, become silver.

53. THE SEAMOUNT

DEPTH:	45-130+ FEET
	(14-39+ M)
LEVEL:	INTERMEDIATE TO
	EXPERIENCED
ACCESS:	BOAT

The seamount at Las Animas is located off the south side of the island. The top of the seamount is at a depth of 45 feet (14 m) and has a relatively flat plateau covered with colorful sea fans and gorgonians. In between the coral fans are an array of reef fishes. Damselfishes, chromis, longnose hawkfish and chameleon wrasses fill the voids between the corals. Large schools of butterflyfishes and king angelfish seem more prevalent around the seamount than at many other sites. The walls of the seamount are quite steep and drop to depths of over 130 feet (39+ m). Along these deeper ledges, divers can usually find hammerhead sharks at between 80 and 130 feet (24-39 m).

The seamount walls are lined with deep depressions. Tidy nudibranchs inch their way along the encrusting corals and sponges. Scorpionfish use coloring as protective camouflage. As they lie quite still they are easy subjects for the photographer to frame. Many varieties of sea stars are also encountered here and include the chocolate-chip, the orange star, the gulf star, the red-spotted star and the multi-armed crown of thorns.

The seamount is a fantastic spot with great photo opportunities. Just off the wall on the seaward side, large schools of crevalle jacks linger. On this seaward side the currents around the seamount can get extremely strong, so always beware. If the surface water is rippling over the top of the seamount like a little river, it's best to choose another dive spot.

Just south beside the seamount which is out of the current run is the protruding **Sea Lion Rock**. Diving here starts in 5 feet (1.5 m) of water dropping to a 60-foot (18 m) sandy bottom. Sea lions frolic and play all around this rock, doing acrobatics for the cameras.

Large schools of tropicals dart around the rock as if carrying on the sea lions' acrobatic dance. This is also a great spot for snorkeling, as the sea lions will float upside down a few feet beneath the divers, observing the slow, cumbersome humans.

54. ISLA SAN DIEGO (S)

DEPTH:	20-50 FEET
	(6-15 M)
LEVEL:	NOVICE TO
	EXPERIENCED
ACCESS:	BOAT

Isla San Diego has a reef structure off its southwest side known as San Diego Reef, which is a long, low-lying rock reef that breaks the surface. A diver can swim around the entire reef in one dive.

On its south side at a depth of 30 feet (9 m) is a labyrinth of caves and grottos. These honeycombed passageways are great to explore as there is always some sunlight penetrating through the cracks and chimneys above. Cave-dwelling fishes that live in these darker waters have extremely large eyes. Sometimes a hundred or more squirrelfishes, cardinalfish, soldierfish, glasseye and bigeye snappers are found bunched up together under the cave ledges. Shimmering schools of thousands of tiny baitfish swirl around the entrance of the caves, opening to form a circle around divers as they enter. Cornetfish, trumpetfish and cortez angelfish are seen lingering close to the reef, darting in and out of the grottos.

At San Diego Reef, there are many small caves and grottos to swim through. The entrances are often swarming with small bait fish. Within the grottos, squirrelfishes, soldierfishes and glasseyes can be found.

The synapted cucumber has a snake-like body with no tube feet but with long feather-like feeding tentacles. They are only seen at night when the reef and sandy bottom are sometimes covered with them. Their long tentacles are used to forage for food. When fully extended, they are at least 3 feet (1 m) long.

An uncommon fish in the Sea of Cortez is the leopard grouper, but it is frequently spotted solo at San Diego Reef. For some reason the ones here have turned golden, and they are simply referred to as the golden grouper. Small schools of guinea puffers, chubs, grunts and surgeonfish are found clustered around the ends of the reef. Regularly seen around San Diego Reef are great schools of the Pacific crevalle jacks. Photographic opportunities are excellent in these schools as hundreds of pairs of eyes, like polished mirrors, move straight towards the camera lens.

The reef's outer walls are sprinkled with beautifully colored gorgonian corals which grow into the shape of oriental fans. The entire reef is nothing less than a three-tiered world of dramatic shapes and colors.

Incredible Night Dive. Night diving on San Diego Reef is equally incredible. The walls are a brilliant gold, covered with golden cup coral open to feed on tiny planktonic animals drifting in the current. Anemones can be found in groups, transforming long vertical ledges into vibrant, living masterpieces. Nestled within the anemones are fish sleeping for the night. Bright-red shrimps, decorator crabs, arrow crabs and nudibranchs are milling about in search of food. Two interesting little creatures are the decorator crab and the sponge crab. Both carry excess baggage on their backs. The decorator crab plants leafy algae on his entire body, while the little sponge crab places only pieces of sponge on his. At night, divers will often spot them when they see pieces of algae and sponges moving slowly across the rocks.

The sandy bottom literally moves with the 3-foot-long (1 m) synapted cucumbers. There is also a very unique worm called a nemertean worm which only appears at night and has the coloring of a red-banded coral snake. They are remarkably elastic and can stretch several times their body length, some to over 6 feet (2 m). They are predators and have a long proboscis which is thrust out to entangle prey, such as small crustaceans and annelid worms, with a paralyzing mucus.

Southeast of the exposed reef, at a depth of 60 to 75 feet (18-23 m) is a section of the reef seldom visited. When the current is flowing north, divers can venture out by panga for an excellent drift dive.

If the current is flowing south, it is possible to dive a flat sandy area in 20 to 40 feet (6-12 m) of water that houses thousands of garden eels.

These dives are only for divers equipped with compasses.

55. THE *SALVATIERRA*

DEPTH:	60 FEET
	(18 M)
LEVEL:	INTERMEDIATE TO
	EXPERIENCED
ACCESS:	BOAT

In 1975 the old La Paz to Topolobampo ferry, the *Salvatierra*, collided with some rocks and sank in the San Lorenzo Channel at a depth of 60 feet (18 m). The cargo consisted of trucks, many of which were salvaged, but much remains to be seen. The props are still attached to the 300-foot-long (91 m) hull which is largely intact, and has been taken over by reef fishes and large grouper. There are really not many places to penetrate, but there are openings in the wreckage to swim through.

On a clear day, this wreck is sensational.

Some of the largest known specimens of cortez angelfish have made this wreck their home. During the fall months, the beautiful iridescent blue- and yellow-striped juvenile cortez angelfish can be seen frolicking through the jumble. The wreck's skeletal cavities harbor green morays, jewel morays and octopus, along with a variety of soft corals. Occasional manta rays and mobulas have also been sighted gliding over the wreckage.

Cargo remains are strewn about the sandy bottom. Divers who look closely can find bullseye stingrays, round stingrays and halibut camouflaged between the debris.

Caution. Currents can really rip across the wreckage as it is not protected by any reefs. So, remember to make your dives when there is no current.

56. LA PAZ SHORE (S)

DEPTH:	6-30 FEET
	(2-9 M)
LEVEL:	NOVICE
ACCESS:	SHORE

The coves in and around the La Paz area were once the center of much pirate activity. Construction on the main road in the 1970's gave credibility to the old pirate stories when a large chest of valuable silver and coins was discovered by workmen during the excavation.

These coves are good spots for shore diving, but marine life is not nearly as abundant as that found around the offshore islands. There is some good snorkeling and shallow diving along the edges of the coves which reveal tropical fish life, along with invertebrate and shell life. Easy entries are made as there is no surf. Drive 10 miles (16 km) north of La Paz and follow the main road to the ferry landing. Continue north along the waterfront and you will find the large **Bay of Pichilingue**. From here there will be another road that will continue on to **Ballandra Bay** which is also a large bay. There are also several dirt roads which lead to coves. Any of the points off the coves can make for interesting explorations.

CHAPTER **X** EAST CAPE

AT A GLANCE

Located halfway between La Paz and Cabo San Lucas, the East Cape area encompasses the southeast portion of the Baja peninsula. At one time this entire region was frequented by Spanish galleons and ravaging pirates. By the middle 1700's, virtually all the Indian population had died either of European diseases or in fighting with the Spanish. Surviving Indians were moved to the missions farther north, but the cape area and San Jose del Cabo remained an important Spanish military outpost until the mid-19th century when the presidio was turned over to Mexican nationals.

Today, sailboats and private yachts can be found bobbing peacefully in the coves along the coastline. Miles of white sand beaches, rocky reefs and protected coves are only a short distance from the main roads.

GETTING THERE

Alaska Airlines and Mexicana Airlines both fly into Los Cabos. There are also airstrips for small private aircraft at several resorts. By vehicle, there is a turnoff from Highway 1 at Las Cuevas, which leads to the coastline and continues north to Punta Pescadero or south to San Jose del Cabo.

WHERE TO STAY

In between, there are several resorts that offer excellent accommodations and food: the spacious **Rancho Leonero Resort** has a compressor, tanks and boats. The restaurant is considered one of the best on the East Cape. Further north on the point is the **Hotel Buena Vista**, which is very nice and has a restaurant, tennis courts and wind surfing rentals. It also has a boat ramp. Still further north is the **Hotel**

Punta Pescadero, which is also nice with tennis courts, a landing strip, scuba rentals and boats. These resorts are approximately a 45-minute to 1-1/2-hour taxi ride from the airport at Los Cabos. At Los Barriles in between these fine resorts are **Hotel Palmas de Cortez** and **Hotel Spa Buenavista**, which are lower in price.

CAMPING

North of **Rancho Leonero** and just south of Los Barriles is a campground and Pemex gas station.

LAUNCH RAMPS

At the present time there are no concrete launch ramps in this area, so all launching is done over sandy beaches. Inflatables and aluminum boats in the 12- to 15-foot (3.6-4.5 m) range are very popular along the East Cape. Larger boats can be launched at the **Martin Verdugos Trailer Park** at Los Barriles and at the **Playa de Oro RV Resort**. Both **Hotel de Cortez** and **Hotel Spa Buenavista** have launching services.

DIVING FACILITIES

Diving services with boats, tanks and weights are available at both **Rancho Leonero Resort** and **Hotel Punta Pescadero**.

At night, red cleaner shrimp come out to forage. Hidden way back in the rocks during the day, these tiny shrimp can be seen all over the reefs during the night hours. They make for great macro photography subjects.

Also, **Amigos del Mar**, located further south in Cabo San Lucas is equipped with a larger boat and offers day trips to dive the East Cape area of Cabo Pulmo Reef, Gorda Bank and the local shipwrecks.

Pepe's Dive Center is a small dive shop equipped with panga boats, tanks, dive equipment and a compressor. They are located on the waterfront, but if you are driving your own vehicle, it could be hard to find the center. Halfway between San Jose del Cabo and Buena Vista on Highway 1 is the sign for the turnoff to Cabo Pulmo. From the turnoff, take the junction road that reads 30 Kil-La Ribera, about 25 miles (40 km) to where the road makes a "T." Turn right. After 10 miles (16 km) this paved road turns into a dirt road for the next 6 miles (10 km). Follow it south to the water and you'll find Pepe's Dive Center. There are several bungalows with kitchenettes near Pepe's to stay at. There is also a small but very good restaurant called **Estellas** next to the dive center. Pepe's is only open from April to late October.

Cabo Pulmo Divers is another small dive shop located by the water near Pepe's. It is equipped with pangas, tanks, some diving equipment and a compressor.

If you are flying to Los Cabos, a taxi can take you out to Cabo Pulmo, but the cost is about $100 which can be split among your group.

DIVING

Diving along the East Cape can be very exciting. To the south is Cabo Pulmo, where the only living hard coral reef exists in the Sea of Cortez. This coral ecosystem has created a beautiful natural aquarium. The rocky points which protrude from the peninsula offer an underwater terrain of large boulders creating a reef chiseled with narrow passageways and deep crevices.

There is a shipwreck whose remains lay strewn across the sandy floor, acting as a natural habitat for marine life. And there is Gorda Bank which lies further south. At certain times of the year Gorda Bank's deep-water plateau attracts large pelagic fish including whale sharks and hammerhead sharks. The entire East Cape area, with its walls, ledges and reef systems, is teeming with a plethora of colorful marine life, which

makes it a potentially rewarding area for photographers. Water visibility ranges from 60 to 100 feet (18-30 m) depending on the dive site. Clarity is better during the spring months. Water temperatures range from 65°F (18°C) in the early winter months to at least 80°F (27°C) in the late summer. The tides in this region are minimal compared to other areas in the Sea of Cortez.

Rocky reefs which line the shore are excellent for snorkeling. Typical local reef fishes are in abundance as are a variety of shellfish, including the pink murex, spiny oysters, spotted cowries and pen scallops.

57. PUNTA PESCADERO (S)

DEPTH:	25-80+ FEET
	(6-24+ M)
LEVEL:	NOVICE TO
	EXPERIENCED
ACCESS:	BOAT

The point of Pescadero offers some great diving. Large fish such as pargo, porgy, rock croaker, snapper and grouper can be encountered swimming over rocky boulders and through a catacomb of reef formations. The rocky bottom has a 20-foot (6 m) depth with a gradual slope which beckons divers to deeper water. Sandy channels cut through the reef like long fingers. Sitting almost motionless in the water, the Mexican barracuda with its sleek body and large mouth can sometimes be spotted hovering just over the sand. Also sitting practically motionless are the beautifully colored hawkfish, which are easily camouflaged with their maze of wavy blue lines. Lizardfish, with their lizard-like bodies, are common here. They have the habit of resting high up on their pelvic fins.

Around the Pescadero point it is not uncommon to witness small schools of manta-like mobulas swimming over the sand just beyond the rocks. There are literally hundreds of tropicals in this area, including butterflyfishes, triggerfishes, tangs and rainbow wrasse. Don't forget to look in the sandy patches, as sculpin, garden eels, stingrays and angel sharks inhabit this granular environment.

It is a good place to try shooting some challenging photographs.

58. CABO PULMO REEF (S)

DEPTH:	25-60 FEET
	(8-18 M)
LEVEL:	INTERMEDIATE TO
	EXPERIENCED
ACCESS:	BOAT

The four finger-shaped reefs which stretch northeast from Pulmo Bay are known as Cabo Pulmo Reef. This is the only hard coral reef system on the western side of North America. Decorated with coral clusters in hues of green and gold, they are home to myriad reef-dwelling animals and marine vegetation.

Clusters of sea fans in shades of red and purple frame the narrow valleys and ledges. The reef is made up of short walls which drop from 25 feet (8 m) to 60 feet (18 m), where a sand-bottom community dwells. Here are stingrays, snake eels and patches of hundreds of garden eels. The reef has some large angular-shaped boulders that play teeter-totter over each other to form small grottos. The reef actually has the appearance of a fallen freeway overpass with chiseled channels zigzagging throughout.

Almost every type of tropical reef fish can be found on Pulmo Reef. This natural setting has

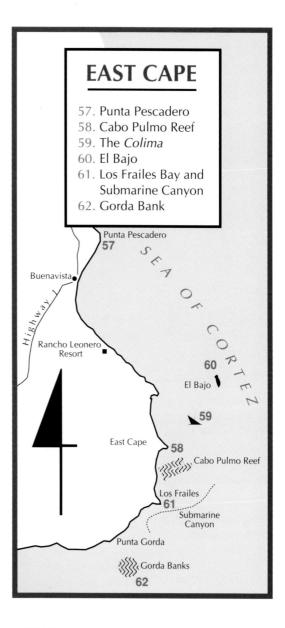

EAST CAPE

57. Punta Pescadero
58. Cabo Pulmo Reef
59. The *Colima*
60. El Bajo
61. Los Frailes Bay and Submarine Canyon
62. Gorda Bank

These blue-and-gold snappers and cortez grunts are shadowed by a trumpetfish.

On the wreck of the Mexican freighter Colima, *divers will encounter large schools of balloonfish. They are found hiding in almost every nook and cranny of the wreckage.*

created an almost aquarium-like environment. Large game fishes are often seen among the outer reef areas, feeding on smaller fishes, while schools of brightly colored tropicals circumnavigate the entire area. The oddly-shaped body of the scrawled filefish, which is covered with blue-green scrawl marks and spots, are found among the coral clusters along with the black durgon, an uncommon triggerfish that can be found at times wedged into tiny rock crevices. Other triggerfishes, such as the blunthead and orangeside, are found in abundance. Also seen here are the large azure parrotfish with green bodies—each scale is outlined with orange and green streaks, and bright colored lines radiate from their eyes.

There is usually a current running across the reef, so Cabo Pulmo is often a drift dive. Winds can pick up in the afternoon, causing waves to break against the shallower reefs, and creating uncomfortable surge and reducing visibility. But even on a bad day,

visibility will usually average around 40 feet (12 m). Pulmo's beautiful montage of reef crests, ledges, deep crevices and drop-offs make this area outstanding.

59. THE *COLIMA*

DEPTH:	50 FEET
	(15 M)
LEVEL:	NOVICE TO
	EXPERIENCED
ACCESS:	BOAT

Approximately 1-1/2 miles (2.4 km) north of Pulmo Point lie the remains of the *Colima*, a large Mexican fishing vessel. The *Colima* hit the point during a storm in 1939 and was carried out to sea. It is now strewn across a sandy sea floor in 50 feet (15 m) of water.

Great masses of fishing net lie in clumps around the wreckage and entangled around the large prop. The rigging and sections of the torn hull harbor hundreds of fishes. This wreck, now an artificial reef, should in fact be renamed "The Puffer Wreck", as almost every square foot of wreckage seems to have slow-moving, glassy-eyed pufferfish in it. They swim over it in schools of 30 or more and can be found in almost every pocket of the wreck.

Also schooling here are elongated trumpetfish. In groups of about 20 or more, they hover over the great balls of fishing net. Schools of goatfishes, each one ranging in the hundreds, linger over the wreck's skeletal remains along with grunts and snapper. Completely surrounding the main part of the dismembered hull are thousands of garden eels. They seem to be much larger and more approachable here than in other locations.

The colorful gray-and-yellow cortez angelfish are usually good models for photographers as they are curious and easy to approach. The juveniles have brilliant gold and deep-blue stripes down their bodies.

This fascinating worm is called a nemertean worm or ribbon worm. They come out only at night and can be found on the reef. Their coloring is very similar to a coral snake and they have been mistaken for sea snakes. Ranging in size from less than an inch to over 12 feet (4 m) in length, they can stretch to over four times their body length. With a long proboscis, they prey on small crustaceans and other worms, using a paralyzing mucus.

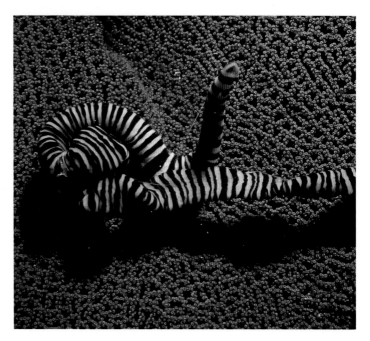

Humpback Whales

Humpback whales first gained widespread public attention when scientists recorded their haunting songs. These complex melodies seem to be unique to each group of humpbacks, though they share certain common threads between groups. Just why they sing is not clear, although most of the vocalizing takes place in or near the mating grounds.

Most of the humpbacks that spend the summer in the Gulf of Alaska migrate to Hawaii in winter. The whales seen in Baja are thought to be part of a population that spends the summer off the coast of central and northern California. The underside of their tail is like the fingerprints of humans—the pattern is different on each of them. In 1900, there were over 100,000 humpback whales. Commercial whaling has reduced that number to about 10,000. The females bear one calf every couple of years, so the humpback's comeback fight will be a long one.

60. EL BAJO (S)

DEPTH:	45 FEET
	(14 M)
LEVEL:	NOVICE TO
	EXPERIENCED
ACCESS:	BOAT

The reef located just northeast of the *Colima* is known as El Bajo. Lying in the middle of a slow-moving current, this reef is a maze of boulders and jagged rocky channels. Brilliant yellow porkfish can be found under ledges, bunched together in groups of dozens. Throughout the reef's long torso are many cortez and king angelfish, chubs, triggerfishes, parrotfishes and massive schools consisting of thousands of goatfishes.

Yellow, purple and red gorgonians cover the rocky terrain, forming an incredibly picturesque setting. This is another area where pufferfish are seen swimming in large groups. The depth of the sandy bottom which outlines the long reef is 45 feet (14 m). There are sandy channels that cut into the reef resembling man-made ditches. Above them are large overhangs that are covered with golden cup coral. Invertebrate life, such as the thick-spined pencil urchins, crown of thorns and sea stars, are grasping tightly inside the cracks. Shellfish are found under overhangs. The beautiful pink-colored murex, spiny oysters, pen scallops and spotted cowries are just a few of the surprises that await divers. The visibility is usually between 60 to 100 feet (18-30 m).

Great Night Dive. El Bajo also makes for a great night dive because the reef is covered with feeding golden cup coral. This area will invariably produce an incredible assortment of nocturnal creatures such as octopuses. Four kinds of lobster are residents of the reef: slipper lobster, blue spiny lobster, socorro lobster and the California spiny lobster. Brightly colored nudibranchs come out of hiding, along with basket stars, red shrimp, and an array of crabs in all sizes and colors. Moray eels can be seen out of their holes hunting for food, and on occasion several small opalescent squid are present.

61. LOS FRAILES BAY AND SUBMARINE CANYON

DEPTH:	15-100+ FEET
	(5-39+ M)
LEVEL:	EXPERIENCED
ACCESS:	BOAT OR SHORE

Los Frailes can be reached by boat or by continuing south about two miles (3.2 km) on the dirt road from Cabo Pulmo. The bay itself is protected from the prevailing northerly winds. The sandy bottom reaches 60 feet (18 m) deep until it converges with a submarine canyon approximately a half mile (.8 km) out from shore. The steep canyon walls plunge to incredible depths. Their sheer sides are naturally carved with spectacular falls of cascading sand.

Divers have seen large grouper, black sea bass, jewfish, tuna, yellowtail, roosterfish, jacks, manta rays and turtles along the canyon walls. Colorful sea fans line the vertical fissures which seem to go on forever.

62. GORDA BANK

DEPTH:	110 FEET
	(33 M)
LEVEL:	EXPERIENCED
ACCESS:	BOAT

Located five miles (8 km) off of Punta Gorda is an underwater seamount which comes to within 110 feet (33 m) of the surface. The top of this huge mountain peak plateau is dotted with black coral bushes. In between these bushes are an abundance of moray eels. During certain times of the year, usually in the late fall, schooling hammerhead sharks are regularly seen here. Depending on the seasons and currents, plenty of action is present in the first few feet of the water column. Whirlpools of jacks, solitary manta rays, large tuna and on occasion sleek marlin have been sighted along with massive whale sharks.

Due to the depth and unpredictable currents, this dive site is recommended for experienced divers only.

A bullseye stingray rests on the sandy bottom. The dark markings on this ray's body form concentric rings appearing like a bullseye. They rarely get larger than 2 feet (62 cm) and can be found on the sand along the outer edges of the reefs.

CHAPTER XI   CABO SAN LUCAS

AT A GLANCE

At the southernmost tip of Mexico's Baja Peninsula is the harbor at San Lucas, which English pirates were known to use as a hiding place from which to attack Manila galleons. Many of the historical incidents ascribed to Cabo San Lucas may actually have taken place near San Jose del Cabo, where ships often took on water from the Rio San Jose.

Today Cabo San Lucas is a tourist hot spot visited by over 250,000 people annually. Manila galleons have since been replaced by private yachts and cruise lines, and sport fishing is a major attraction. The area has good restaurants and hotels amidst an array of gift and native craft stores, and a backdrop of rolling desert mountains and beautiful beaches with warm water.

The main attractions include an underwater nature preserve and the naturally sculptured Land's End rock formations at one end of the bay. With the Pacific Ocean on Cabo's west side and the Sea of Cortez on its east side, Cabo's tropical waters attract sun seekers and watersport enthusiasts of all kinds.

GETTING THERE

The major airlines flying into Los Cabos are Alaska Airlines and Mexicana Airlines. If arriving by vehicle, Cabo San Lucas is the last stop on Highway 1.

WHERE TO STAY

Cabo San Lucas offers a wide variety of hotels and condos in all price ranges. The higher end hotels are the **Hotel Solmar**, the **Finisterra**, the **Hacienda**, the **Giggling Marlin Inn**, the **Aston Terrasol Cabo**, and the **Plaza Las Glorius**, to name a few.

Lower end hotels are the **Los Cabos Inn**, the **Medusa Suites**, the **Hotel Mar de Cortez** and the **Hotel Dos Mares** among others. A good dive shop or travel agent can recommend more.

There is an excellent restaurant for seafood dishes called **The Trailer Park**.

CAMPING

Camping and RV parks are located at **El Faro Viejo Trailer Park** in the northwest section of town, and the **El Marlin Trailer Park** on Boulevard Marina. Just northeast of town off Highway 1 is the **Vagabundos del Mar RV Park**. Also northeast at Km 4 on the south side of Highway 1 is the **Cabo Cielo RV Park**. Beach camping is possible on beaches farther northeast along Highway 1 or northwest along Mexico Highway 19.

LAUNCH RAMPS

To reach the **Cabo Isla Marina ramp**, enter Cabo San Lucas on Highway 1 and go past the gas station half mile (.8 km) to the stop light. The ramp is to your left. It is 40 feet (12 m) wide, made of concrete and has good traction.

There is also a **public ramp** which is 14 feet (4.2 m) wide, made of concrete and has good traction. When entering Cabo San Lucas on Highway 1, turn left one block past the stop light. Follow the road to the small traffic circle and turn left. The ramp is next to the Panga Hotel fleet.

The long slender arms covered with short spines, and the red and tan colors easily identify the sea star. About 8 inches (21 cm) across, these brightly colored stars are found on the shallow reefs.

Pirates of the Sea of Cortez

English privateers left behind a colorful legacy in Baja. In spite of Spain's repeated attempts to colonize the peninsula, the pirates probably gained more wealth in the Californias than the Spanish themselves. For 250 years they plagued the Manila galleons off the coast of the Californias, finding the bays of Baja's Cape Region perfect hideouts.

The most notorious of the Pacific privateers was Sir Thomas Cavendish, whose biggest capture took place at Cabo San Lucas in 1587. After a sea battle, he looted the Spanish galleon *Santa Ana*, sent its crew and passengers ashore, then proceeded to set it on fire. The treasure was divided between his two English vessels, *Desire* and *Content*. The two ships set sail for England, but during the night the *Content* disappeared. Cavendish reported in England that the captain and crew must have taken the ship to a nearby island and disappeared with the loot. Neither the wreckage of the vessel nor the treasure was ever discovered.

Daniel Defoe's Robinson Crusoe was inspired by the famed pirate Woodes Rogers when he landed in La Paz after rescuing a seaman who had been marooned five years on a deserted island off Chile's coast. The rescued man was named Alexander Selkirk, whose island adventure gave life to Robinson Crusoe. Selkirk was aboard Rogers's ship *Dover* when the crew captured the Spanish galleon *Encarnacion* off Cabo San Lucas in 1709. He then served as sailing master on the ship's return voyage to England the following year.

DIVING FACILITIES

There are several dive operations in Cabo San Lucas, and many of the major hotels offer diving services.

Amigos del Mar is a PADI dive center with experienced operators. They have equipment rentals, mid-sized boats that take about 10 divers, and a larger six-pack boat. They offer one day excursions to Cabo Pulmo Reef and Gorda Bank, as well as local Cabo dives. Also offered through Amigos del Mar is the 110-foot (33 m) liveaboard boat, the *Solmar V*. Equipped with 12 staterooms, this vessel runs four- to seven-day dive trips to the Cabo Pulmo Reef, outer islands and the Socorro Islands. Scuba instruction is also offered. Amigos del Mar is located across from the sportfishing dock on the bay.

Cabo Acuadeportes is a NAUI facility. They offer a range of services and scuba equipment, including scuba instruction and boat dives. They are located on the beach in front of the Hacienda Hotel.

Dive Adventures is a PADI facility equipped with a boat and scuba equipment. They are located in the shopping mall of Plaza Bonita.

Another shop is **J & R Baja Divers** located at Guerrero near Tacos Chidos.

DIVING

The Cabo San Lucas Bay has been declared an underwater park and marine sanctuary. No marine life may be removed from the bay. The diving opportunities are varied and include suitable sites for all experience levels. Most of the diving is around the leeward side of the

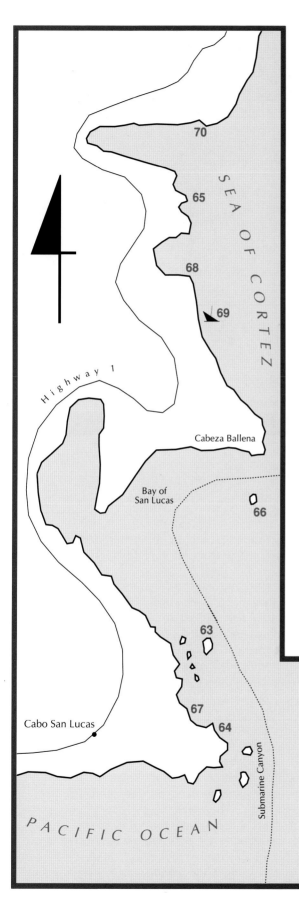

famous granite peninsula that divides the Sea of Cortez from the Pacific Ocean. A 1,000-foot (303 m) submarine canyon lies 50 yards (45 m) off the protected shoreline of the bay, which creates a unique environment for large numbers of tropical fishes, invertebrates and plant life. The unusual sandfalls are one of Cabo's most popular dive sites.

Other classic dives off the cape are found at the end of the peninsula where the famous granite pillars and giant arch, both landmarks of Cabo San Lucas, are located. The scattered remains of a Japanese shipwreck lie just off Finisterra, meaning Land's End. Most of the sites are protected from the wind and currents, and the tides in this area are minimal. From June through October, there can be occasional heavy storms known as *chubascos*. Water temperature generally ranges from high 60'sF (19-21°C) in the early winter months to 85°F (29°C) in the late summer. Water visibility can exceed 100 feet (30 m).

Territorial reef fishes common throughout the region include angelfishes, butterflyfishes, triggerfishes, puffers, damselfishes, moorish idols, parrotfishes, perch and grouper. During the early spring months, the chances of seeing the California gray whale and the humpback whale are excellent but not guaranteed. Coming south from cold northern waters, the whales are in their calving season.

Northeast of Cabo San Lucas on the way to San Jose del Cabo are a number of uncrowded, relatively pristine beaches suitable for swimming, camping, snorkeling and scuba diving.

CABO SAN LUCAS

63. Anegada Rock
64. Land's End
65. The Blowhole
66. The Pinnacle and Rookery
67. Lover's Cove
68. Santa Maria Cove
69. Shipwreck Beach
70. Chileno Beach

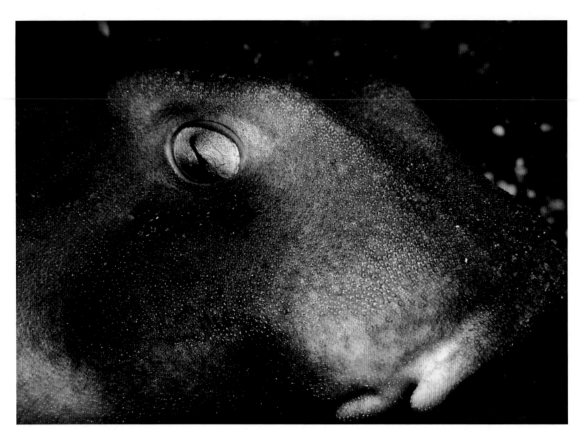

Harmless except for the little thorn on their dorsal fin, horn sharks are found lying in rocky crevices and on sandy sea floors.

63. ANEGADA ROCK (S)

DEPTH:	20-100+ FEET (6-30+ M)
LEVEL:	NOVICE TO EXPERIENCED
ACCESS:	BOAT

Anegada Rock, also known as Pelican Rock, sits on the south side of the bay. On the sandy bottom at 20 feet (6 m), schools of barberfish, goatfishes and king angelfish move back and forth on the shallow side of Anegada Rock. On bright days, flickering rays of sunlight bounce off this shallow sand area beside this great rock where reef fishes seem to congregate. On these sunny days, the rock makes a beautiful backdrop for photos. By swimming south around the arch, divers will reach a year-round sea lion colony. The depth here is 40 feet (12 m).

Over the sandy 20-foot (6 m) ledge at Anegada Rock is a wall which drops down 1,000 feet (303 m) into a submarine canyon. Between a depth of 50 and 100 feet (15-30 m), horizontal rocky outcroppings line the steep sloping wall, giving it the appearance of large jagged stairsteps. The wall provides divers the opportunity to see an array of local tropical fishes and a chance encounter with manta rays, whales or sea turtles.

At 90 feet (27 m) there is the **Sandfalls** made famous by Jacques Cousteau in a television documentary. At certain times of the year, large amounts of sand build up in shallower depths. When there is strong surge, the sand starts spilling down this sand valley resembling a giant white slide. It moves down the rocky wall to a depth of 100 feet (30 m) where the white granules meet a sheer granite wall. Here the sand drops straight down for hundreds of feet. The billions of falling granules resemble a waterfall in slow motion.

Caution. Because of the depth, the Sandfalls should be dived by experienced divers only.

64. LAND'S END

DEPTH:	60 FEET
	(18 M)
LEVEL:	INTERMEDIATE TO
	EXPERIENCED
ACCESS:	BOAT

Cabo's famous naturally-carved arch is at Land's End, where years of wind and weather have hollowed out a beautiful archway through which the waves of the Pacific Ocean break, meeting the waters of the Sea of Cortez. This dramatic topside setting extends beneath the water's surface into a beauty all its own.

Giant angular rocks cascade down to a depth of 60 feet (18 m) where there is a sandy bottom. The short walls along the rocks are full of small ledges and indentations which create homes for large eels, reef fishes and invertebrates. Beautiful moorish idols can be spotted swimming around in pairs, as can king angelfish and longnose butterflyfish. The rarely-seen bright-orange Clarion angelfish is found at Land's End. This elegant-looking fish is normally a resident of the Clarion Islands and also the Socorro Islands much farther south.

The years of intense wave and weather action have formed some very exotic-looking, naturally sculpted rocks on both the east and west side of Baja's tip. Here is the arch at Cabo's famous Land's End, where the Pacific Ocean meets the Sea of Cortez.

*The elegant-looking moorish idols
are found throughout Land's End
and on the shallow reefs in many
other areas.*

There is a surge on the point at Land's End, but it is worth the swim as divers have had encounters with manta rays here. Other frequent visitors are sea turtles, large sea bass and Mexican barracuda.

Several yards off the point's rocky outcropping is the skeletal remains of a Japanese fishing boat which met its doom in 1948. Today the wreckage is strewn across the sandy bottom in about 50 feet (15 m) of water. Fishes and invertebrates have made multi-condominium levels throughout the structure's remains.

65. THE BLOWHOLE

DEPTH:	40-100+ FEET (12-30+ M)
LEVEL:	NOVICE TO EXPERIENCED
ACCESS:	BOAT

This great rock sculpture gets its name from a blowhole in the rocks, where a small water surge is forced through a hole in the rock. The backside of this huge formation forms a wall which is filled with twisted crevices, rugged tunnels and deep ravines. Depths start at about 40 feet (12 m) and drop quickly to over 100 feet (30+ m). Red and yellow gorgonians, along with sea fans, cover the area. Hard encrusting coral blankets the rocks in clumps.

Frequently encountered in the shallower depths are hogfish, surgeonfish, croaker and porgies. Nurse sharks, sea turtles, jacks and guitarfish have been noted in this area along with a few large grouper.

Divers should be wary of the sharp spines of the sea urchin.

66. THE PINNACLE AND ROOKERY

DEPTH:	50-80 FEET (15-24 M)
LEVEL:	INTERMEDIATE TO EXPERIENCED
ACCESS:	BOAT

This is a good area to look for large fish. On occasion, divers have seen lone mantas swimming around the pinnacle. The pinnacle also harbors a community of sea lions which are always great fun to dive with. An entire dive can be spent just playing and photographing these jovial, fun-loving mammals. This area is alive with tropicals and invertebrate life. Look closely in the holes and rock fissures for the zebra moray. It is the only moray in the gulf with white-striped bands on a reddish brown body. Growing in length to a little over 2 feet (62 cm), these morays differ from others by having blunt, molar-like teeth instead of sharp canine teeth.

The bottom terrain levels off at a plateau around 50 feet (15 m), then slopes down to 80 feet (24 m). Currents have been known to pick up around the pinnacles, so the area is recommended for experienced divers.

67. LOVER'S COVE (S)

DEPTH:	10-40 FEET (3-12 M)
LEVEL:	NOVICE TO EXPERIENCED
ACCESS:	SHORE OR BOAT

Lover's Cove is located almost at the point of Land's End. It is most easily accessed by boat as water taxis shuttle between San Lucas and the cove every 20 minutes. To get there by foot, walk towards Land's End on the beach

Lover's Cove at Cabo San Lucas is a good spot for snorkeling and can be reached by water taxi.

behind the Solmar Hotel. The cove doesn't have a lot to offer scuba divers, but there are some interesting rocks along the shoreline to snorkel around. There is one rock where several sea lions are always hanging out, basking in the sun.

68. SANTA MARIA COVE (S)

DEPTH:	15-60+ FEET (5-18+ M)
LEVEL:	NOVICE TO EXPERIENCED
ACCESS:	SHORE

Located 7 miles (11 km) north of Cabo San Lucas, in front of the Twin Dolphin Hotel, is an excellent cove for shore diving. Parking is available in the hotel parking lot, and there is a pathway on the left which leads to the mouth of the cove. The north point of Santa Maria Cove is made up of large rocks and finger ridges. Further out are deep canyons. The southern point of the cove is also fringed with large rocks and small caverns. Corals and sea fans are interspersed among the ridges, along with a kaleidoscope of tropical fish life. Small bright-red coral hawkfish, longnose hawkfish, chameleon wrasses, sand perch, jawfish, and royal blue and yellow chromis are scattered in shallow water at 15 to 25 feet (5-8 m). Large game fish occasionally frequent the deeper areas by the tip of the points.

Caution. Currents can pick up around the points.

69. SHIPWRECK BEACH (S)

DEPTH:	30 FEET (9 M)
LEVEL:	NOVICE TO EXPERIENCED
ACCESS:	SHORE

Just south of the Twin Dolphins Hotel is Shipwreck Beach. In 1966 the Japanese freighter *Inari Maru* was wrecked on the shoreline. Part of the rusted hull lies on the shore, while the rest of the remains are scattered offshore in about 30 feet (9 m) of water. Easily reached from the beach, this is a good snorkeling and shallow scuba diving spot.

The Twin Dolphins Hotel is on the main highway. From the highway, turn at the Barco Varado sign which leads to the beach.

Just beyond the beached remains of the wreckage, there is a series of long finger reefs. Being full of cubby holes and pockets, the rocky structure is home to an array of marine life. It is a good area for fish portraits if you are a photographer, as a variety of wrasses, blennys, trunkfish and triggerfish live throughout the reef. Also some of the best snorkeling areas that can be reached from shore are from Shipwreck Beach to Santa Maria Cove.

70. CHILENO BEACH (S)

DEPTH:	10-50 FEET (3-15 M)
LEVEL:	NOVICE TO EXPERIENCED
ACCESS:	SHORE

Located north of the Twin Dolphins Hotel is Chileno Beach, which is next to the Cabo San Lucas Hotel. It is accessible by turning at the Cabo Real sign. The Cabo San Lucas Hotel does have a diving operation on the premises. Easy shore entries can be made in front of the hotel.

Protected finger reefs start right at the shore of Chileno Beach and jut out into the bay for about a half mile (.8 km). Divers will usually see a broad assortment of tropicals and eels, such as the zebra, tiger reef, tiger snake, jewel and green moray eel which hide in the deep fissures of the reef. A wide variety of invertebrates stalk the outer fringes of the rocks, including the multi-petaled lavender flower urchin, brightly-colored sea stars, hydroids and feather duster worms.

This is also a very appealing area for snorkelers due to the shallower depths.

CHAPTER **XII** SOCORRO ISLANDS

AT A GLANCE

Located 220 miles (355 km) south of Baja's tip sits a small group of volcanic islands, virtually in the middle of nowhere. There are four islands in the chain of which Isla San Benedicto is the closest to Baja. Isla Socorro is 22 miles (36 km) further south, while Isla Partida sits to the southwest. Isla Clarion lies the furthest in the Pacific, being 370 miles (597 km) from Baja's tip.

In 1952, Isla San Benedicto erupted, forming a prominent cone about 1,000 feet (303 m) high, along with a large lava flow area which can be seen on its southern end. In January 1993, Isla Socorro awoke from 145 years of dormancy when a fissure opened on the ocean floor, spewing huge rocks as large as 10 feet (3 m) in diameter. These rocks were filled with gas and floated on the surface until the gas dissipated. Except for a small Mexican naval base and a village on the southern tip of Isla Socorro, the islands are uninhabited.

This archipelago has been referred to as the Mexican Galapagos. The birds seem fearless and many are endemic to the area, as are several plants. A story by one biologist who was doing research was that when he was napping, a Socorro wren landed on his belly, hopped up to his chest, and looked intently at the folds in his shirt and even up his nose for morsels to eat.

Almost every hurricane that originates in the Pacific and heads for Mexico and Central America moves through this archipelago. Because of the unpredictable weather, these islands are only visited by long-range boats and commercial tuna vessels. All boats traveling to these islands need special permits from the Mexican government. The hurricane months are from June to October, with occasional storms in May and November. During the winter months from late October through May, the weather conditions can, at times, exhibit strong winds and heavy seas. The most stable weather conditions are in November to early December, and in April and May. In the fall, the water temperature is around 80°F (27°C), while in the spring it is about 70°F (21°C).

A presidential decree in 1994 declared the Socorro Island chain a national protected area. No collecting or fishing is allowed within several miles of the inland waters. There has been much controversy over the commercial fishing here, and after a dive boat videotaped the slaughter of some of the giant manta rays at The Boilers in February of 1994, a public demand to protect the Socorro Islands grew. But the entire Sea of Cortez is in need of more legal protection as well as adequate patrolling to enforce fishing laws.

GETTING THERE

The best way to get to the Socorro Island chain is by boat. There is a small airstrip on Socorro, but is not commonly used. From Baja's tip at Cabo San Lucas, most dive boats take approximately 24 hours to arrive at Isla Benedicto. Dive boats that make this journey include the following:

The *Solmar V*, based out of Cabo San Lucas, is a 112-foot (34 m) luxury liveaboard with 12 cabins. The spacious and well laid-out boat can accommodate up to 24 divers. Bookings can be made through Solmar Resorts.

Along Isla San Benedicto's pinnacle called The Boilers, schools of elegant moorish idols weave in and out of the rock outcroppings.

The brilliant orange clarion angelfish is outlined in iridescent blue. Seen only occasionally in the southern part of the Sea of Cortez, this fish appears in huge schools around the Socorro Islands where they live along the shallow rocky reefs.

The dive boat *Copper Sky* is a 72-foot (22 m) schooner that is based out of La Paz. It can accommodate up to eight divers. Bookings and more information can be obtained through Baja Expeditions.

The *Baja Treasure* is a 116-foot (35 m) dive boat out of Guaymas that can accommodate up to 20 divers. More information and bookings can be obtained through See & Sea Travel.

DIVING

The most visited islands by the liveaboard dive boats are Isla San Benedicto and Isla Socorro because they are closest to Baja, and they are closest to each other. The diving around these two islands is excellent and you can expect to see large schools of the brightly-colored clarion angelfish and the elegant redtail triggerfish. Larger pelagics, such as tuna, wahoo, schools of jacks, a variety of sharks and huge manta rays tend to come more often into shallower water than elsewhere. In the spring months, divers have a good chance to see humpback whales.

Being of volcanic origin and because of the swift hurricanes that move through this area, the topside terrain is quite barren. Likewise,

the underwater terrain is void of gorgonians and soft corals.

ISLA SAN BENEDICTO

71. THE BOILERS (S)

DEPTH:	25-100+ FEET
	(8-30+ M)
LEVEL:	ADVANCED
ACCESS:	BOAT

One of the most picturesque dive sites at Isla San Benedicto is known as The Boilers, located at the northwest end. It is an underwater pinnacle that starts in 25 feet (8m) of water. This shallow plateau extends approximately 100 feet (30 m) across.

The sides of the pinnacle are vertical walls that drop to a 120-foot (36 m) sandy bottom. The top of the pinnacle is absolutely alive with color as are its side walls. The exotic-looking black and gold moorish idols can be found here in schools of great numbers. Neon orange clarion angelfish, pufferfish, wrasses, hogfish and redtail triggers are also abundant. Whale

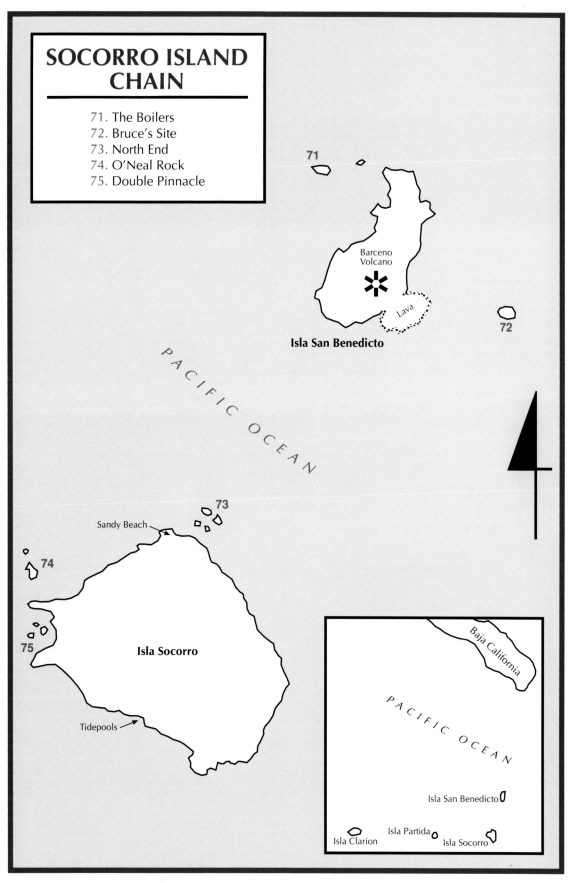

SOCORRO ISLAND CHAIN

71

Barceno
Volcano

Lava

Isla San Benedicto

72

PACIFIC OCEAN

73

Sandy Beach

74

75

Isla Socorro

Tidepools

Baja California

PACIFIC OCEAN

Isla San Benedicto

Isla Partida

Isla Clarion

Isla Socorro

One of the most graceful creatures in the sea is the manta ray. Very large ones have been seen near Isla Benedicto. With a wingspan sometimes over 18 feet (6 m), these majestic beauties somersault and glide effortlessly. They appear to really enjoy interaction with divers.

Manta rays seem to always have some tag-alongs. Here two remoras hold tightly to the manta with their suckers.

In 1952, Isla San Benedicto erupted forming a prominent cone about 1,000 feet (303 m) high along with a large lava flow area. The island looks barren, but beneath its surface life abounds.

sharks have been known to linger around the pinnacle during both fall and spring months.

But the main attraction of this seamount is the likelihood of seeing the giant manta rays. With 18-foot (5 m) wing spans, these exquisite creatures seem to be as curious about divers as the divers are about them. Being one of the most docile animals in the sea, these eminent beauties seem to really enjoy human contact. After spending a good amount of time with these creatures, it is easy to see why studies are beginning to show their intelligence. It is suspected that they will soon be high on the list of respected and protected animals, as are the dolphins and whales.

Around the seamount are columns of silver swirls, which are hundreds of both amberjacks and horse-eyed jacks. Occasionally solo tuna and wahoo dart by. Beyond the seamount in deeper water, divers can sometimes spot hammerhead sharks. A little closer to the island, approximately 75 yards (68 m) from the shore is another seamount that comes to within 80 feet of the surface. It is a good spot to find larger fish weaving their way across the reeftop.

72. BRUCE'S SITE

DEPTH:	40-100+ FEET
	(12-30+ M)
LEVEL:	ADVANCED
ACCESS:	BOAT

There appears to be more shark activity at the southern end of this island which is made up of rocky terrain. At 40 feet (12 m), there are some rock formations that descend to over 100 feet (30+ m). Sharks that frequent this area are hammerheads, silkys, tigers, whitetip, Galapagos and gray reef sharks. The depths range from approximately 40 feet (12 m) at the shallowest, down to below 100 feet (30+ m). In the deeper depths is where schooling hammerheads can be seen.

The sharks here at San Benedicto are less spooked by divers, and are fairly easy to approach. The Galapagos, whitetip and hammerhead are the most commonly seen. Both the south end and east side are still virgin sites for diving and are a shark photographer's paradise.

Isla Socorro

73. NORTH END

DEPTH:	30-100+ FEET
	(9-30+ M)
LEVEL:	ADVANCED
ACCESS:	BOAT

The island of Socorro is larger than San Benedicto. On the northeast side of the island divers can usually find a fair amount of shark activity. The area can get some pretty strong currents, so drift diving is often the choice.

At the north end, there are some protruding rocks that jut out from the island. Underwater at about 50 feet (15 m) and deeper, the terrain is made up of large, flat and oblong boulders. Here, there are great schools of clarion angelfish and redtail triggerfish. As you ascend to about 30 feet (9 m), the terrain takes on a whole new appearance. The incredible volcanic earth formations look like something you might expect to see on the moon. There are great angular channels in the reef to swim through which are dotted with pockets. These pockets make perfect homes for eels, octopus, urchins, starfish and large socorro lobster.

74. O'NEAL ROCK

DEPTH:	40-100+ FEET
	(12-30+ M)
LEVEL:	ADVANCED
ACCESS:	BOAT

This site on the northwest side of the island has several different names depending on the dive boat you're on, but the most common are Old Man Rock and O'Neal Rock. Depths start in about 40 feet (12 m) of water and drop to well over 100 feet (30+ m). There is a large, rocky plateau at 40 feet (12 m) where big lobsters, rays, eels and myriad tropical fishes can be found throughout. On the outer edge of the plateau is a drop-off. Below the drop-off on the wall at 90 feet (27 m), there is a cavern with a large arch above it, which is a dramatic backdrop for photographers. Along the wall is a good area to look for schooling hammerhead sharks. Sometimes they will be seen in pairs or small groups swimming gracefully over the shallower plateau.

75. DOUBLE PINNACLE

DEPTH:	30-100+ FEET
	(9-30+ M)
LEVEL:	ADVANCED
ACCESS:	BOAT

On the west side of the island high above the water's surface, there is a double set of rocks which resemble a manta ray's horns. Named the Double Pinnacle, or sometimes called Manta Rock, the great boulders that make up this reef formation lie between 30 to 50 feet (9-15 m) in depth. The crevices among the boulders are great places to find large moray eels and lobsters. There also seem to be many juvenile whitetip sharks in this area. At a 50-foot (15 m) depth, the boulder-covered plateau plunges to over 100 feet (30+ m). Along this wall there is an array of fish life, including trumpetfish, triggerfishes, large jacks and schools of chubs.

The large green moray eel, growing to over 5 feet (1.5 m) in length, is seen in the daylight hours in holes and under crevices in the reef. Being nocturnal creatures, they forage for food at night. Intimidating-looking with their mouths open for oxygen exchange, they are actually shy animals, usually withdrawing back into their holes when approached.

Rarely seen in the Sea of Cortez, the incredibly marked redtail triggerfish flourishes throughout the Socorro Islands. The most exquisite-looking of all triggerfishes, it is easily recognized by the reddish tail of the adults, and a gold body with blue streaks across its face.

This brown colored Galapagos shark can get more aggressive than hammerheads or whitetips. But they are mainly curious, and move in slowly to check out the reef and then leave. Usually seen in deeper water of about 100 feet (30 m), these sharks move into the shallows along with the bottlenose dolphin, feeding on flying fish at night.

CHAPTER **XIII**   MARINE LIFE

The northern and central Pacific shores of Baja California are known for their kelp forests and the animals that inhabit that ecosystem. However, Baja is mainly known for the marine life found in the Sea of Cortez.

The Sea of Cortez is unusual because it is an enclosed body of water with two distinct ecological regions. North of Bahia de Los Angeles, the shallow waters are strongly influenced by the climate of the surrounding Sonoran Desert, and as a result there are extreme seasonal variations in water temperature. The waters of the northern Gulf are essentially cool during the winter, but warm in the summer. In this area, certain tropical species disappear in the winter months while others disappear in the summer.

The southern part of the Gulf, with its larger area, numerous deep canyons and proximity to the open sea, is more under the influence of the ocean, making it a more stable environment. Seasonally, however, certain species are more prevalent than others.

Following are some of the more interesting animals found in the waters surrounding the Baja Peninsula.

Balloonfish (Diodon holocanthus).

Balloonfish

The balloonfish (*Diodon holocanthus*) is most easily recognized by the dark bar over the forehead that extends down past the eye, and the long spines that cover the body. When touched, balloonfish blow up with water to increase their size as protection from predators. They are found along the reefs and sandy bottoms, sometimes in schools as many as 30. They grow to about 18 inches (46 cm).

Barberfish

About 8 inches (21 cm) in length, barberfish (*Johnrandallia nigrirostris*) are recognized by their black forehead and the silvery-yellow body with a black stripe under their dorsal fin. They are usually found hovering in small schools around the shallow reefs, picking at algae growth on the rocks.

Blunthead Triggerfish

This triggerfish (*Pseudobalistes naufragium*) can reach up to 3 feet (1 m) in length. They are best recognized by dark bars on their bluish-gray to brownish-gray bodies and by their prominent foreheads. They are found around reefs and over sandy bottoms. Triggerfish make crater-like nests in which to lay their eggs by blowing the sand away with jets of water. Many times divers can see them shaking over these holes as if doing a little dance.

*California gray whale
(Rhachianectes glaucus).*

*Bottlenose dolphin (*Tursiops truncatus*).*

Bottlenose Dolphin

The bottlenose dolphin (*Tursiops truncatus*) is the most common dolphin in this area and can be seen roaming in schools, sometimes consisting of hundreds of animals. One of the larger species, they will occasionally interact with divers. They are playful and curious, but also quite cautious. Fully grown they can reach 13 feet (4 m) in length and weigh 600 pounds (273 kg). They usually stay within 100 miles (161 km) of land, and can often be seen in bays and inlets. These are dolphins most used by man as performers.

Bullseye Stingray

The bullseye stingray (*Urolophus concentricus*) has dark markings that form concentric rings. Their average size is about 2 feet (62 cm) across. They are found on shallow, sandy areas around reefs and in bays.

California Gray Whale

The gray whale (*Rhachianectes glaucus*) is one of ten species of baleen whales believed to be the oldest of all the living species of whales. Though they are 40-50 feet (12-15 m) long,

their nourishment comes from some of the smallest creatures on earth—plankton, krill, small fish, crustaceans and kelp. Despite their slaughter to near-extinction twice in the last 120 years, they were removed from the endangered species list in 1994. Though they are mostly found on Baja's Pacific side during January through April, many come around the point and up into the Sea of Cortez. Some have been reported as far south as the Socorro Islands. Their yearly migrational journey to bear young and mate originates in the Bering Sea.

*Cortez angelfish (*Pomacanthus zonipectus*).*

California Sea Lion

The California sea lion (*Zalophus Californianus*) is found throughout Baja's coastlines and offshore islands. From the Pacific to the Sea of Cortez, these playful sea dogs are curious and will investigate divers. Large bulls keep a harem of females and are quite territorial during mating season. Sea lion pups are born in late spring and early summer. By early fall they are frolicking in the depths. Sea lions differ from seals in that they have external ears.

Colonial Cup Coral

These yellow to orange corals (*Tubastraea tenuilamellosa*) live in colonies anchored to rocky reefs at depths from 10 to at least 250 feet (3-76 m). In small clusters, they are found in the darker areas, such as under ledges and overhangs. At night they open to filter-feed. Certain species of shrimp and the longnose hawkfish live among these corals.

Cortez Angelfish

Cortez angelfish (*Pomacanthus zonipectus*) are prolific throughout the Sea of Cortez. The adults have gray bodies with yellow and black bands on the head and body. Juveniles are striped with brilliant blue and gold bands. They are found along the reefs to depths of at least 100 feet (30 m).

Cortez Garden Eels

These small eels (*Taeniconger diguiti*) live in holes burrowed in the sand. Their communities often consist of hundreds of animals. They are very shy and difficult to approach. Unlike morays they have small mouths, pectoral fins and a lateral line. Their heads seem to always be poking out of the sand, just watching. They eat plankton floating by in the current. When spooked, they disappear into their holes in unison.

Golden Grouper

The golden grouper (*Mycteroperca rosacea*) is actually a leopard grouper which is gray with reddish spots. A few of the leopard grouper turn golden. Not commonly seen, they are usually sighted alone on rocky reefs. They grow to 3 feet (1 m) in length.

Green Sea Turtle

The green sea turtle's (*Chelonia mydas*) shell is mottled with brown and green. Their name actually comes from the color of their body fat. They can be distinguished by the single pair of scales on the front of their head. Most are about 40 inches (103 cm) in length, but have been known to grow as large as 5 feet (1.5 m). At times they can be encountered in the open sea, but are more frequently seen on seamounts and pinnacles.

Green sea turtle (Chelonia mydas*).*

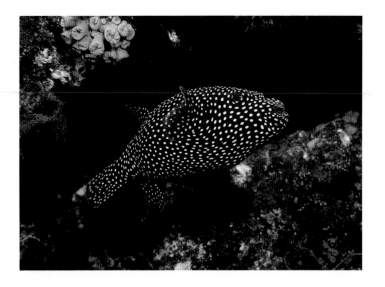

Guineafowl pufferfish (Arothron meleagris).

King angelfish (Holocanthus passer).

Pacific crevalle jack (Caranx caninus).

Guineafowl Pufferfish

The guineafowl pufferfish (*Arothron meleagris*) look like little painted clowns. They have black bodies with small white polka dots. When touched, they puff up with water so tightly that their faces almost disappear. Unlike the balloonfish, their bodies are smooth. They are found in shallow reef areas and grow to approximately 1 foot (31 cm) in length.

Jewel Moray

This beautifully decorated moray eel (*Muraena lentiginosa*), which grows to about 2 feet (62 cm) in length, can be recognized by the chain-like rows of light spots ringed by dark brown halos. They are nocturnal foragers and can be found during the day under rocky overhangs and in crevices.

King Angelfish

These colorful angelfish (*Holocanthus passer*) are found throughout reef areas. They are a rich blue in color with a white stripe extending from their dorsal to their pectoral fin. Their fins are gold. The juveniles have much more gold on their bodies than the adults. The king angelfish are often seen clustered on the reef in small schools. They reach a length of about 14 inches (36 cm).

Longnose Butterflyfish

The longnose butterflyfish (*Forcipiger flavissimus*) is easily recognized by its long snout and gold-and-black body. This 6-inch (15 cm) reef fish ranges from the Sea of Cortez to the Indo-Pacific region.

Manta Rays

This exquisite animal (*Manta alfredi*) is easily recognized by the two large flaps beneath its head, which are used to funnel plankton into its mouth. This elegant creature has a wingspan that can exceed 20 feet (6 m). They are usually spotted off the outer islands or cruising near the surface along drop-offs around submerged pinnacles, but have occasionally been seen inside bays.

Moorish Idol

The moorish idol (*Zanclus cornutus*) reaches about 9 inches (23 cm) in length. These fish are rarely found alone. They are usually seen in pairs or schools, and their black vertical bands, long nose and dorsal fin identify them.

Pacific Crevalle Jack

These magnificent-looking fish (*Caranx caninus*) are seen in groups of hundreds, hanging out just beyond reefs and seamounts. They are identified by the black spot on the rear of the gills, and the white tip on the dorsal and anal fins. They are a pelagic inshore fish. During mating, the males will turn black. After the courting season, they will turn silver again. Adults reach about 30 inches (77 cm) in length.

Panamic Green Moray

The panamic green moray (*Gymnothorax castaneus*) is one of the larger species of moray in the Sea of Cortez. They can grow to over 4 feet (1.2 m) in length. They are found poking their heads out of crevices and holes in the daytime, and at night may be seen any place on the reef or over sand bottoms, hunting for food.

*Panamic green moray (*Gymnotorax castaneus*).*

*Panamic sergeant major (*Abudefduf troschelii*).*

*Scalloped hammerhead shark (*Sphyrna lewini*). Photo: Marty Snyderman.*

Panamic Sergeant Major

Sergeant majors (*Abudefduf troschelii*) are found throughout the Sea of Cortez. They can be identified by black stripes on a silver to yellow body. They are about 9 inches (23 cm) long and are found over reefs and wrecks to depths of around 100 feet (30 m) from the Sea of Cortez to Peru.

Scalloped Hammerhead Shark

The scalloped hammerhead shark (*Sphyrna lewini*), which are well known to the Sea of Cortez, can exceed over 12 feet (4 m) in length, but are usually seen between 6 and 8 feet (2-2.5 m). They are regularly spotted over seamounts and deeper pinnacles, either in large scools, in pairs or alone. They are shy animals, and don't appear curious about divers.

Scissortail Damselfish

These small fish (*Chromis atrilobata*) grow to about 5 inches (13 cm) in length. They are best identified by their deeply forked tail and the white spot below their dorsal fin. They congregate in large numbers around reefs and are found to depths of about 250 feet (76 m).

Scorpionfish

These fish (*Scorpaena mystes*) are so well camouflaged that they are often missed by divers. They lie very still on sandy bottoms and reef structures. They are more easily spotted at night when they are likely to be out in the open on top of the reef. Their dorsal fins have venomous spines which can cause a painful injury. They reach a length of up to 17 inches (44 cm).

Spottail Grunt

Distinguished by spots on their scales that form stripes on their sides, these grunts (*Haemulon maculicauda*) school around reefs during the day, and at night move off the reef to feed over sandy bottoms usually at depths of at least 100 feet (30 m). They are about 12 inches (31 cm) in length and can be found as far south as Ecuador.

Synapted Sea Cucumber

The synapted sea cucumber (*Euapta godeffroyi*) only comes out at night to feed along the shallow reefs and rocks. It has a soft snake-like body that lacks tube feet. When touched, they will contract. Its long appendages protruding from the mouth will move around looking for food. At times the sandy bottom can be covered with them. They are approximately 12 inches (31 cm) when contracted, and up to 50 inches (128 cm) when stretched out. This sea cucumber clings to the skin when handled and are easily fragmented.

Yellow Polyp Black Coral

Black coral (*Antipathes galapagensis*) can still be found growing in depths as shallow as 30 feet (9 m), but it is more commonly seen growing on deep banks and walls at depths of over 100 feet (30+ m). They appear to be small yellow bushes almost resembling a tumbleweed. The bright yellow polyps on the slender, branching skeleton are distinctive. This species is currently harvested commercially for jewelry in La Paz and Cabo San Lucas.

Yellow polyp black coral (Antipathes galapagensis).

Whale shark (Rhineodon typus).
Photo: Marty Snyderman.

Whale Shark

Reaching over 60 feet (18 m) in length, the whale shark (*Rhineodon typus*) is the largest known fish in the ocean. Migrating seasonally, these peaceful giants are seen occasionally on the seamounts, over deep-water banks, and in the bays throughout the Sea of Cortez. They are gray-brown with round white-yellow spots on their body. Their mouths are almost always open, forming a gap as much as 6 feet (2 m) wide. They feed on plankton and small fish, as do whales. They are often covered with a number of remoras and surrounded by myriad pilot fish. Although huge, the whale shark is considered harmless and is fairly curious about divers. Although not likely to harm a diver, a stroke of their powerful tail could have unpleasant consequences.

Yellowtail Surgeonfish

The yellow tail and gray body with black spots of this fish (*Prionurus punctatus*) make it easy to recognize underwater. Growing to a length of about 2 feet (62 cm), these fish are seen in small groups moving over the reef. They are distinguished from the very similar common yellowtail surgeonfish found around the Socorros and Galapagos Islands, which lack black spots.

Yellowtail surgeonfish (Prionurus punctatus).

APPENDIX 1

EMERGENCY NUMBERS

The United States Coast Guard monitors VHF radio channel 16, and can pick up transmissions as far south as the Ensenada area. In the north end of the Sea of Cortez, the Cholla Bay Sportsmen's Club in Lukesville, Arizona can respond to pleas for emergency assistance on VHF 16 with their own search and rescue team. In other areas along the Baja coastline, many Mexican agencies also monitor this channel, including the Mexican Navy and commercial ships. Citizen-band (CB) radio is commonly used as a substitute for a telephone in many of the remote areas. It is also used by the Green Angels, boaters and many travelers. Besides channel 9, which is widely used in the United States, channels 1, 3, 4, 7, 9 and 10 are also used. Special permits for radio use by foreign visitors are no longer required for CB radios with a transmission power of five watts or less.

DIVERS ALERT NETWORK (DAN)

The Divers Alert Network (DAN) operates a 24-hour emergency number **(919) 684-8111** (collect calls accepted if necessary) to provide divers and physicians with medical advice on treating diving injuries and assist in coordinating treatment, evacuation and insurance verification. In addition, they can organize air evacuation to the nearest recompression chamber.

Since many emergency room physicians do not know how to properly treat diving injuries, it is highly recommended that in the event of an accident, you have the physician consult a DAN doctor specializing in diving medicine.

DAN is a not-for-profit organization affiliated with Duke University Medical Center and supported by a membership of more than 115,000 divers. Membership is $25 a year and includes the DAN Dive and Travel Medical Guide, the dive safety magazine, *Alert Diver*, and Travel Assist emergency medical evacuation assistance. Travel Assist provides all DAN members with guaranteed emergency evacuation from anywhere for a medically necessary reason whether dive related or not. They provide multi-lingual, medically trained operators 24 hours a day at many locations throughout the world. DAN members are also able to purchase dive accident medical insurance. DAN offers three policies which cover hospitalization, air ambulance and recompression chamber treatment for diving injuries.

DAN's address is Divers Alert Network, Box 3823, Duke University Medical Center, Durham, NC 27710. Their non-emergency number is (919) 684-2948. To join the Divers Alert Network call (800) 446-2671.

Appendix 2

Useful Numbers

To call a number in Mexico from outside the United States, dial 011 + 52 + area code + number.

Discover Baja Travel Club
(*general information and insurance*)
3065 Clairemont Dr.
San Diego, CA 92117
Tel: (800) 727-2252

Mike Overcast
(*weather*)
Tel: (619) 470-1890

Mexican Tourism Office
Tijuana
Tel: 668-19492

Los Angeles
Tel: (310) 203-8191

Mexican Consulate
San Diego
Tel: (619) 231-8427

Ferry Office
La Paz
Tel: 112-53833 or 55117

Appendix 3

Scuba Diving Centers and Dive Charters

Pacific

Dale's La Bufadora Dive
APDO Post #102
Maneadero, B.C. Mexico
Tel: 617-32092

Baja Tennis Club & Dive Expeditions
Tel: 617-30220 or 30225

Sea of Cortez

Mulege Divers
Madero #45
Mulege, B.C.S. Mexico

Arturo's Sport Fishing Fleet
Hidalgo St.
P.O. Box 5
Loreto, B.C.S. Mexico
Tel: 113-50409
Fax: 113-50022

Baja Buceo y Servicio (Baja Dive Service)
Independencia 107-B
La Paz, B.C.S. Mexico
Tel: 112-21826 or 52575
Fax: 112-28644

Deportiva La Paz
AP. Postal 263
La Paz, B.C.S. Mexico
Tel: 112-21090 or 21408

Hotel Buena Vista
P.O. Box 574
La Paz, B.C.S. Mexico
Tel: 112-21962

Rancho Leonero Hotel
East Cape
Tel: (800) 696-2164
    (714) 375-3720

Pepe's Dive Center
P.O. Box 532
Cabo San Lucas, B.C.S. Mexico
Tel: (619) 489-7001

Amigos Del Mar
P.O. Box 43
Cabo San Lucas, B.C.S. Mexico
Tel: 114-30505
Fax: 114-30887

Cabo Acuadeportes
Apartado Postal 136
Cabo San Lucas, B.C.S Mexico
Tel/Fax: 114-30117

Dive Adventures
Plaza Bonita
Cabo San Lucas, B.C.S. Mexico
Tel/Fax: 114-32630

J&R Baja Divers
Cabo San Lucas, B.C.S. Mexico
Tel: 114-31570

U.S. Contacts

Baja Expeditions
2656 Garnet Ave.
San Diego, CA 92109
Tel: (800) 843-6967
       (619) 581-3311

Dolphin Dive Center
11 W. Duarte Rd.
Arcadia, CA 91007
Tel: (818) 447-5536
Fax: (818) 447-8685

Scuba Voyages
595 Fairbanks St.
Corona, CA 91719
Tel: (800) 544-7631
Fax: (909) 279-0478

Sea Safaris
3770 Highland Ave. Ste. 102
Manhattan Beach, CA 90266
Tel: (213) 546-2464
       (800) 262-6670 (CA only)
       (800) 821-6670 (US & Canada)
Fax: (310) 545-1672

See & Sea Travel
50 Francisco St. Ste. 205
San Francisco, CA 94133
Tel: (800) 348-9778
Fax: (415) 434-3409

Solmar Resorts
P.O. Box 383
843 Via de la Paz
Pacific Palisades, CA 90272
Tel: (800) 344-3349
Fax: (310) 454-1686

INDEX

A **boldface** page number denotes a picture caption.
An <u>underlined</u> page number indicates detailed treatment.

DIVING
BAJA CALIFORNIA

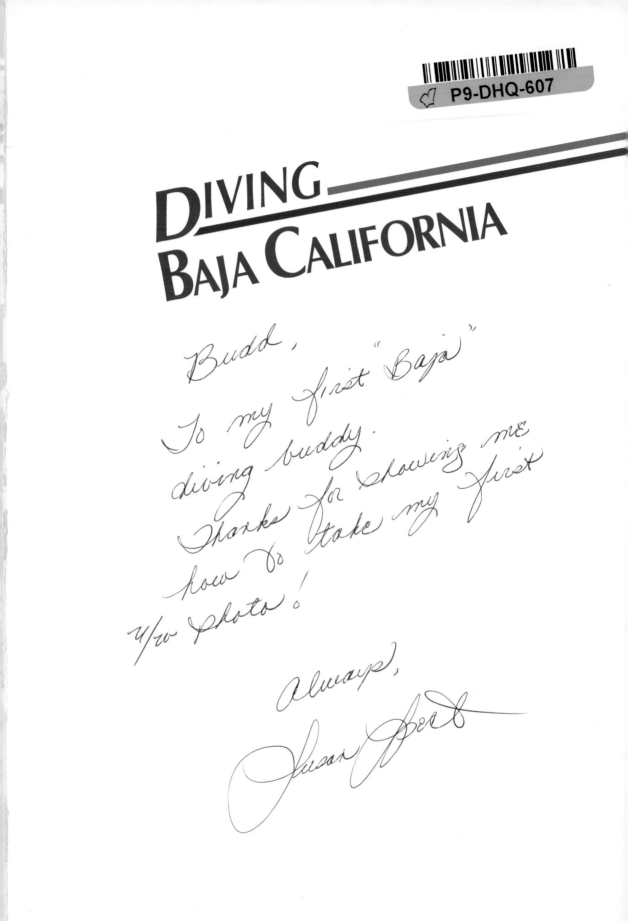

Budd,

To my first "Baja"
diving buddy.
Thanks for showing me
how to take my first
U/W photo!

Always,

Susan Speck

170 Calories — Thai Beef-Noodle Bowls, page 73

Lemony Asparagus-Prosciutto Ravioli, page 79 — **300** Calories

Angel Hair Pasta with Basil, Avocado and Tomatoes, page 94 — **260** Calories

230 Calories — Healthified Spicy Tostadas, page 95

C-3

260 Calories **Country French Chicken and Rice**, page 101

Roasted Butternut Squash-Stuffed Shells, page 110 **190** Calories

Easy Italian Artichoke-Bacon Pie, page 120 **280** Calories

Healthified Creamy Ricotta-Artichoke Lasagna, page 127

290
Calories

C-5

Healthified Rice and Bean Burgers, page 144

300 Calories

170 calories Lasagna Cupcakes, page 129

Tilapia Tacos, page 147

220 Calories

C-6

240 Calories

Falafel Sandwiches with Yogurt Sauce, page 152

Steak Salad with Creamy Dressing, page 162

170 Calories

Asian Shrimp and Noodle Salad, page 166

250 Calories

lasagna cupcakes

Prep Time: 15 Minutes   **Start to Finish:** 1 Hour   **Makes:** 12 servings   (photo on page C6)

170 Calories

1 cup ricotta cheese	2 cups frozen Italian sausage-style soy-protein crumbles
½ cup grated Parmesan cheese	
1 egg	36 round pot sticker (gyoza) wrappers
1 jar (25.5 oz) tomato pasta sauce (any variety)	1 cup shredded mozzarella cheese (4 oz)

1. Heat oven to 375°F. Spray 12 regular-size muffin cups with cooking spray. In small bowl, mix ricotta cheese, Parmesan cheese and egg. In another small bowl, mix pasta sauce and soy-protein crumbles.

2. Place 1 round wrapper in bottom of each muffin cup; top each with 1 heaping tablespoon pasta sauce mixture and 1 tablespoon cheese mixture. Repeat layers, ending with pasta sauce mixture. Sprinkle each with mozzarella cheese.

3. Spray large sheet of foil with cooking spray; place sprayed side down over pan. Bake 15 minutes. Uncover; bake 15 minutes longer. Let stand 15 minutes before serving.

1 Serving: Calories 170 (Calories from Fat 60); Total Fat 7g (Saturated Fat 3g; Trans Fat 0g); Cholesterol 30mg; Sodium 500mg; Total Carbohydrate 13g (Dietary Fiber 2g); Protein 12g **% Daily Value:** Vitamin A 8%; Vitamin C 4%; Calcium 20%; Iron 8% **Exchanges:** 1 Starch, 1 Medium-Fat Meat **Carbohydrate Choices:** 1

Quick Meal Idea Freeze these fantastic little casseroles to have on hand for a fast dinner—or to take to work for lunch. Microwave one frozen lasagna cupcake uncovered on Medium (50%) 5 to 6 minutes or until hot.

Try This

If you have some fresh basil on hand, layer some of the small leaves in the center of each lasagna cupcake.

sage and garlic vegetable bake

Prep Time: 25 Minutes   **Start to Finish:** 1 Hour 40 Minutes   **Makes:** 6 servings (1½ cups each)

1 medium butternut squash, peeled, cut into 1-inch pieces (3 cups)	1 medium onion, coarsely chopped (½ cup)
2 medium parsnips, peeled, cut into 1-inch pieces (2 cups)	½ cup uncooked quick-cooking barley
2 cans (14.5 oz each) stewed tomatoes, undrained	½ cup water
2 cups frozen cut green beans (from 12-oz bag)	1 teaspoon dried sage leaves
	½ teaspoon seasoned salt
	2 cloves garlic, finely chopped

1. Heat oven to 375°F. In ungreased 3-quart casserole, mix all ingredients, breaking up large pieces of tomatoes.

2. Cover; bake 1 hour to 1 hour 15 minutes or until vegetables and barley are tender.

1 Serving: Calories 170 (Calories from Fat 0); Total Fat 0g (Saturated Fat 0g; Trans Fat 0g); Cholesterol 0mg; Sodium 410mg; Total Carbohydrate 37g (Dietary Fiber 8g); Protein 4g **% Daily Value:** Vitamin A 150%; Vitamin C 30%; Calcium 8%; Iron 10% **Exchanges:** ½ Starch, 1½ Other Carbohydrate, 1½ Vegetable **Carbohydrate Choices:** 2½

Health Smart Butternut squash is chock-full of fiber and nutrients. The peanut-shaped squash has a peel that ranges from cream to yellow, and the flesh inside is bright orange.

asian stuffed portabellas

250 Calories

Prep Time: 55 Minutes **Start to Finish:** 1 Hour 10 Minutes **Makes:** 4 servings

¾ cup uncooked regular brown rice	½ cup cut-up snow pea pods
1½ cups water	¼ cup sliced green onions
4 large portabella mushroom caps (4 to 5 inches), stems removed	1 tablespoon finely chopped gingerroot
1 tablespoon canola oil	1 clove garlic, finely chopped
1½ cups coleslaw mix (shredded cabbage and carrots)	¼ cup reduced-sodium soy sauce
	2 teaspoons sesame oil
	4 teaspoons sesame seed

1. In 1½-quart saucepan, heat brown rice and water to boiling; reduce heat. Cover; simmer 45 to 50 minutes or until water is absorbed.

2. Heat oven to 400°F. Spray 15x10x1-inch pan with cooking spray. Place mushroom caps, gill sides down, in pan. Bake 5 minutes or until tender and beginning to brown.

3. Meanwhile, in 10-inch nonstick skillet, heat canola oil over medium-high heat. Add coleslaw mix, pea pods, onions, gingerroot and garlic; cook 2 to 3 minutes, stirring frequently, until coleslaw mix is wilted and vegetables are crisp-tender. Stir in cooked rice; sprinkle with soy sauce and sesame oil. Cook rice mixture, tossing gently with soy sauce and oil, until thoroughly heated; remove from heat.

4. Turn mushrooms gill sides up. Spoon rice mixture evenly into mushroom caps, about ¾ cup each; sprinkle each with 1 teaspoon sesame seed.

5. Bake 13 to 15 minutes or until sesame seed begins to turn brown.

1 Serving: Calories 250 (Calories from Fat 80); Total Fat 9g (Saturated Fat 1g; Trans Fat 0g); Cholesterol 0mg; Sodium 560mg; Total Carbohydrate 35g (Dietary Fiber 6g); Protein 7g **% Daily Value:** Vitamin A 15%; Vitamin C 15%; Calcium 4%; Iron 10% **Exchanges:** 2 Starch, 1 Vegetable, 1½ Fat **Carbohydrate Choices:** 2

Health Smart Keep sodium under control by cooking rice in water instead of broth and without salt. The soy sauce in this recipe provides plenty of flavor.

ratatouille-polenta bake

Prep Time: 25 Minutes   **Start to Finish:** 1 Hour 15 Minutes   **Makes:** 6 servings

1 medium onion, coarsely chopped (½ cup)	1 can (14.5 oz) Italian-style stewed tomatoes, undrained
1 medium bell pepper, coarsely chopped (1 cup)	1 roll (1 lb) refrigerated plain or flavored polenta
1 small unpeeled eggplant (1 lb), chopped (2 cups)	2 tablespoons shredded Parmesan cheese
1 medium zucchini, chopped (1 cup)	¾ cup finely shredded mozzarella cheese (3 oz)
½ teaspoon salt	¼ cup chopped fresh parsley
¼ teaspoon pepper	

1. Heat oven to 375°F. Spray 11x7-inch (2-quart) glass baking dish with cooking spray.

2. Spray 12-inch skillet with cooking spray; heat over medium-high heat. Add onion and bell pepper; cook 2 minutes, stirring occasionally. Stir in eggplant, zucchini, salt and pepper. Cook 3 to 4 minutes, stirring occasionally, until vegetables are tender. Stir in tomatoes, breaking up with spoon. Reduce heat to low. Cook 3 minutes, stirring occasionally. Remove from heat.

3. Cut polenta into ¼-inch slices. Arrange slices in bottom of baking dish, overlapping and cutting to fit as necessary. Sprinkle with Parmesan cheese. Spoon vegetable mixture evenly over top.

4. Cover; bake 30 minutes. Uncover; sprinkle with mozzarella cheese and parsley. Bake about 15 minutes longer or until bubbly and cheese is melted. Let stand 5 minutes before serving.

1 Serving: Calories 260 (Calories from Fat 65); Total Fat 7g (Saturated Fat 3g; Trans Fat 0g); Cholesterol 10mg; Sodium 830mg; Total Carbohydrate 45g (Dietary Fiber 6g); Protein 10g **% Daily Value:** Vitamin A 18%; Vitamin C 26%; Calcium 24%; Iron 16% **Exchanges:** 2 Starch, 3 Vegetable, ½ Fat **Carbohydrate Choices:** 3

Health Smart Eggplant is an exceptional choice for a lower-calorie eating plan. There are only about 20 calories in each ½ cup of this vegetable. Keep in mind that 1 pound of uncooked eggplant will yield about ½ pound when cooked.

chili-cheese sweet potato fries

270 Calories

Prep Time: 5 Minutes   **Start to Finish:** 30 Minutes   **Makes:** 6 servings

1   package (20 oz) frozen julienne-cut sweet potato fries
    Butter-flavor cooking spray
1   can (15 oz) vegetarian chili with beans

½   cup shredded reduced-fat sharp Cheddar cheese (2 oz)
4   medium green onions, sliced (¼ cup)

1. Heat oven to 450°F. Arrange fries in single layer in 15x10x1-inch pan. Spray fries with cooking spray. Bake 18 to 22 minutes or until crisp.

2. In small saucepan, heat chili over medium heat 3 minutes or until thoroughly heated.

3. Transfer fries to serving platter or individual plates. Spoon chili over fries; sprinkle with cheese and onions. Serve immediately.

1 Serving: Calories 270 (Calories from Fat 110); Total Fat 12g (Saturated Fat 2.5g; Trans Fat 0g); Cholesterol 10mg; Sodium 510mg; Total Carbohydrate 35g (Dietary Fiber 5g); Protein 7g **% Daily Value:** Vitamin A 60%; Vitamin C 2%; Calcium 10%; Iron 10% **Exchanges:** 2 Starch, ½ Other Carbohydrate, 2 Fat **Carbohydrate Choices:** 2

CHAPTER 5

Sandwiches & Salads

mediterranean chicken panini

Prep Time: 30 Minutes   **Start to Finish:** 50 Minutes   **Makes:** 4 sandwiches

¼ cup dry-pack sun-dried tomatoes	1 clove garlic, finely chopped
2 tablespoons boiling water	Dash pepper
¼ cup drained roasted red bell peppers (from 7-oz jar)	2 boneless skinless chicken breasts (4 oz each)
1 tablespoon balsamic vinegar	1 small zucchini
¾ teaspoon chopped fresh or ¼ teaspoon dried oregano leaves	4 multigrain ciabatta rolls or whole wheat bagel flatbreads, split
	Olive oil cooking spray

1. In small bowl, stir tomatoes and boiling water. Cover; let stand 5 minutes. In food processor, place undrained tomato mixture, roasted peppers, vinegar, oregano, garlic and pepper. Cover; process until smooth. Set aside.

2. Heat closed contact grill or panini maker for 5 minutes. Place chicken on grill. Close grill; cook 6 to 7 minutes or until chicken is no longer pink. Cool chicken slightly; cut crosswise into 2-inch slices. Wipe grill with damp paper towel, if necessary.

3. Using vegetable peeler, cut zucchini into very thin lengthwise strips. Spread reserved tomato mixture on cut sides of rolls. On roll bottoms, place chicken slices and zucchini strips; cover with roll tops. Lightly spray top and bottom of each sandwich with olive oil cooking spray.

4. Place sandwiches on grill (in batches, if necessary). Close grill, pressing down lightly; cook 2 to 3 minutes or until bread is toasted and sandwiches are hot.

1 Sandwich: Calories 240 (Calories from Fat 30); Total Fat 3.5g (Saturated Fat 0.5g; Trans Fat 0g); Cholesterol 35mg; Sodium 460mg; Total Carbohydrate 34g (Dietary Fiber 1g); Protein 17g **% Daily Value:** Vitamin A 8%; Vitamin C 25%; Calcium 0%; Iron 15% **Exchanges:** 1½ Starch, ½ Other Carbohydrate, 1 Vegetable, 1½ Very Lean Meat, ½ Fat **Carbohydrate Choices:** 2

Quick Meal Idea Serve these sandwiches with a side of homemade coleslaw—½ cup of coleslaw mix or shredded cabbage with 1 tablespoon fat-free coleslaw dressing adds only about 20 calories and a lot of crunch to your meal.

fontina panini with spinach

260 Calories

Prep Time: 15 Minutes   **Start to Finish:** 15 Minutes   **Makes:** 4 sandwiches

8 slices (½ inch thick) crusty Italian bread	½ cup drained roasted red bell peppers (from 7-oz jar), cut into strips
2 tablespoons honey mustard	4 oz Fontina cheese, cut into ⅛-inch-thick slices
2 medium green onions, sliced (2 tablespoons)	
1 cup loosely packed fresh spinach leaves	

1. Heat closed contact grill or panini maker for 5 minutes. Spread 1 side of each bread slice with honey mustard; sprinkle onions over 4 slices of bread. Layer with spinach, roasted peppers, cheese and remaining bread slices.

2. Place sandwiches on grill. Close grill; cook 2 to 3 minutes or until bread is toasted and cheese is melted. Cut each sandwich in half to serve.

1 Sandwich: Calories 260 (Calories from Fat 110); Total Fat 13g (Saturated Fat 6g; Trans Fat 0.5g); Cholesterol 35mg; Sodium 570mg; Total Carbohydrate 25g (Dietary Fiber 2g); Protein 11g **% Daily Value:** Vitamin A 20%; Vitamin C 2%; Calcium 20%; Iron 8% **Exchanges:** 1½ Starch, 1 Medium-Fat Meat, 1½ Fat **Carbohydrate Choices:** 1½

Try This

For great flavor and crunch, add a few chopped pecans with the green onions.

Substitute Gouda cheese if Fontina is not available.

fast 'n' fresh
chicken sandwiches

Prep Time: 10 Minutes   **Start to Finish:** 10 Minutes   **Makes:** 4 sandwiches

8 slices rustic raisin-nut or cranberry-nut bread	4 teaspoons chopped fresh dill weed
½ cup mascarpone cheese or cream cheese, softened	1 package (9 oz) thinly slice cooked chicken breast
4 medium green onions, chopped (¼ cup)	

1. On 1 side of each bread slice, spread 1 tablespoon cheese. On 4 slices, evenly sprinkle onions.

2. On remaining 4 slices, evenly sprinkle dill. Divide chicken among onion-topped bread slices; cover with dill-topped bread slices.

1 Sandwich: Calories 260 (Calories from Fat 40); Total Fat 4.5g (Saturated Fat 1g; Trans Fat 0.5g); Cholesterol 35mg; Sodium 1000mg; Total Carbohydrate 34g (Dietary Fiber 3g); Protein 20g **% Daily Value:** Vitamin A 4%; Vitamin C 6%; Calcium 10%; Iron 15% **Exchanges:** 1½ Starch, 1 Other Carbohydrate, 2 Very Lean Meat, ½ Fat **Carbohydrate Choices:** 2

Try This

These sandwiches can be prepared up to 2 hours ahead of time and chilled until ready to serve.

california chicken sandwiches

270 Calories

Prep Time: 10 Minutes   **Start to Finish:** 10 Minutes   **Makes:** 6 sandwiches

3 tablespoons reduced-fat mayonnaise	12 thin slices sourdough bread, toasted
1 medium green onion, finely chopped (1 tablespoon)	6 large slices tomato (¼ inch thick)
1 teaspoon smoked paprika	2 cups shredded skinless smoked chicken
½ teaspoon grated lemon peel	1 medium ripe avocado, pitted, peeled and cut into 12 slices
1 clove garlic, finely chopped	

1. In small bowl, stir together mayonnaise, onion, paprika, lemon peel and garlic with whisk.

2. On 1 side of 6 bread slices, evenly spread mayonnaise mixture; layer with tomato, chicken and avocado. Top with remaining 6 bread slices. Serve immediately.

1 Sandwich: Calories 270 (Calories from Fat 0); Total Fat 9g (Saturated Fat 2g; Trans Fat 0g); Cholesterol 0mg; Sodium 360mg; Total Carbohydrate 26g (Dietary Fiber 2g); Protein 20g **% Daily Value:** Vitamin A 10%; Vitamin C 4%; Calcium 4%; Iron 20% **Exchanges:** 2 Starch, 2 Very Lean Meat, 1½ Fat **Carbohydrate Choices:** 2

Try This

The mayonnaise mixture can be prepared ahead of time; cover and refrigerate until ready to assemble the sandwiches.

260 Calories

greek chicken burgers with tzatziki sauce

Prep Time: 30 Minutes   **Start to Finish:** 30 Minutes   **Makes:** 4 burgers

TZATZIKI SAUCE
- 1 medium peeled or unpeeled cucumber
- ½ cup plain Greek yogurt (from 6-oz container)
- 2 tablespoons chopped onion
- 2 teaspoons chopped fresh mint

BURGERS
- 1 lb lean ground chicken
- 1 cup chopped fresh spinach

- ¼ cup chopped pitted kalamata olives
- 1 tablespoon cornstarch
- 1 tablespoon chopped fresh oregano leaves
- 2 cloves garlic, chopped
- ¼ teaspoon salt
- ¼ teaspoon pepper
- 2 whole wheat pita (pocket) breads (6 inch), cut in half to form pockets
- ½ cup chopped tomato

1. Set oven control to broil. Chop enough cucumber to equal ½ cup; cut 12 slices from cucumber for sandwiches. Add all remaining sauce ingredients to chopped cucumber; refrigerate until serving time.

2. In large bowl, mix chicken, spinach, olives, cornstarch, oregano, garlic, salt and pepper. Shape into 4 oval patties, each about ½ inch thick. Place patties on broiler pan. Broil with tops about 5 inches from heat 10 to 12 minutes, turning once, until thermometer inserted in center of patties reads at least 165°F.

3. Place burgers in pita pocket halves; add tomato, 3 cucumber slices and about 3 tablespoons sauce to each.

1 Burger: Calories 260 (Calories from Fat 80); Total Fat 8g (Saturated Fat 2g; Trans Fat 0g); Cholesterol 65mg; Sodium 460mg; Total Carbohydrate 25g (Dietary Fiber 3g); Protein 20g **% Daily Value:** Vitamin A 25%; Vitamin C 6%; Calcium 10%; Iron 15% **Exchanges:** 1 Starch, ½ Other Carbohydrate, ½ Vegetable, 1 Very Lean Meat, 1½ Lean Meat, ½ Fat **Carbohydrate Choices:** 1½

Try This

Serve with a lemon wedge to squeeze over the filling in the pita halves. Lemon juice enhances the flavor of food without adding salt or carbs.

asian turkey burgers

Prep Time: 25 Minutes **Start to Finish:** 25 Minutes **Makes:** 5 burgers

300 Calories

1 cup Fiber One original bran cereal	½ teaspoon ground ginger
1 lb lean (at least 93%) ground turkey	⅛ teaspoon pepper
1 small onion, finely chopped (⅓ cup)	5 whole wheat burger buns, split
¼ cup reduced-sodium teriyaki marinade and sauce (from 10-oz bottle)	5 leaves leaf lettuce
¼ cup chopped fresh parsley	5 slices tomato

1. Heat gas or charcoal grill. Place cereal in resealable food-storage plastic bag; seal bag and crush with rolling pin or meat mallet.

2. In large bowl, mix crushed cereal, turkey, onion, teriyaki marinade, parsley, ginger and pepper until well mixed. Shape mixture into 5 (4-inch) patties.

3. Carefully brush oil on grill rack. Place patties on grill over medium heat. Cover grill; cook 11 to 15 minutes, turning once, until meat thermometer inserted in center of patties reads at least 165°F.

4. On bun bottoms, place lettuce, tomato and burgers; cover with bun tops.

1 Burger: Calories 300 (Calories from Fat 60); Total Fat 7g (Saturated Fat 1.5g; Trans Fat 0.5g); Cholesterol 60mg; Sodium 560mg; Total Carbohydrate 32g (Dietary Fiber 9g); Protein 26g **% Daily Value:** Vitamin A 15%; Vitamin C 8%; Calcium 10%; Iron 20% **Exchanges:** 2 Starch, ½ Vegetable, 2½ Very Lean Meat, 1 Fat **Carbohydrate Choices:** 2

Broiling Directions: To broil patties, set oven control to broil. Place patties on broiler pan; broil with tops about 5 inches from heat 11 to 15 minutes, turning once.

Kitchen Tip Look for teriyaki marinade and sauce in the Asian foods section in your supermarket. Don't confuse teriyaki baste and glaze, which is thick like molasses, with the teriyaki marinade and sauce, which is watery.

turkey burgers with chutney

Prep Time: 15 Minutes   **Start to Finish:** 15 Minutes   **Makes:** 4 burgers

BURGERS

1	lb ground turkey breast
1	egg white
¼	teaspoon salt
¼	teaspoon freshly ground pepper
4	whole wheat burger buns, split
4	leaves green leaf lettuce

CHUTNEY

⅓	cup cranberry chutney
⅓	cup finely chopped fresh peach
1	medium green onion, finely chopped (1 tablespoon)

1. In medium bowl, mix turkey, egg white, salt and pepper. Shape mixture into 4 patties, ½ inch thick.

2. Spray 12-inch skillet with cooking spray; heat over medium heat. Add patties; cook 6 to 8 minutes, turning once, until meat thermometer inserted in center of patties reads at least 165°F.

3. Meanwhile, in small bowl, mix chutney ingredients until well blended.

4. On bun bottoms, place lettuce and burgers. Spoon 2 tablespoons chutney on each burger. Cover with bun tops.

1 Burger: Calories 300 (Calories from Fat 0); Total Fat 4g (Saturated Fat 1g; Trans Fat 0g); Cholesterol 0mg; Sodium 450mg; Total Carbohydrate 36g (Dietary Fiber 3g); Protein 31g **% Daily Value:** Vitamin A 10%; Vitamin C 6%; Calcium 6%; Iron 15% **Exchanges:** 1 Starch, 4 Lean Meat **Carbohydrate Choices:** 2

Quick Meal Idea Serve these dressed-up turkey burgers with vegetable chips and red grapes.

blts with pimiento cheese

230 Calories

Prep Time: 10 Minutes   **Start to Finish:** 10 Minutes   **Makes:** 4 sandwiches

½	cup reduced-fat pimiento cheese spread
8	slices whole wheat or white bread
8	slices reduced-fat bacon, crisply cooked
4	leaves green leaf lettuce
12	slices tomato (¼ inch thick)
¼	teaspoon freshly ground pepper

1. Spread 1 tablespoon pimiento cheese over 1 side of each bread slice.

2. On each of 4 bread slices, layer 2 bacon slices, 1 lettuce leaf and 3 tomato slices. Sprinkle with pepper. Top with remaining 4 bread slices. Cut sandwiches in half; secure each half with toothpick, if desired.

1 Sandwich: Calories 230 (Calories from Fat 0); Total Fat 8g (Saturated Fat 2g; Trans Fat 0g); Cholesterol 0mg; Sodium 690mg; Total Carbohydrate 30g (Dietary Fiber 8g); Protein 12g **% Daily Value:** Vitamin A 25%; Vitamin C 15%; Calcium 15%; Iron 15% **Exchanges:** 2 Starch, 1 Medium-Fat Meat **Carbohydrate Choices:** 2

healthified rice and bean burgers

Prep Time: 30 Minutes   **Start to Finish:** 30 Minutes   **Makes:** 4 burgers   (photo on page C6)

1	can (15 oz) kidney beans, drained, rinsed	½	teaspoon ground cumin
1	medium onion, finely chopped (½ cup)	¼	teaspoon pepper
¼	cup finely chopped celery	⅛	teaspoon salt
¼	cup soft whole wheat bread crumbs	¾	cup cooked brown rice
2	tablespoons chopped fresh cilantro	4	whole wheat burger buns, split, toasted
1	clove garlic, finely chopped	2	tablespoons fat-free mayonnaise
½	teaspoon dried oregano leaves		Fresh spinach leaves, sliced tomato and red onion, if desired

1. In medium bowl, coarsely mash beans with potato masher or fork. Stir in chopped onion, celery, bread crumbs, cilantro, garlic, oregano, cumin, pepper and salt. Stir in rice. Shape mixture into 4 patties, ½ inch thick.

2. Heat grill pan or large skillet over medium heat. Add patties; cook 10 to 12 minutes, turning once, until thoroughly heated.

3. Spread cut sides of bun bottoms with mayonnaise; top with burgers, spinach, tomato and red onion. Cover with bun tops.

1 Burger: Calories 300 (Calories from Fat 25); Total Fat 3g (Saturated Fat 0.5g; Trans Fat 0g); Cholesterol 0mg; Sodium 580mg; Total Carbohydrate 53g (Dietary Fiber 10g); Protein 14g **% Daily Value:** Vitamin A 0%; Vitamin C 4%; Calcium 10%; Iron 20% **Exchanges:** 3½ Starch, ½ Vegetable, ½ Very Lean Meat **Carbohydrate Choices:** 3½

pizza joes

Prep Time: 25 Minutes   **Start to Finish:** 25 Minutes   **Makes:** 8 sandwiches

290 Calories

1 lb extra-lean (at least 90%) ground beef	2 cups pizza sauce (from two 15-oz jars or cans)
1 large onion, coarsely chopped (1 cup)	8 burger buns, split, toasted
1 medium green bell pepper, coarsely chopped (about 1 cup)	1 cup shredded mozzarella cheese (4 oz)

1. Heat 12-inch nonstick skillet over medium-high heat. Add beef, onion and bell pepper; cook 7 to 9 minutes, stirring occasionally, until beef is thoroughly cooked.

2. Stir in pizza sauce. Reduce heat to medium; simmer uncovered about 5 minutes or until thoroughly heated.

3. Spoon beef mixture into buns; top with cheese.

1 Sandwich: Calories 290 (Calories from Fat 90); Total Fat 10g (Saturated Fat 4.5g; Trans Fat 0.5g); Cholesterol 45mg; Sodium 420mg; Total Carbohydrate 30g (Dietary Fiber 3g); Protein 20g **% Daily Value:** Vitamin A 10%; Vitamin C 15%; Calcium 20%; Iron 20% **Exchanges:** 2 Starch, 1 Vegetable, 1 Lean Meat, 1 Fat **Carbohydrate Choices:** 2

Try This

To save time, you can substitute 2 cups frozen diced onion and green bell pepper for the fresh onion and bell pepper, or look for chopped fresh vegetables in the produce department.

steak sandwiches with carrot slaw

Prep Time: 30 Minutes   **Start to Finish:** 35 Minutes   **Makes:** 4 sandwiches

2 teaspoons rice vinegar	¼ cup shredded radishes
1 teaspoon grated gingerroot	1 tablespoon chopped fresh cilantro
2 cloves garlic, finely chopped	4 frozen ciabatta rolls (1.5 oz each; from 12-oz bag)
4 teaspoons olive oil	
½ teaspoon salt	1 flank steak (1 lb), trimmed of fat
½ teaspoon freshly ground pepper	1 teaspoon five-spice powder
1 cup shredded carrots (from 10-oz bag)	2 cups fresh baby spinach leaves

1. In medium bowl, mix vinegar, gingerroot, garlic, 1 teaspoon of the oil and ¼ teaspoon each of the salt and pepper. Add carrots, radishes and cilantro; toss to coat. Cover; refrigerate until serving time.

2. Heat gas or charcoal grill. Meanwhile, bake rolls as directed on package.

3. Rub steak with 2 teaspoons oil; sprinkle with five-spice powder and remaining ¼ teaspoon each salt and pepper. Carefully brush remaining 1 teaspoon oil on grill rack. Place steak on grill over medium-high heat. Cover grill; cook 12 minutes, turning once, until of desired doneness. Transfer steak from grill to cutting board. Cover loosely; let stand 5 minutes. Cut steak diagonally across grain into thin slices.

4. Cut rolls in half horizontally. On roll bottoms, place spinach, steak and carrot slaw. Cover with roll tops.

1 Sandwich: Calories 300 (Calories from Fat 0); Total Fat 10g (Saturated Fat 2.5g; Trans Fat 0g); Cholesterol 0mg; Sodium 580mg; Total Carbohydrate 23g (Dietary Fiber 2g); Protein 29g **% Daily Value:** Vitamin A 13%; Vitamin C 10%; Calcium 4%; Iron 25% **Exchanges:** 1½ Starch, ½ Vegetable, 3 Lean Meat **Carbohydrate Choices:** 1½

tilapia tacos

Prep Time: 20 Minutes   **Start to Finish:** 20 Minutes   **Makes:** 5 servings (2 tacos each)
(photo on page C6)

220
Calories

1	box (8.8 oz) taco shells that stand on their own dinner kit
1	lb tilapia fillets, cut into 1-inch pieces
2½	cups coleslaw mix (from 16-oz bag)

¼	cup coleslaw dressing
1	ripe avocado, pitted, peeled and diced
	Lime wedges, if desired

1. Heat oven to 375°F. Spray large cookie sheet with cooking spray.

2. In large resealable food-storage plastic bag, place seasoning mix (from dinner kit) and fish pieces. Seal bag; shake to coat fish with seasoning. Place fish on one half of cookie sheet. Bake 8 to 10 minutes or until fish flakes easily with fork. For last 4 minutes of bake time, place taco shells on other half of cookie sheet.

3. Meanwhile, in medium bowl, toss coleslaw mix and dressing.

4. Divide coleslaw evenly among warmed taco shells. Top each with fish, avocado and 2 teaspoons taco sauce (from dinner kit). Serve with lime wedges.

1 Serving: Calories 220 (Calories from Fat 100); Total Fat 11g (Saturated Fat 2g; Trans Fat 0g); Cholesterol 50mg; Sodium 350mg; Total Carbohydrate 11g (Dietary Fiber 3g); Protein 18g **% Daily Value:** Vitamin A 15%; Vitamin C 15%; Calcium 4%; Iron 2% **Exchanges:** ½ Starch, 2½ Very Lean Meat, 2 Fat **Carbohydrate Choices:** 1

Try This

Tilapia is a mild whitefish available year-round. Other whitefish like cod, pollack or halibut would be good substitutes.

salsa-shrimp tacos

Prep Time: 15 Minutes   **Start to Finish:** 15 Minutes   **Makes:** 6 servings (2 tacos each)
(photo on page C7)

¾	cup chunky-style salsa	1	box (4.6 oz) taco shells (12 shells)
½	cup chopped green bell pepper	¾	cup shredded Mexican cheese blend (3 oz)
¾	lb uncooked deveined peeled medium shrimp, thawed if frozen, tail shells removed	¾	cup shredded lettuce
		¼	cup taco sauce

1. In 10-inch nonstick skillet, heat salsa and bell pepper over medium-high heat, stirring frequently, until warm.

2. Stir in shrimp. Cook 3 to 4 minutes, turning shrimp occasionally, until shrimp are pink.

3. Fill each taco shell with about ¼ cup shrimp mixture. Top with cheese, lettuce and taco sauce.

1 Serving: Calories 210 (Calories from Fat 80); Total Fat 9g (Saturated Fat 5g; Trans Fat 0g); Cholesterol 95mg; Sodium 570mg; Total Carbohydrate 16g (Dietary Fiber 1g); Protein 13g **% Daily Value:** Vitamin A 10%; Vitamin C 10%; Calcium 15%; Iron 10% **Exchanges:** 1 Starch, 1½ Lean Meat, 1 Fat **Carbohydrate Choices:** 1

mexican potato tacos

Prep Time: 35 Minutes   **Start to Finish:** 35 Minutes   **Makes:** 4 tacos

200 Calories

2 large unpeeled Yukon Gold or 3 or 4 medium red potatoes (½ lb), cut into ¼- to ½-inch pieces
2 tablespoons vegetable oil
1 medium onion, chopped (½ cup)
½ medium green bell pepper, finely chopped (½ cup)
½ cup salsa verde
2½ teaspoons taco seasoning mix (from 1-oz package)

4 taco shells that stand on their own (from 4.7-oz box), heated as directed on box
1 cup shredded lettuce
1 medium tomato, seeded, chopped
½ cup taco sauce
½ cup crumbled queso fresco cheese or shredded Mexican cheese blend (2 oz)

1. Place potatoes in microwavable bowl; cover with microwavable plastic wrap. Microwave on High 5 minutes or until tender.

2. In 10-inch skillet, heat oil over medium-high heat. Add potatoes, onion and bell pepper; cook 5 to 7 minutes, stirring frequently, until onion and bell pepper are crisp-tender. Reduce heat to medium-low. Stir in salsa verde and taco seasoning mix; cook 3 to 5 minutes, stirring occasionally.

3. Divide filling evenly among taco shells. Top each with lettuce, tomato, taco sauce and cheese.

1 Taco: Calories 200 (Calories from Fat 90); Total Fat 11g (Saturated Fat 3.5g; Trans Fat 0g); Cholesterol 10mg; Sodium 700mg; Total Carbohydrate 20g (Dietary Fiber 2g); Protein 5g **% Daily Value:** Vitamin A 15%; Vitamin C 20%; Calcium 10%; Iron 6% **Exchanges:** 1 Starch, 1 Vegetable, 2 Fat **Carbohydrate Choices:** 1

Kitchen Tip Salsa verde is a green salsa, often made of tomatillos, cilantro and green chiles. It is now commonly available at the grocery store. Of course, other types of salsas can be substituted and used in this recipe.

greek tuna salad pita sandwiches with feta cheese

Prep Time: 20 Minutes   **Start to Finish:** 20 Minutes   **Makes:** 6 sandwiches

1	tablespoon olive oil
1	tablespoon lemon juice
1	clove garlic, finely chopped
¼	teaspoon salt
1	medium cucumber, peeled, seeded and finely chopped
1	medium tomato, seeded, diced
½	cup crumbled feta cheese (2 oz)

12	kalamata or other large ripe olives, pitted, coarsely chopped (¼ cup)
2	cans (5 oz each) tuna in water, drained, flaked
3	leaves romaine lettuce, torn in half
6	pita (pocket) breads (6 inch), cut in half to form pockets

1. In small bowl, stir together oil, lemon juice, garlic and salt with whisk. In medium bowl, toss cucumber, tomato, cheese, olives and tuna. Pour dressing over salad; toss until coated.

2. Place 1 lettuce leaf half in each pita pocket; add ½ cup tuna salad to each. Serve immediately.

1 Sandwich: Calories 270 (Calories from Fat 60); Total Fat 7g (Saturated Fat 2.5g; Trans Fat 0g); Cholesterol 25mg; Sodium 610mg; Total Carbohydrate 33g (Dietary Fiber 2g); Protein 19g **% Daily Value:** Vitamin A 10%; Vitamin C 4%; Calcium 15%; Iron 15% **Exchanges:** 2 Starch, ½ Vegetable, 1½ Lean Meat, ½ Fat **Carbohydrate Choices:** 2

dilled shrimp and egg salad wraps

290 Calories

Prep Time: 10 Minutes   **Start to Finish:** 10 Minutes   **Makes:** 4 wraps

4 hard-cooked eggs, chopped
1 cup chopped cooked shrimp
1 tablespoon chopped fresh dill weed
2 tablespoons finely chopped red onion
3 tablespoons creamy Dijon mustard–mayonnaise spread

¼ teaspoon salt
4 flour tortillas for burritos (8 inch; from 11-oz package)
2 cups shredded lettuce

1. In medium bowl, mix all ingredients except tortillas and lettuce. Spread shrimp mixture evenly on each tortilla; top with lettuce.

2. Fold in sides of tortilla and roll up; cut in half. Serve immediately, or wrap in plastic wrap and refrigerate up to 24 hours.

1 Wrap: Calories 290 (Calories from Fat 100); Total Fat 11g (Saturated Fat 3g; Trans Fat 1g); Cholesterol 335mg; Sodium 740mg; Total Carbohydrate 24g (Dietary Fiber 0g); Protein 22g **% Daily Value:** Vitamin A 10%; Vitamin C 4%; Calcium 10%; Iron 20% **Exchanges:** 1½ Starch, ½ Vegetable, 1 Very Lean Meat, 1 Medium-Fat Meat, 1 Fat **Carbohydrate Choices:** 1½

Try This

Using shredded lettuce instead of leaves makes rolling the wraps easier. To shred lettuce, cut the leaves into thin strips with a sharp knife. Or save time by buying bagged shredded lettuce.

falafel sandwiches with yogurt sauce

Prep Time: 1 Hour   **Start to Finish:** 1 Hour   **Makes:** 8 sandwiches   (photo on page C8)

SANDWICHES

- ¾ cup water
- ¼ cup uncooked bulgur
- 1 can (15 oz) garbanzo beans, drained, rinsed
- ¼ cup chopped fresh cilantro
- ¼ cup sliced green onions (4 medium)
- 1 tablespoon all-purpose flour
- 3 tablespoons water
- 2 teaspoons ground cumin
- ¾ teaspoon baking powder
- ½ teaspoon salt
- 2 cloves garlic, finely chopped
- 4 pita (pocket) breads (6 inch), cut in half to form pockets
- 2 tablespoons vegetable oil
- 8 slices tomato
- 16 slices cucumber

SAUCE

- 1 cup plain fat-free yogurt
- 2 tablespoons chopped fresh mint leaves
- ¼ teaspoon ground cumin

1. In 1-quart saucepan, heat ¾ cup water to boiling. Stir in bulgur; remove from heat. Cover; let stand about 30 minutes or until tender. Drain; set aside.

2. Meanwhile, in food processor, place beans, cilantro, onions, flour, 3 tablespoons water, 2 teaspoons cumin, the baking powder, salt and garlic. Cover; process with on-and-off pulses 10 times or until well blended and coarsely chopped (mixture will be wet). Spoon mixture into large bowl.

3. Stir bulgur into bean mixture. Divide mixture into 8 equal portions, about ¼ cup each; shape each portion into oval patty, ¼ inch thick.

4. In 10-inch nonstick skillet, heat 1 tablespoon of the oil over medium heat. Add 4 patties; cook 8 minutes, turning once, until golden brown. Transfer patties to platter; cover with foil to keep warm. Repeat with remaining 1 tablespoon oil and 4 patties.

5. Meanwhile, in small bowl, stir together sauce ingredients. Spread 2 tablespoons sauce in each pita pocket half. Fill each with tomato slices, cucumber slices and falafel patty.

1 Sandwich: Calories 240 (Calories from Fat 50); Total Fat 5g (Saturated Fat 1g; Trans Fat 0g); Cholesterol 0mg; Sodium 370mg; Total Carbohydrate 39g (Dietary Fiber 5g); Protein 10g **% Daily Value:** Vitamin A 6%; Vitamin C 4%; Calcium 15%; Iron 15% **Exchanges:** 2½ Starch, ½ Vegetable, ½ Fat **Carbohydrate Choices:** 2½

Try This

The falafel patties can be baked at 400°F for 20 minutes on a greased cookie sheet turning once, but they won't have the crisp crust that comes from cooking on the stovetop.

crunchy oriental chicken salad

300 Calories

Prep Time: 15 Minutes   **Start to Finish:** 15 Minutes   **Makes:** 6 servings (about 1¼ cups each)

2 tablespoons butter	½ teaspoon pepper
1 package (3 oz) oriental-flavor ramen noodle soup mix	2 cups cut-up cooked chicken
2 tablespoons sesame seed	¼ cup dry-roasted peanuts, if desired
¼ cup sugar	4 medium green onions, sliced (¼ cup)
¼ cup white vinegar	1 bag (16 oz) coleslaw mix (8 cups)
1 tablespoon dark sesame oil	1 can (11 oz) mandarin orange segments, drained

1. In 10-inch skillet, melt butter over medium heat. Stir in seasoning packet from soup mix. Break block of noodles into bite-size pieces over skillet; stir into butter mixture. Cook noodles 2 minutes, stirring occasionally. Stir in sesame seed. Cook about 2 minutes longer, stirring occasionally, until noodles are golden brown; remove from heat.

2. In large glass or plastic bowl, mix sugar, vinegar, oil and pepper. Add noodle mixture and all remaining ingredients; toss. Serve immediately.

1 Serving: Calories 300 (Calories from Fat 110); Total Fat 12g (Saturated Fat 4g; Trans Fat 1g); Cholesterol 45mg; Sodium 320mg; Total Carbohydrate 30g (Dietary Fiber 4g); Protein 17g **% Daily Value:** Vitamin A 40%; Vitamin C 40%; Calcium 8%; Iron 8% **Exchanges:** 2 Starch, 1½ Lean Meat, 1 Fat **Carbohydrate Choices:** 2

280 Calories

southwest layered chicken salad

Prep Time: 35 Minutes   **Start to Finish:** 35 Minutes   **Makes:** 12 servings

¾ cup mayonnaise
¾ cup sour cream
1 envelope (1 oz) taco seasoning mix
⅓ cup chopped fresh cilantro
1 teaspoon grated lime peel
3 tablespoons fresh lime juice
8 cups chopped romaine lettuce

½ medium jicama, peeled, cut into matchstick pieces (about 1 cup)
3 cups chopped cooked chicken
1 can (15.25 oz) whole-kernel corn, drained
2 large red bell peppers, chopped (about 2½ cups)
2 ripe avocados, pitted, peeled and chopped (about 3 cups)

1. In medium bowl, mix mayonnaise, sour cream, taco seasoning mix, cilantro, lime peel and lime juice until well blended.

2. In 4-quart glass serving bowl, layer all remaining ingredients except avocados. Just before serving, top salad with avocados. Serve with dressing.

1 Serving: Calories 280 (Calories from Fat 180); Total Fat 20g (Saturated Fat 4.5g; Trans Fat 0g); Cholesterol 45mg; Sodium 430mg; Total Carbohydrate 13g (Dietary Fiber 4g); Protein 12g **% Daily Value:** Vitamin A 80%; Vitamin C 80%; Calcium 4%; Iron 8% **Exchanges:** 1 Starch, 1½ Lean Meat, 3 Fat **Carbohydrate Choices:** 1

Try This

Leave the chopped cilantro out of the dressing and serve it on the side in a separate small bowl, so guests can sprinkle it on their salads if they choose.

italian chicken salad

Prep Time: 10 Minutes   **Start to Finish:** 10 Minutes   **Makes:** 12 servings (1½ cups each)

170 Calories

4 cups cut-up cooked chicken	2 cans (4¼ oz each) chopped ripe olives, drained
2 bags (10 oz each) Italian-blend (romaine and radicchio) salad greens (about 12 cups)	½ cup zesty Italian dressing
2 cans (14 oz each) artichoke hearts, drained, chopped	

1. In very large (9-quart) bowl, mix chicken, salad greens, artichoke hearts and olives.

2. Just before serving, drizzle dressing over salad; toss until coated.

1 Serving: Calories 170 (Calories from Fat 50); Total Fat 6g (Saturated Fat 1g; Trans Fat 0g); Cholesterol 40mg; Sodium 480mg; Total Carbohydrate 12g (Dietary Fiber 7g); Protein 16g **% Daily Value:** Vitamin A 60%; Vitamin C 10%; Calcium 6%; Iron 10% **Exchanges:** ½ Starch, 1 Vegetable, 1½ Very Lean Meat, 1 Fat **Carbohydrate Choices:** 1

Try This

Use a balsamic vinaigrette dressing instead of the zesty Italian.

chicken bulgur salad

230 Calories

Prep Time: 20 Minutes   **Start to Finish:** 20 Minutes   **Makes:** 4 servings (1¼ cups each)

1 cup water
½ cup uncooked bulgur
1½ cups cubed cooked chicken breast
1 can (14 oz) artichoke hearts, drained, coarsely chopped

1 cup finely chopped fresh parsley
1 cup grape tomatoes, cut in half
⅓ cup light Northern Italian dressing with basil and Romano cheese
2 tablespoons lemon juice

1. In 2-quart saucepan, heat water to boiling; stir in bulgur. Return to boiling; reduce heat. Cover; simmer 8 minutes or until liquid is absorbed. Rinse with cold water; drain well.

2. In large bowl, stir together all remaining ingredients. Add bulgur; toss gently to coat.

1 Serving: Calories 230 (Calories from Fat 0); Total Fat 6g (Saturated Fat 1g; Trans Fat 0g); Cholesterol 0mg; Sodium 440mg; Total Carbohydrate 23g (Dietary Fiber 4g); Protein 21g **% Daily Value:** Vitamin A 35%; Vitamin C 30%; Calcium 6%; Iron 15% **Exchanges:** 1 Starch, 1 Vegetable, 2 Very Lean Meat, 1 Fat **Carbohydrate Choices:** 1½

Try This

Adding freshly squeezed lemon juice to a bottled dressing makes it taste like it was made from scratch.

gazpacho-style chicken salad

240 Calories

Prep Time: 25 Minutes **Start to Finish:** 25 Minutes **Makes:** 2 servings (photo on page C8)

SALAD

- 4 cups packed torn green and/or red leaf lettuce
- 1 package (6 oz) refrigerated grilled chicken breast strips
- 1 medium tomato, chopped (¾ cup)
- 1 cup chopped peeled cucumber
- ¾ cup chopped yellow bell pepper
- ⅓ cup thinly sliced red onion

DRESSING

- ½ cup spicy Bloody Mary mix
- 3 tablespoons red wine vinegar
- 2 tablespoons olive oil
- ½ teaspoon salt
- ¼ teaspoon pepper
- ¼ teaspoon red pepper sauce
- 1 clove garlic, finely chopped

1. Arrange lettuce on serving platter. Arrange chicken in center of lettuce. Place tomato, cucumber, bell pepper and onion on top of lettuce, around the chicken.

2. In tightly covered container, shake all dressing ingredients. Spoon ¼ cup dressing over salad; gently toss to coat. Serve immediately. Reserve remaining dressing for another use.

1 Serving: Calories 240 (Calories from Fat 70); Total Fat 8g (Saturated Fat 1.5g; Trans Fat 0g); Cholesterol 70mg; Sodium 720mg; Total Carbohydrate 13g (Dietary Fiber 3g); Protein 29g **% Daily Value:** Vitamin A 130%; Vitamin C 110%; Calcium 8%; Iron 15% **Exchanges:** 3 Vegetable, 3 Lean Meat **Carbohydrate Choices:** 1

Try This

Change up the flavor of the dressing by experimenting with different types of vinegar. Try white wine vinegar or cider vinegar.

220 Calories

grilled chicken and vegetable salad

Prep Time: 20 Minutes   **Start to Finish:** 20 Minutes   **Makes:** 4 servings (2¾ cups each)

1   lb uncooked chicken breast tenders (not breaded)
7   tablespoons light balsamic vinaigrette dressing
1   medium zucchini (8 oz), cut lengthwise in half

1   medium red onion, cut into ¼-inch slices
4   plum (Roma) tomatoes, cut in half
6   cups baby arugula
¼   cup crumbled feta cheese (1 oz)

1. Heat gas or charcoal grill. Brush chicken with 1 tablespoon of the dressing. Carefully brush oil on grill rack. Place chicken, zucchini and onion on grill over medium-high heat. Cover grill; cook 6 to 8 minutes, turning once, or until chicken is no longer pink in center and vegetables are tender. Add tomato halves to grill for last 4 minutes of cooking time.

2. Remove chicken and vegetables from grill. Cut chicken crosswise into thin slices; coarsely chop vegetables.

3. In large bowl, toss chicken, vegetables and remaining 6 tablespoons dressing. Add arugula and cheese; toss gently.

1 Serving: Calories 220 (Calories from Fat 0); Total Fat 8g (Saturated Fat 2g; Trans Fat 0g); Cholesterol 0mg; Sodium 510mg; Total Carbohydrate 11g (Dietary Fiber 2g); Protein 27g **% Daily Value:** Vitamin A 25%; Vitamin C 20%; Calcium 10%; Iron 10% **Exchanges:** 2 Vegetable, 3 Very Lean Meat, 1 Fat **Carbohydrate Choices:** ½

chicken, edamame and rice salad

240 Calories

Prep Time: 20 Minutes   **Start to Finish:** 20 Minutes   **Makes:** 4 servings

1 package (8.8 oz) microwavable long-grain white rice	1 tablespoon grated gingerroot
1¼ cups frozen shelled edamame (from 10- to 12-oz bag)	2 tablespoons rice vinegar
1 cup chopped cooked chicken breast	1 tablespoon canola oil
2 tablespoons finely chopped fresh mint leaves	¼ teaspoon salt
	4 leaves radicchio

1. Cook rice in microwave as directed on package.

2. In small microwavable bowl, place edamame and 3 tablespoons water. Cover with microwavable plastic wrap. Microwave on High 3 minutes. Let stand 2 minutes; drain.

3. In large bowl, mix rice, edamame, chicken, mint, gingerroot, vinegar, oil and salt. Spoon about ¾ cup salad onto each radicchio leaf.

1 Serving: Calories 240 (Calories from Fat 0); Total Fat 8g (Saturated Fat 0.5g; Trans Fat 0g); Cholesterol 0mg; Sodium 330mg; Total Carbohydrate 24g (Dietary Fiber 3g); Protein 19g **% Daily Value:** Vitamin A 2%; Vitamin C 4%; Calcium 6%; Iron 15% **Exchanges:** 2 Starch, 2 Lean Meat, 1 Fat **Carbohydrate Choices:** 2

Kitchen Tip If you've never tried edamame, here is your chance! These soybeans look much like lima beans and have a wonderful mild, nutty flavor.

healthified italian chopped salad

Prep Time: 30 Minutes   **Start to Finish:** 30 Minutes   **Makes:** 8 servings (1²/₃ cups each)

SALAD

- 6 cups chopped romaine lettuce
- 2 cups shredded cooked chicken breast
- 1 medium yellow or green bell pepper, coarsely chopped
- 1 medium unpeeled cucumber, chopped
- 3 plum (Roma) tomatoes, chopped
- 2 oz Genoa salami, chopped (⅓ cup)
- 1 can (15 oz) garbanzo beans, drained, rinsed
- ½ cup pitted kalamata olives, halved
- ¼ cup very thinly sliced red onion
- ½ cup torn fresh basil leaves
- 1 oz Parmesan cheese, shaved

DRESSING

- 3 tablespoons olive oil
- 3 tablespoons balsamic vinegar
- 1 teaspoon Dijon mustard
- 1 teaspoon sugar
- ⅛ teaspoon coarse ground black pepper
- 1 clove garlic, finely chopped

1. In large bowl, toss all salad ingredients except cheese.

2. In small bowl, beat all dressing ingredients with whisk until blended. Pour dressing over salad mixture; toss to coat. Top with cheese.

1 Serving: Calories 250 (Calories from Fat 110); Total Fat 12g (Saturated Fat 2.5g; Trans Fat 0g); Cholesterol 40mg; Sodium 320mg; Total Carbohydrate 19g (Dietary Fiber 4g); Protein 18g **% Daily Value:** Vitamin A 50%; Vitamin C 70%; Calcium 10%; Iron 15% **Exchanges:** 1 Starch, 2 Lean Meat, 1 Fat **Carbohydrate Choices:** 1

Kitchen Tip We've called for Genoa salami because it's a traditional Italian favorite, but you could use any salami that you like in this restaurant-style salad.

Health Smart Parmesan cheese is used instead of provolone because it packs a punch of flavor in a smaller amount. You won't miss the extra cheese!

asian steak salad

Prep Time: 20 Minutes **Start to Finish:** 20 Minutes **Makes:** 6 servings

1	lb cut-up lean beef for stir-fry	1	cup fresh snow pea pods, strings removed, cut diagonally in half
1	package (3 oz) oriental-flavor ramen noodle soup mix	½	cup julienne carrots (from 10-oz bag)
½	cup reduced-fat Asian marinade and dressing	1	can (11 oz) mandarin orange segments, drained
1	bag (10 oz) romaine and leaf lettuce mix		

1. Spray 12-inch skillet with cooking spray; heat over medium-high heat. Add beef to skillet; sprinkle with 1 teaspoon seasoning mix from soup mix. (Discard remaining seasoning mix.) Cook beef 4 to 5 minutes, stirring occasionally, until browned. Stir in 1 tablespoon of the dressing.

2. In large bowl, break block of noodles from soup mix into small pieces. Add lettuce, pea pods, carrots, and orange segments. Add remaining dressing; toss until well coated. Divide mixture among individual serving plates. Top with beef strips.

1 Serving: Calories 240 (Calories from Fat 60); Total Fat 7g (Saturated Fat 2.5g; Trans Fat 1g); Cholesterol 30mg; Sodium 990mg; Total Carbohydrate 25g (Dietary Fiber 2g); Protein 19g **% Daily Value:** Vitamin A 130%; Vitamin C 30%; Calcium 4%; Iron 15% **Exchanges:** 1½ Starch, 1 Vegetable, 2 Lean Meat **Carbohydrate Choices:** 1½

steak salad with creamy dressing

Prep Time: 30 Minutes   **Start to Finish:** 30 Minutes   **Makes:** 4 servings   (photo on page C8)

2 beef tenderloin steaks, ¾ to 1 inch thick (6 oz each), trimmed of fat	¾ cup fat-free sour cream
¼ teaspoon salt	¼ cup chopped red onion
½ teaspoon freshly ground pepper	2 teaspoons chopped fresh chives
1 bag (6.5 oz) sweet butter lettuce blend	2½ teaspoons prepared horseradish
1 cup cherry tomatoes, cut in half	½ teaspoon fresh lemon juice
½ cup thinly sliced English (seedless) cucumber	

1. Heat gas or charcoal grill. Sprinkle steaks with salt and ¼ teaspoon of the pepper. Carefully brush oil on grill rack. Place steaks on grill over medium-high heat. Cover grill; cook 10 minutes, turning once, or until of desired doneness. Remove steaks from grill. Cover loosely; let stand 10 minutes.

2. Meanwhile, in large bowl, toss lettuce, tomatoes and cucumber; divide salad among 4 serving plates. In small bowl, stir sour cream, onion, chives, horseradish, lemon juice and remaining ¼ teaspoon pepper with whisk until well blended.

3. Cut steaks across grain into thin slices; arrange over salads. Drizzle with dressing.

1 Serving: Calories 170 (Calories from Fat 0); Total Fat 5g (Saturated Fat 1.5g; Trans Fat 0g); Cholesterol 0mg; Sodium 240mg; Total Carbohydrate 12g (Dietary Fiber 1g); Protein 20g **% Daily Value:** Vitamin A 40%; Vitamin C 8%; Calcium 8%; Iron 15% **Exchanges:** ½ Other Carbohydrate, 1 Vegetable, 2½ Lean Meat **Carbohydrate Choices:** 1

grilled pork 'n' nectarine spinach salad

Prep Time: 25 Minutes   **Start to Finish:** 25 Minutes   **Makes:** 6 servings

1	peppercorn-flavored pork tenderloin (1 lb)	¼	cup light balsamic vinaigrette dressing
3	nectarines, cut in half	¼	cup crumbled feta cheese (1 oz)
2	bags (6 oz each) fresh baby spinach leaves		Black pepper, if desired

1. Heat gas or charcoal grill. Using sharp knife, cut tenderloin in half horizontally, cutting to, but not through, other side; open flat as you would a book.

2. Carefully brush oil on grill rack. Place nectarine halves, cut sides down, and pork on grill over medium heat. Cover grill; cook 8 to 10 minutes, turning once, until nectarines are thoroughly heated and meat thermometer inserted into center of pork reads at least 145°F. Remove nectarines and pork from grill. Cover pork; let stand 3 minutes.

3. Cut nectarine halves into slices. Thinly slice pork. In large bowl, gently toss spinach and dressing.

4. On each of 6 plates, evenly divide spinach, nectarine slices, pork slices and cheese. Sprinkle with pepper.

1 Serving: Calories 160 (Calories from Fat 45); Total Fat 5g (Saturated Fat 2g; Trans Fat 0g); Cholesterol 40mg; Sodium 210mg; Total Carbohydrate 11g (Dietary Fiber 2g); Protein 18g **% Daily Value:** Vitamin A 110%; Vitamin C 15%; Calcium 10%; Iron 10% **Exchanges:** ½ Starch, 1 Vegetable, 2 Lean Meat **Carbohydrate Choices:** 1

290 Calories

chipotle taco salad

Prep Time: 25 Minutes   **Start to Finish:** 25 Minutes   **Makes:** 6 servings

1	lb ground beef sirloin	2	medium tomatoes, chopped (1½ cups)
1	cup chipotle salsa	½	cup fat-free sour cream
2	tablespoons water	4	medium green onions, sliced (¼ cup)
6	cups shredded iceberg lettuce	¼	cup shredded reduced-fat Mexican cheese blend (1 oz)
4	cups baked tortilla chips		

1. In 10-inch nonstick skillet, cook beef over medium heat 8 to 10 minutes, stirring occasionally, until thoroughly cooked; drain. Stir in ½ cup of the salsa and the water; cook 1 minute.

2. Place 1 cup lettuce in each of 6 bowls or shallow plates; top evenly with tortilla chips, tomatoes, beef mixture, remaining ½ cup salsa, the sour cream, onions and cheese.

1 Serving: Calories 290 (Calories from Fat 0); Total Fat 8g (Saturated Fat 3g; Trans Fat 0g); Cholesterol 0mg; Sodium 570mg; Total Carbohydrate 27g (Dietary Fiber 3g); Protein 28g **% Daily Value:** Vitamin A 20%; Vitamin C 10%; Calcium 10%; Iron 15% **Exchanges:** 1 Starch, 2 Vegetable, 3 Lean Meat, nc Medium-Fat Meat **Carbohydrate Choices:** 2

Try This

For added color, use red and blue baked tortilla chips instead of the traditional yellow variety.

tuna, artichoke and pepper salad

280 Calories

Prep Time: 10 Minutes   **Start to Finish:** 10 Minutes   **Makes:** 4 servings (1¼ cups salad and 4 crackers each)

2 jars (6 oz each) marinated artichoke hearts	2 cups chopped fresh baby spinach leaves
¼ cup chopped fresh dill weed	2 cans (5 oz each) albacore tuna in water, drained, flaked
1 tablespoon olive oil	
1 tablespoon lemon juice	1 jar (12 oz) roasted red bell peppers, drained, chopped
½ teaspoon freshly ground pepper	
2 cloves garlic, finely chopped	16 whole wheat reduced-fat crackers

1. Drain artichokes, reserving 2 tablespoons marinade. Coarsely chop artichokes.

2. In large bowl, stir together artichokes, reserved marinade, dill, oil, lemon juice, pepper and garlic. Add spinach, tuna and roasted peppers; toss well. Serve with crackers.

1 Serving: Calories 280 (Calories from Fat 0); Total Fat 10g (Saturated Fat 1g; Trans Fat 0g); Cholesterol 0mg; Sodium 600mg; Total Carbohydrate 28g (Dietary Fiber 6g); Protein 20g **% Daily Value:** Vitamin A 70%; Vitamin C 200%; Calcium 6%; Iron 15% **Exchanges:** 1 Starch, 2 Vegetable, 2 Very Lean Meat, 1½ Fat **Carbohydrate Choices:** 2

Quick Meal Idea This Mediterranean-inspired dish can be prepared in advance for a lunch-to-go or made for dinner. Just add the spinach and toss before serving.

asian shrimp and noodle salad

Prep Time: 15 Minutes **Start to Finish:** 15 Minutes **Makes:** 4 servings (2 cups each)
(photo on page C8)

3 oz uncooked rice stick noodles	2 cloves garlic, finely chopped
3 tablespoons lime juice	5 cups thinly sliced Chinese (napa) cabbage
1½ teaspoons fish sauce	¾ lb cooked deveined peeled large shrimp
4½ teaspoons creamy peanut butter	1½ cups fresh snow pea pods, strings removed, cut diagonally in half
2 teaspoons sugar	Thinly sliced green onions, if desired
2 teaspoons grated gingerroot	Chopped fresh cilantro, if desired
2 teaspoons reduced-sodium soy sauce	
2 teaspoons dark sesame oil	

1. Cook noodles in boiling water 2 to 3 minutes; drain and rinse with cold water. Drain well.

2. Meanwhile, in small bowl, stir lime juice, fish sauce, peanut butter, sugar, gingerroot, soy sauce, oil and garlic with whisk until smooth; set aside.

3. In large bowl, stir together noodles, cabbage, shrimp and pea pods. Add dressing; toss well. Sprinkle individual servings with onions and cilantro.

1 Serving: Calories 250 (Calories from Fat 0); Total Fat 6g (Saturated Fat 1g; Trans Fat 0g); Cholesterol 0mg; Sodium 290mg; Total Carbohydrate 21g (Dietary Fiber 2g); Protein 27g **% Daily Value:** Vitamin A 20%; Vitamin C 45%; Calcium 20%; Iron 10% **Exchanges:** ½ Starch, 2 Vegetable, 3½ Very Lean Meat, ½ Fat **Carbohydrate Choices:** 1

prosciutto and olive pasta salad

250 Calories

Prep Time: 20 Minutes   **Start to Finish:** 20 Minutes   **Makes:** 4 servings (about 1½ cups each)

1¾ cups uncooked multigrain penne pasta
2   cups fresh baby spinach leaves
8   jalapeño-stuffed green olives, sliced
2   oz thinly sliced prosciutto, chopped

2   tablespoons chopped fresh oregano leaves
1   tablespoon olive oil
⅓   cup crumbled reduced-fat feta cheese

1. Cook pasta as directed on package, omitting salt and oil; drain. Rinse with cold water to cool; drain well.

2. In large bowl, stir together spinach, olives, prosciutto, oregano and oil. Add pasta and cheese; toss well.

1 Serving: Calories 250 (Calories from Fat 0); Total Fat 8g (Saturated Fat 1.5g; Trans Fat 0g); Cholesterol 0mg; Sodium 510mg; Total Carbohydrate 33g (Dietary Fiber 5g); Protein 11g **% Daily Value:** Vitamin A 35%; Vitamin C 4%; Calcium 8%; Iron 15% **Exchanges:** 1½ Starch, ½ Other Carbohydrate, 1 Medium-Fat Meat **Carbohydrate Choices:** 2

Quick Meal Idea Sweet and juicy cantaloupe makes a delicious accompaniment to this tangy dish.

healthified vegetarian thai salad with peanut dressing

Prep Time: 40 Minutes   **Start to Finish:** 40 Minutes   **Makes:** 4 servings

SALAD
- 1 cup reduced-sodium chicken broth
- ½ cup uncooked bulgur
- 1 bag (10 oz) frozen shelled edamame
- 1 medium red bell pepper, cut into thin bite-size strips
- ½ cup coarsely shredded carrots
- ½ cup thinly sliced red onion
- 2 tablespoons chopped fresh cilantro
- 4 cups fresh spinach leaves
- 2 tablespoons finely chopped honey-roasted peanuts

DRESSING
- ⅓ cup water
- 3 tablespoons reduced-fat creamy peanut butter
- 2 tablespoons reduced-sodium soy sauce
- 1 teaspoon sugar
- ¼ teaspoon ground ginger
- ⅛ teaspoon crushed red pepper flakes
- 1 clove garlic, finely chopped

1. In 2-quart saucepan, heat broth to boiling; add bulgur. Return to boiling; reduce heat. Cover; simmer about 15 minutes or until bulgur is tender and most of the liquid is absorbed. Drain, if necessary. Meanwhile, cook edamame as directed on package.

2. In large bowl, stir together bulgur, edamame, bell pepper, carrots, onion and cilantro. Set aside.

3. In 1-quart saucepan, mix all dressing ingredients with whisk. Cook over medium-low heat about 3 minutes, stirring constantly, until smooth and slightly thickened (mixture will appear curdled at first but will become smooth as it's heated and stirred).

4. Divide spinach among 4 serving plates; top evenly with bulgur mixture. Drizzle with dressing; sprinkle with peanuts.

1 Serving: Calories 290 (Calories from Fat 100); Total Fat 11g (Saturated Fat 1.5g; Trans Fat 0g); Cholesterol 0mg; Sodium 550mg; Total Carbohydrate 35g (Dietary Fiber 10g); Protein 17g **% Daily Value:** Vitamin A 130%; Vitamin C 100%; Calcium 15%; Iron 20% **Exchanges:** 1½ Starch, ½ Other Carbohydrate, 1 Vegetable, 1½ Lean Meat, 1½ Fat **Carbohydrate Choices:** 2

Health Smart With 50% less saturated fat and 46% less sodium than the original recipe, this fresh and filling main-dish salad provides a whopping 10 grams of fiber per serving.

crab salad with buttermilk dressing

140 Calories

Prep Time: 10 Minutes **Start to Finish:** 10 Minutes **Makes:** 4 servings

½ cup fat-free buttermilk
¼ cup reduced-fat sour cream
2 teaspoons grated lemon peel
1 teaspoon chopped fresh dill weed
¼ teaspoon freshly ground pepper
⅛ teaspoon salt

1 lb cooked jumbo lump crabmeat, drained, shell pieces removed
4 large leaves Bibb lettuce
2 cups multicolored cherry tomatoes (about 12 oz), quartered

1. In small bowl, beat buttermilk, sour cream, lemon peel, dill, pepper and salt with whisk.

2. In medium bowl, toss crabmeat and dressing until coated. Place lettuce leaves on 4 serving plates. Top with crab salad and tomatoes. Serve immediately.

1 Serving: Calories 140 (Calories from Fat 0); Total Fat 3g (Saturated Fat 1g; Trans Fat 0g); Cholesterol 0mg; Sodium 500mg; Total Carbohydrate 8g (Dietary Fiber 1g); Protein 19g **% Daily Value:** Vitamin A 25%; Vitamin C 30%; Calcium 15%; Iron 6% **Exchanges:** ½ Other Carbohydrate, 2½ Very Lean Meat **Carbohydrate Choices:** ½

Try This

Serve the salad with whole wheat crackers on the side.

tabbouleh

Prep Time: 10 Minutes   **Start to Finish:** 35 Minutes   **Makes:** 6 servings (about 1 cup each)

1½ cups water
1 cup uncooked bulgur
1 can (15 oz) garbanzo beans, drained, rinsed
1½ cups grape tomatoes, cut in half
1 cup diced cucumber
8 medium green onions, thinly sliced (½ cup)
⅓ cup crumbled feta cheese

⅓ cup chopped fresh parsley
2 tablespoons finely chopped fresh mint leaves
½ teaspoon salt
¼ cup lemon juice
1 tablespoon olive oil

1. In 2-quart saucepan, heat water to boiling over medium-high heat. Add bulgur; reduce heat. Cover; simmer 13 to 15 minutes or until water is absorbed. Transfer to large bowl; cool completely.

2. Add garbanzo beans, tomatoes, cucumber, onions, cheese, parsley, mint and salt to bulgur; toss gently. In small bowl, stir lemon juice and oil with whisk. Pour over bulgur mixture; toss gently to coat.

1 Serving: Calories 190 (Calories from Fat 0); Total Fat 5g (Saturated Fat 1.5g; Trans Fat 0g); Cholesterol 0mg; Sodium 350mg; Total Carbohydrate 31g (Dietary Fiber 7g); Protein 7g **% Daily Value:** Vitamin A 20%; Vitamin C 15%; Calcium 10%; Iron 10% **Exchanges:** 2 Starch, 1 Fat **Carbohydrate Choices:** 2

Try This

Pair this crunchy salad with warm pita wedges.

mediterranean panzanella

300 Calories

Prep Time: 10 Minutes **Start to Finish:** 10 Minute **Makes:** 4 servings (about 2⅔ cups each)

1 tablespoon canola oil	¼ cup pitted kalamata olives
3 tablespoons white balsamic vinegar	½ cup fresh basil leaves, torn
¼ teaspoon pepper	4 cups torn whole wheat country-style bread (8 oz)
⅛ teaspoon salt	⅓ cup crumbled feta cheese
6½ cups chopped tomatoes (about 3 very large)	
1½ cups cubed English (seedless) cucumbers	

1. In large bowl, mix oil, vinegar, pepper and salt with whisk.

2. Stir in tomatoes, cucumbers, olives and basil. Add bread and cheese; toss gently. Serve immediately.

1 Serving: Calories 300 (Calories from Fat 0); Total Fat 11g (Saturated Fat 2.5g; Trans Fat 0g); Cholesterol 0mg; Sodium 630mg; Total Carbohydrate 42g (Dietary Fiber 7g); Protein 11g **% Daily Value:** Vitamin A 50%; Vitamin C 70%; Calcium 20%; Iron 15% **Exchanges:** 2 Starch, 2 Vegetable, 2 Fat **Carbohydrate Choices:** 2½

Kitchen Tip White balsamic vinegar offers the sweetness of regular balsamic but won't discolor the salad. You can use regular balsamic vinegar if white isn't available.

pea, carrot and tofu salad

Prep Time: 25 Minutes **Start to Finish:** 25 Minutes **Makes:** 4 servings

1 package (14 oz) water-packed firm lite tofu, drained	1 can (8 oz) sliced water chestnuts, drained
2 tablespoons sesame oil	½ cup thinly sliced red onion
½ cup reduced-fat sesame-ginger dressing	¼ teaspoon freshly ground pepper
1 bag (1 lb) frozen baby sweet peas, cooked, drained	1 medium head Bibb lettuce, torn
1 cup julienne carrots (from 10-oz bag)	4 teaspoons roasted unsalted sunflower nuts

1. Place tofu on several layers of paper towels. Cover tofu with additional paper towels; gently press out moisture. Cut tofu into 1-inch cubes.

2. In 10-inch nonstick skillet, heat oil over medium-high heat. Add tofu; cook 10 to 12 minutes, stirring occasionally, until golden on all sides.

3. In large bowl, gently toss tofu, dressing, cooked peas, carrots, water chestnuts, onion and pepper. Divide lettuce among 4 serving plates; top evenly with tofu mixture. Sprinkle with sunflower nuts.

1 Serving: Calories 250 (Calories from Fat 0); Total Fat 9g (Saturated Fat 1g; Trans Fat 0g); Cholesterol 0mg; Sodium 630mg; Total Carbohydrate 32g (Dietary Fiber 8g); Protein 14g **% Daily Value:** Vitamin A 18%; Vitamin C 15%; Calcium 10%; Iron 25% **Exchanges:** 1 Starch, ½ Other Carbohydrate, 2 Vegetable **Carbohydrate Choices:** 2

chickpea, feta and orzo salad

300 Calories

Prep Time: 15 Minutes   **Start to Finish:** 15 Minutes   **Makes:** 4 servings (1½ cups each)

1 cup uncooked orzo or rosamarina pasta (6 oz)	½ teaspoon salt
4½ teaspoons lemon juice	¼ teaspoon freshly ground pepper
1 tablespoon olive oil	1 large tomato, chopped (1 cup)
½ cup chopped English (seedless) cucumber	1 can (15 oz) chickpeas (garbanzo beans), drained, rinsed
2 tablespoons finely chopped red onion	⅓ cup crumbled tomato-basil feta cheese
1 tablespoon chopped fresh thyme leaves	

1. Cook pasta as directed on package, omitting salt and oil; drain. Rinse with cold water to cool; drain well.

2. Meanwhile, in medium bowl, stir lemon juice and oil with whisk. Stir in cucumber, onion, thyme, ¼ teaspoon of the salt and the pepper.

3. In large bowl, gently toss tomato and chickpeas. Stir in pasta, remaining ¼ teaspoon salt and the cucumber mixture. Add cheese; toss gently.

1 Serving: Calories 300 (Calories from Fat 0); Total Fat 8g (Saturated Fat 1.5g; Trans Fat 0g); Cholesterol 0mg; Sodium 490mg; Total Carbohydrate 47g (Dietary Fiber 5g); Protein 11g **% Daily Value:** Vitamin A 10%; Vitamin C 10%; Calcium 10%; Iron 15% **Exchanges:** 3 Starch, 1 Fat **Carbohydrate Choices:** 3

Soups, Stews & Chilies

chicken-tortilla soup

Prep Time: 15 Minutes   **Start to Finish:** 35 Minutes   **Makes:** 4 servings   (photo on page C9)

3 teaspoons vegetable oil	1 can (10 oz) diced tomatoes with green chiles, undrained
4 soft corn tortillas (6 inch), cut into 2 x ½-inch strips	1½ cups shredded cooked chicken
1 medium onion, chopped (½ cup)	1 tablespoon lime juice
3½ cups chicken broth	1 tablespoon chopped fresh cilantro or parsley

1. In 2-quart nonstick saucepan, heat 2 teaspoons of the oil over medium-high heat. Add tortilla strips; cook 30 to 60 seconds, stirring constantly, until crisp and light golden brown. Remove from saucepan; drain on paper towels.

2. In same saucepan, cook onion in remaining 1 teaspoon oil over medium-high heat, stirring occasionally, until tender. Stir in broth and tomatoes. Heat to boiling; reduce heat. Simmer uncovered 20 minutes. Stir in chicken; heat until hot.

3. Stir in lime juice. Sprinkle tortilla strips on top of soup or spoon soup over tortilla strips. Sprinkle with cilantro.

1 Serving: Calories 230 (Calories from Fat 70); Total Fat 8g (Saturated Fat 1.5g; Trans Fat 0g); Cholesterol 45mg; Sodium 1100mg; Total Carbohydrate 17g (Dietary Fiber 3g); Protein 22g **% Daily Value:** Vitamin A 6%; Vitamin C 6%; Calcium 6%; Iron 8% **Exchanges:** 1 Starch, 2½ Very Lean Meat, 1 Fat **Carbohydrate Choices:** 1

Try This

Offer sour cream, shredded Monterey Jack cheese and avocado chunks as toppings.

chicken-tomato-basil soup

290 Calories

Prep Time: 30 Minutes   **Start to Finish:** 30 Minutes   **Makes:** 5 servings

½   lb boneless skinless chicken breasts, cut into ½-inch pieces

½   teaspoon garlic-pepper blend

2   cans (19 oz each) tomato-basil soup

½   cup uncooked orzo or rosamarina pasta (3 oz)

1   small zucchini, diced

¼   cup shredded Parmesan cheese (1 oz)

1. Heat 3-quart nonstick saucepan over medium heat. Add chicken; sprinkle with garlic-pepper blend. Cook 3 to 5 minutes, stirring frequently, until browned.

2. Add soup and orzo; mix well. Heat to boiling; reduce heat to medium-low. Simmer uncovered 10 to 15 minutes or until chicken is no longer pink in center and orzo is tender.

3. Stir in zucchini. Cook 2 to 3 minutes, stirring occasionally. Sprinkle each serving with 1 tablespoon cheese.

1 Serving: Calories 290 (Calories from Fat 50); Total Fat 6g (Saturated Fat 2g; Trans Fat 0g); Cholesterol 30mg; Sodium 960mg; Total Carbohydrate 42g (Dietary Fiber 2g); Protein 17g **% Daily Value:** Vitamin A 20%; Vitamin C 8%; Calcium 10%; Iron 10% **Exchanges:** 1½ Starch, 1 Other Carbohydrate, ½ Vegetable, 1½ Very Lean Meat, 1 Fat **Carbohydrate Choices:** 3

Try This

If you don't have garlic-pepper blend, you can substitute ¼ teaspoon each garlic powder and coarse ground black pepper.

230 Calories

chicken and spinach tortellini soup

Prep Time: 30 Minutes **Start to Finish:** 30 Minutes **Makes:** 5 servings

1 tablespoon olive or vegetable oil	2 cups shredded cooked chicken
5 medium green onions, chopped (⅓ cup)	1 cup frozen small cheese-filled tortellini
⅓ cup julienne carrots (from 10-oz bag)	¼ teaspoon ground nutmeg, if desired
2 cloves garlic, finely chopped	⅛ teaspoon pepper
6 cups chicken broth	3 cups chopped fresh spinach

1. In 4½- to 5-quart Dutch oven or saucepan, heat oil over medium-high heat. Cook onions, carrots and garlic in oil 3 to 4 minutes, stirring frequently, until onions are softened.

2. Stir in broth and chicken. Heat to boiling. Stir in tortellini; reduce heat to medium. Cover; cook 3 to 5 minutes or until tortellini is tender.

3. Stir in nutmeg, pepper and spinach. Cover; cook 2 to 3 minutes or until spinach is hot.

1 Serving: Calories 230 (Calories from Fat 80); Total Fat 9g (Saturated Fat 3g; Trans Fat 0g); Cholesterol 80mg; Sodium 1310mg; Total Carbohydrate 11g (Dietary Fiber 1g); Protein 26g **% Daily Value:** Vitamin A 60%; Vitamin C 6%; Calcium 8%; Iron 15% **Exchanges:** ½ Starch, ½ Vegetable, 3½ Very Lean Meat, 1½ Fat **Carbohydrate Choices:** 1

Try This

Dried cheese-filled tortellini can be used in place of the frozen tortellini by adjusting the cooking time according to the package instructions. You can also substitute shredded carrots for the julienne carrots.

cheesy chicken enchilada soup

270 Calories

Prep Time: 20 Minutes   **Start to Finish:** 20 Minutes   **Makes:** 6 servings (1 cup each)

2   cans (10¾ oz each) condensed 98% fat-free cream of chicken soup
1   can (10 oz) enchilada sauce
2   cups milk
1   cup shredded reduced-fat Cheddar cheese (4 oz)

1   package (9 oz) frozen cooked southwestern-seasoned chicken breast strips, thawed, chopped (2 cups)
¾   cup crushed tortilla chips

1. In 3-quart saucepan, mix all ingredients except tortilla chips. Cook over medium heat, stirring occasionally, until thoroughly heated and cheese is melted.

2. Top each serving with tortilla chips.

1 Serving: Calories 270 (Calories from Fat 110); Total Fat 12g (Saturated Fat 3.5g; Trans Fat 0.5g); Cholesterol 35mg; Sodium 1150mg; Total Carbohydrate 22g (Dietary Fiber 0g); Protein 19g **% Daily Value:** Vitamin A 8%; Vitamin C 0%; Calcium 25%; Iron 4% **Exchanges:** 1½ Starch, 2 Lean Meat, 1 Fat **Carbohydrate Choices:** 1½

Quick Meal Idea This easy soup is a great choice for dinner any night. Serve bowls of the soup with warm breadsticks and cantaloupe wedges.

creamy chicken noodle soup with pesto drizzle

Prep Time: 35 Minutes   **Start to Finish:** 35 Minutes   **Makes:** 6 servings (1½ cups each)

2 tablespoons butter	2½ cups milk
2 medium carrots, sliced (1 cup)	1 box (6.4 oz) Betty Crocker Tuna Helper® creamy broccoli
2 medium stalks celery, sliced (1 cup)	
1 medium onion, chopped (½ cup)	2 cups cut-up cooked chicken
1 carton (32 oz) reduced-sodium chicken broth (4 cups)	1 dried bay leaf
	2 tablespoons basil pesto

1. In 5-quart Dutch oven or saucepan, melt butter over medium heat. Cook carrots, celery and onion in butter about 5 minutes, stirring frequently, until carrots are crisp-tender.

2. Stir in broth, milk, uncooked pasta and sauce mix from Tuna Helper box, chicken and bay leaf. Heat to boiling; reduce heat. Simmer uncovered 12 to 15 minutes, stirring occasionally, until pasta and vegetables are tender.

3. Remove bay leaf; ladle soup into bowls. Place pesto in small resealable food-storage plastic bag; seal bag. Cut off tiny corner of bag; drizzle pesto over soup.

1 Serving: Calories 280 (Calories from Fat 130); Total Fat 15g (Saturated Fat 6g; Trans Fat 0g); Cholesterol 60mg; Sodium 660mg; Total Carbohydrate 16g (Dietary Fiber 1g); Protein 19g **% Daily Value:** Vitamin A 80%; Vitamin C 4%; Calcium 15%; Iron 6% **Exchanges:** 1 Starch, 2½ Lean Meat, 1 Fat **Carbohydrate Choices:** 1

Try This

Use any type of cooked chicken in this recipe; it's a terrific and tasty way to use up leftover chicken.

chicken-vegetable-barley soup

160 Calories

Prep Time: 20 Minutes   **Start to Finish:** 25 Minutes   **Makes:** 8 servings (1 cup each)

5 cups reduced-sodium chicken broth	1 bag (16 oz) frozen vegetables for soup with tomatoes
2 cups shredded deli rotisserie chicken breast (from 2-lb chicken)	¾ cup uncooked quick-cooking barley
½ teaspoon kosher (coarse) salt	2 cups chopped fresh baby spinach leaves
½ teaspoon freshly ground pepper	

1. In 5-quart Dutch oven or saucepan, stir together broth, chicken, salt, pepper and frozen vegetables. Heat to boiling. Stir in barley; reduce heat. Cover; simmer 10 minutes, stirring occasionally.

2. Remove from heat; stir in spinach. Let stand 5 minutes before serving.

1 Serving: Calories 160 (Calories from Fat 0); Total Fat 3g (Saturated Fat 1g; Trans Fat 0g); Cholesterol 0mg; Sodium 490mg; Total Carbohydrate 18g (Dietary Fiber 3g); Protein 16g **% Daily Value:** Vitamin A 20%; Vitamin C 4%; Calcium 4%; Iron 8% **Exchanges:** 1 Starch, 1 Vegetable, 1½ Lean Meat **Carbohydrate Choices:** 1

Kitchen Tip Be sure to use the quick-cooking barley in this recipe. The longer-cooking variety will not be tender in the short cooking time.

210
Calories

chicken-vegetable soup

Prep Time: 25 Minutes   **Start to Finish:** 25 Minutes   **Makes:** 6 servings (1½ cups each)

1	carton (32 oz) reduced-sodium chicken broth (4 cups)
2½	cups diced cooked chicken breast
1	container (8 oz) refrigerated chopped celery, onion and bell pepper mix
1	cup frozen sliced carrots (from 16-oz bag)
1	bag (14 oz) frozen baby potato and vegetable blend
1	teaspoon roasted garlic (from 4-oz jar)

½	teaspoon Italian seasoning
½	teaspoon curry powder
½	teaspoon freshly ground pepper
¼	teaspoon salt
1½	cups coarsely chopped fresh baby spinach leaves
1	can (12 oz) evaporated fat-free milk
	Additional freshly ground pepper, if desired

1. In 5-quart Dutch oven or saucepan, stir together broth, chicken, celery mixture and carrots. Cover; heat to boiling.

2. Meanwhile, place potato-vegetable blend in microwavable bowl. Cover with microwavable plastic wrap, folding back one edge or corner ¼ inch to vent steam. Microwave on High 5 minutes. Add garlic, Italian seasoning, curry powder, ½ teaspoon pepper and the salt to broth mixture; cover and continue to cook.

3. Using kitchen scissors, cut cooked potato-vegetable blend into bite-size pieces; add to broth mixture. Stir in spinach and milk. Cover; cook over high heat 5 minutes or until carrots are tender. Sprinkle individual servings with additional pepper.

1 Serving: Calories 210 (Calories from Fat 25); Total Fat 3g (Saturated Fat 1g; Trans Fat 0g); Cholesterol 50mg; Sodium 610mg; Total Carbohydrate 20g (Dietary Fiber 3g); Protein 25g **% Daily Value:** Vitamin A 100%; Vitamin C 15%; Calcium 25%; Iron 10% **Exchanges:** ½ Starch, ½ Skim Milk, 1½ Vegetable, 2½ Very Lean Meat **Carbohydrate Choices:** 1

asian mushroom-chicken soup

150 Calories

Prep Time: 20 Minutes **Start to Finish:** 30 Minutes **Makes:** 6 servings (photo on page C10)

1½ cups water	3 cups reduced-sodium chicken broth
1 package (1 oz) dried portabella or shiitake mushrooms	1 can (8 oz) sliced bamboo shoots, drained
1 tablespoon canola oil	2 tablespoons reduced-sodium soy sauce
¼ cup thinly sliced green onions (4 medium)	½ teaspoon sriracha sauce
2 tablespoons finely chopped gingerroot	1 cup shredded cooked chicken breast
3 cloves garlic, finely chopped	1 cup cooked brown rice
1 jalapeño chile, seeded, finely chopped	4 teaspoons lime juice
1 cup fresh snow pea pods, strings removed, cut diagonally in half	½ cup thinly sliced fresh basil leaves

1. In medium microwavable bowl, heat water uncovered on High 30 seconds or until hot. Add mushrooms; let stand 5 minutes or until soft. Drain mushrooms (reserve liquid). Slice any mushrooms that are large. Set aside.

2. In 4-quart saucepan, heat oil over medium heat. Add 2 tablespoons of the onions, the gingerroot, garlic and chile; cook about 3 minutes, stirring occasionally, until vegetables are tender. Add pea pods; cook 2 minutes, stirring occasionally.

3. Stir in mushrooms, mushroom liquid, broth, bamboo shoots, soy sauce, sriracha, chicken and brown rice. Heat to boiling; reduce heat. Cover; simmer 10 minutes or until hot. Stir in lime juice.

4. Divide soup evenly among 6 bowls. Top with basil and remaining 2 tablespoons onions.

1 Serving: Calories 150 (Calories from Fat 35); Total Fat 4g (Saturated Fat 0.5g; Trans Fat 0g); Cholesterol 20mg; Sodium 490mg; Total Carbohydrate 16g (Dietary Fiber 3g); Protein 11g **% Daily Value:** Vitamin A 8%; Vitamin C 15%; Calcium 4%; Iron 8% **Exchanges:** ½ Starch, 1½ Vegetable, 1 Very Lean Meat, ½ Fat **Carbohydrate Choices:** 1

Kitchen Tip Boneless skinless chicken breasts are great to use in this recipe. Purchased rotisserie chicken is another option that is quick and easy to use.

turkey-wild rice soup

Prep Time: 10 Minutes **Start to Finish:** 35 Minutes **Makes:** 6 servings

3 tablespoons butter	2 cups water
½ cup all-purpose flour	2 tablespoons dried chopped onion
3½ cups reduced-sodium chicken broth	1 box (6 oz) original long-grain and wild rice mix
1 package (8 oz) 98% fat-free oven-roasted turkey breast, cubed (about 2 cups)	2 cups fat-free half-and-half

1. In 5-quart Dutch oven or saucepan, melt butter over medium heat. Stir in flour with whisk until well blended. Slowly stir in broth with whisk. Stir in turkey, water, dried chopped onion, rice and contents of seasoning packet from rice mix.

2. Heat to boiling over high heat, stirring occasionally. Reduce heat to medium-low. Cover; simmer about 25 minutes or until rice is tender.

3. Stir in half-and-half; heat just to boiling.

1 Serving: Calories 290 (Calories from Fat 70); Total Fat 8g (Saturated Fat 4.5g; Trans Fat 0g); Cholesterol 40mg; Sodium 1200mg; Total Carbohydrate 40g (Dietary Fiber 1g); Protein 14g **% Daily Value:** Vitamin A 4%; Vitamin C 0%; Calcium 10%; Iron 10% **Exchanges:** 2 Starch, ½ Other Carbohydrate, 1 Lean Meat, 1 Fat **Carbohydrate Choices:** 2½

Kitchen Tip Wild rice is really the seed of an aquatic grass, and it is considered a whole grain. It has a delicious nutty flavor and slightly chewy texture.

smoked turkey-lentil soup

140 Calories

Prep Time: 10 Minutes   **Start to Finish:** 8 Hours 10 Minutes   **Makes:** 8 servings (1 cup each)

6	cups vegetable broth
1	cup dried lentils (8 oz), sorted, rinsed
1	container (8 oz) refrigerated prechopped celery, onion and bell pepper mix
2	teaspoons chopped fresh or ½ teaspoon dried oregano leaves

½	teaspoon freshly ground pepper
1	smoked turkey leg (8 oz)
	Fat-free Greek plain yogurt, if desired
	Fresh oregano sprigs, if desired

1. Spray 3- to 4-quart slow cooker with cooking spray. In slow cooker, stir together broth, lentils, prechopped vegetables, chopped oregano and pepper; add turkey leg.

2. Cover; cook on Low heat setting 8 to 10 hours or until lentils are tender and turkey falls off bone.

3. Remove turkey leg from slow cooker. Remove and discard skin. Shred meat; discard bone. Return meat to slow cooker; stir well.

4. Ladle soup into 8 bowls; garnish with yogurt and oregano sprigs.

1 Serving: Calories 140 (Calories from Fat 10); Total Fat 1g (Saturated Fat 0g; Trans Fat 0g); Cholesterol 20mg; Sodium 730mg; Total Carbohydrate 20g (Dietary Fiber 5g); Protein 12g **% Daily Value:** Vitamin A 10%; Vitamin C 8%; Calcium 40%; Iron 20% **Exchanges:** 1 Other Carbohydrate, ½ Vegetable, 1½ Very Lean Meat **Carbohydrate Choices:** 1

Health Smart Fresh oregano provides lots of flavor and eliminates the need to add extra salt, but you can use dried oregano if you prefer.

chunky vegetable-beef-barley soup

Prep Time: 30 Minutes   **Start to Finish:** 2 Hours 15 Minutes   **Makes:** 8 servings

1 tablespoon canola oil	¼ teaspoon pepper
¾ lb lean beef stew meat, cut into 1-inch cubes	1 dried bay leaf
7 cups reduced-sodium beef broth	1 cup frozen mixed vegetables (from 12-oz bag)
1 large onion, chopped (1 cup)	1 can (14.5 oz) no-salt-added diced tomatoes, undrained
½ cup chopped celery	1 cup ½-inch slices peeled parsnip or ½-inch cubes peeled potato
1 teaspoon dried oregano or basil leaves, crushed	⅔ cup uncooked quick-cooking barley
2 cloves garlic, finely chopped	

1. In 5- to 6-quart Dutch oven or saucepan, heat oil over medium heat. Cook beef in oil, stirring frequently, until browned. Stir in broth, onion, celery, oregano, garlic, pepper and bay leaf. Heat to boiling; reduce heat. Cover; simmer 1 hour 30 minutes.

2. Stir in frozen vegetables, tomatoes, parsnip and barley. Heat to boiling; reduce heat. Cover; simmer about 15 minutes longer or until meat and vegetables are tender. Remove and discard bay leaf before serving.

1 Serving: Calories 210 (Calories from Fat 60); Total Fat 7g (Saturated Fat 2g; Trans Fat 0g); Cholesterol 25mg; Sodium 420mg; Total Carbohydrate 23g (Dietary Fiber 4g); Protein 13g **% Daily Value:** Vitamin A 10%; Vitamin C 8%; Calcium 4%; Iron 10% **Exchanges:** 1½ Starch, ½ Vegetable, 1 Lean Meat, ½ Fat **Carbohydrate Choices:** 1½

Slow Cooker Directions: Thaw the frozen mixed vegetables, and substitute regular pearl barley for quick-cooking barley. In 12-inch skillet, heat oil over medium heat. Cook beef in oil, stirring frequently, until browned; drain. Spray 5- to 6-quart slow cooker with cooking spray. In slow cooker, mix beef and all remaining ingredients. Cover; cook on Low heat setting 8 to 10 hours (or on High heat setting 4 to 5 hours).

easy vegetable-beef soup

210 Calories

Prep Time: 35 Minutes   **Start to Finish:** 35 Minutes   **Makes:** 6 servings (1½ cups each)

SEASONING BLEND
1	large onion, chopped (1 cup)
4½	teaspoons finely chopped garlic
1	teaspoon Italian seasoning
½	teaspoon pepper
¼	teaspoon salt

SOUP
1	lb ground beef sirloin
2½	cups water
1	bag (16 oz) frozen mixed vegetables
1	can (14.5 oz) Italian-style stewed tomatoes, undrained, chopped
1	can (8 oz) tomato sauce

1. In small bowl, mix all seasoning blend ingredients.

2. In 5-quart Dutch oven or saucepan, cook beef and seasoning blend over medium-high heat 5 to 7 minutes, stirring occasionally, until beef is thoroughly cooked; drain.

3. Stir in all remaining ingredients. Heat to boiling over medium-high heat; reduce heat. Cover; simmer 20 minutes, stirring occasionally, until hot.

1 Serving: Calories 210 (Calories from Fat 80); Total Fat 9g (Saturated Fat 3.5g; Trans Fat 0.5g); Cholesterol 45mg; Sodium 730mg; Total Carbohydrate 16g (Dietary Fiber 4g); Protein 16g **% Daily Value:** Vitamin A 45%; Vitamin C 35%; Calcium 6%; Iron 15% **Exchanges:** ½ Other Carbohydrates, 1 Vegetable, 2 Medium-Fat Meat **Carbohydrate Choices:** 1½

Kitchen Tip If you don't feel like chopping the onion, they are often available already chopped in the refrigerator area or frozen section of the supermarket.

easy chili mole

Prep Time: 30 Minutes   **Start to Finish:** 30 Minutes   **Makes:** 8 servings (about 1 cup chili and 1 tortilla each)

1   lb extra-lean (at least 90%) ground beef
1   medium onion, chopped (½ cup)
1   package (1.25 oz) Tex-Mex chili seasoning mix
1   can (28 oz) diced tomatoes, undrained
1   can (28 oz) crushed tomatoes

1   can (15 oz) spicy chili beans, undrained
1   oz unsweetened baking chocolate, coarsely chopped
8   soft corn tortillas (6 inch), heated as directed on package

1. In 4-quart Dutch oven or saucepan, cook beef and onion over medium heat 8 to 10 minutes, stirring occasionally, until beef is thoroughly cooked; drain.

2. Stir in seasoning mix, both tomatoes and beans. Heat to boiling; reduce heat to low. Cover; cook 15 minutes, stirring occasionally, to blend flavors. Stir in chocolate just until melted. Serve with tortillas.

1 Serving: Calories 270 (Calories from Fat 70); Total Fat 8g (Saturated Fat 3g; Trans Fat 0g); Cholesterol 35mg; Sodium 830mg; Total Carbohydrate 32g (Dietary Fiber 7g); Protein 18g **% Daily Value:** Vitamin A 10%; Vitamin C 15%; Calcium 10%; Iron 110% **Exchanges:** 1½ Starch, ½ Other Carbohydrate, 1 Vegetable, 1½ Lean Meat, ½ Fat **Carbohydrate Choices:** 2

Quick Meal Idea Serve the chili with a crisp green salad and warm wedges of cornbread instead of the tortillas.

Try This

Regular chili seasoning mix and 1 teaspoon finely chopped jalapeño chile can be substituted for the Tex-Mex seasoning mix.

sirloin three-bean chili

Prep Time: 30 Minutes   **Start to Finish:** 50 Minutes   **Makes:** 10 servings

300 Calories

1	tablespoon vegetable oil	1	can (15 to 16 oz) kidney beans, drained, rinsed
2	lb boneless beef sirloin steak, trimmed of fat, cut into 1-inch cubes	1	can (15 oz) black beans, drained, rinsed
1	large onion, coarsely chopped (1 cup)	1	cup beef broth
1	medium bell pepper (any color), coarsely chopped (1 cup)	4½	teaspoons ground cumin
2	cans (28 oz each) diced tomatoes, undrained	3	teaspoons chili powder
1	can (15 to 16 oz) pinto beans, drained, rinsed		

1. In 4-quart Dutch oven or saucepan, heat oil over medium-high heat. Cook half of the beef at a time in oil, stirring occasionally, until brown; remove from Dutch oven.

2. Add onion and bell pepper to Dutch oven. Cook 2 to 3 minutes, stirring occasionally, until crisp-tender. Stir in all remaining ingredients except beef.

3. Cover; cook over medium heat 10 minutes. Stir in beef. Cook 3 to 8 minutes or until beef is tender.

1 Serving: Calories 300 (Calories from Fat 40); Total Fat 4.5g (Saturated Fat 1g; Trans Fat 0g); Cholesterol 45mg; Sodium 320mg; Total Carbohydrate 35g (Dietary Fiber 11g); Protein 28g **% Daily Value:** Vitamin A 15%; Vitamin C 10%; Calcium 8%; Iron 30% **Exchanges:** 2 Starch, 1 Vegetable, 1½ Very Lean Meat, 1 Lean Meat **Carbohydrate Choices:** 2

Health Smart This chili packs a hefty amount of fiber, at 11 grams per serving! Beans of all varieties are high in fiber, but the three varieties in this recipe—kidney, pinto and black—are some of the highest.

beefy corn and black bean chili

Prep Time: 15 Minutes   **Start to Finish:** 25 Minutes   **Makes:** 6 servings (about 1 cup each)
(photo on page C10)

1 lb ground beef round	1 can (14 oz) reduced-sodium beef broth
2 teaspoons salt-free chili powder blend	1 can (15 oz) seasoned tomato sauce for chili
1 package (14 oz) frozen seasoned corn and black beans	Reduced-fat sour cream, if desired
	Sliced green onions, if desired

1. In 4-quart Dutch oven or saucepan, cook beef and chili powder blend over medium-high heat 5 to 7 minutes, stirring occasionally, until beef is thoroughly cooked; drain.

2. Stir in frozen corn and beans, broth and tomato sauce. Heat to boiling; reduce heat. Cover; simmer 10 minutes. Uncover; simmer 5 minutes longer, stirring occasionally.

3. Top individual servings with sour cream and onions.

1 Serving: Calories 210 (Calories from Fat 60); Total Fat 6g (Saturated Fat 1.5g; Trans Fat 0g); Cholesterol 55mg; Sodium 680mg; Total Carbohydrate 13g (Dietary Fiber 3g); Protein 25g **% Daily Value:** Vitamin A 10%; Vitamin C 6%; Calcium 2%; Iron 20% **Exchanges:** 1 Starch, 3 Very Lean Meat, ½ Fat **Carbohydrate Choices:** 1

Quick Meal Idea Serve this piping-hot chili with cornbread, or spoon it over hot baked potatoes and top with reduced-fat sour cream.

caldillo

Prep Time: 20 Minutes   **Start to Finish:** 50 Minutes   **Makes:** 6 servings (1⅓ cups each)

200 Calories

1	lb boneless beef sirloin steak (about ½ inch thick), cut into 1-inch cubes
	Cooking spray
1	large onion, chopped (1 cup)
3	cups water
2	cans (14.5 oz each) diced tomatoes with green chiles, undrained
1	teaspoon ground cumin
3	cups cubed (½ inch) unpeeled Yukon Gold or red potatoes
¼	cup chopped fresh cilantro, if desired

1. Spray 5-quart Dutch oven or saucepan with cooking spray; heat over high heat. Spray beef with cooking spray. Add to Dutch oven; cook 3 minutes, stirring frequently. Add onion. Cook 5 minutes longer, stirring frequently, until liquid is evaporated and beef and onion are browned.

2. Stir in water, tomatoes and cumin. Heat to boiling; reduce heat to medium. Cover; simmer 20 minutes. Add potatoes. Cover; simmer 10 minutes longer or until potatoes are tender. Remove from heat. Stir in cilantro.

1 Serving: Calories 200 (Calories from Fat 25); Total Fat 2.5g (Saturated Fat 1g; Trans Fat 0g); Cholesterol 45mg; Sodium 440mg; Total Carbohydrate 23g (Dietary Fiber 4g); Protein 22g **% Daily Value:** Vitamin A 10%; Vitamin C 15%; Calcium 8%; Iron 15% **Exchanges:** 1½ Starch, ½ Vegetable, 2½ Very Lean Meat **Carbohydrate Choices:** 1½

Try This

Serve this spicy stew with peeled orange slices sprinkled with cinnamon sugar. Bottled cinnamon sugar can be found with the other spices at the supermarket, or make your own by mixing granulated sugar with ground cinnamon.

beef-barley stew

Prep Time: 15 Minutes   **Start to Finish:** 1 Hour 25 Minutes   **Makes:** 6 servings

1	lb extra-lean (at least 90%) ground beef
1	medium onion, chopped (½ cup)
2	cups beef broth
⅔	cup uncooked pearl barley
2	teaspoons chopped fresh or ½ teaspoon dried oregano leaves
¼	teaspoon salt

¼	teaspoon pepper
1	can (14.5 oz) whole peeled tomatoes, undrained
1	can (8 oz) sliced water chestnuts, undrained
2	cups frozen mixed vegetables (from 12-oz bag)

1. Heat oven to 350°F. Heat 10-inch nonstick skillet over medium heat; add beef and onion. Cook 7 to 8 minutes, stirring occasionally, until beef is brown; drain.

2. In ungreased 3-quart casserole, mix beef mixture and all remaining ingredients except frozen vegetables, breaking up tomatoes.

3. Cover; bake 30 minutes. Stir in frozen vegetables. Cover; bake 30 to 40 minutes longer or until barley is tender.

1 Serving: Calories 250 (Calories from Fat 60); Total Fat 7g (Saturated Fat 2.5g; Trans Fat 0g); Cholesterol 45mg; Sodium 600mg; Total Carbohydrate 28g (Dietary Fiber 6g); Protein 19g **% Daily Value:** Vitamin A 15%; Vitamin C 15%; Calcium 6%; Iron 15% **Exchanges:** 1½ Starch, ½ Vegetable, 2 Lean Meat **Carbohydrate Choices:** 2

sweet potato bisque

Prep Time: 35 Minutes **Start to Finish:** 50 Minutes **Makes:** 6 servings (1 cup each)

220 Calories

⅓ cup finely chopped pancetta (about 2¼ oz)

1½ cups cubes (1 inch) sourdough bread

1 teaspoon chopped fresh or ¼ teaspoon dried rosemary leaves

2 large sweet onions, chopped (2 cups)

4 cups cubed peeled sweet potatoes (2 medium)

1 can (12 oz) evaporated low-fat milk

2 cups water

½ teaspoon freshly ground pepper

¼ teaspoon salt

1. In 12-inch nonstick skillet, cook ¼ cup of the pancetta over medium-low heat 4 minutes or until golden brown and crisp. Drain pancetta on paper towels. Add bread cubes to drippings; cook 7 minutes, stirring frequently, until golden and crisp. Stir in rosemary; cook 1 minute. Return pancetta to skillet. Remove from heat; set aside until serving time.

2. In 4-quart Dutch oven or saucepan, cook remaining pancetta over medium-low heat 4 minutes or until golden brown and crisp. Add onions; cook 5 minutes, stirring occasionally. Add sweet potatoes, milk, water, pepper and salt. Heat to boiling; reduce heat. Cover; simmer 15 minutes.

3. In blender or food processor, place 3 cups soup. Cover; blend until smooth. Pour blended soup into large bowl; cover to keep warm. Repeat procedure with remaining soup. Sprinkle individual servings with crouton-pancetta mixture.

1 Serving: Calories 220 (Calories from Fat 50); Total Fat 6g (Saturated Fat 3g; Trans Fat 0g); Cholesterol 15mg; Sodium 430mg; Total Carbohydrate 34g (Dietary Fiber 3g); Protein 8g **% Daily Value:** Vitamin A 260%; Vitamin C 6%; Calcium 20%; Iron 6% **Exchanges:** ½ Starch, 1 Other Carbohydrate, ½ Low-Fat Milk, 1 Vegetable, ½ Fat **Carbohydrate Choices:** 2

280 Calories

baked potato soup

Prep Time: 20 Minutes   **Start to Finish:** 20 Minutes   **Makes:** 6 servings (about 1 cup each)

1   package (24 oz) frozen steam-and-mash potatoes
2½ cups evaporated fat-free milk
1   cup shredded reduced-fat extra-sharp Cheddar cheese (4 oz)

1   cup reduced-fat sour cream
¼   teaspoon salt
½   cup thinly sliced green onion tops
    Freshly ground pepper, if desired
    Crumbled cooked bacon, if desired

1. Microwave potatoes as directed on package.

2. In large microwavable bowl, mix hot potatoes and 2 cups of the milk; mash until smooth. Add ¾ cup of the cheese; stir until melted. Stir in remaining ½ cup milk, the sour cream and salt. Cover; microwave on High 2 to 3 minutes or until thoroughly heated.

3. Ladle soup into 6 bowls; sprinkle evenly with remaining ¼ cup cheese and the onions. Garnish with pepper and bacon.

1 Serving: Calories 280 (Calories from Fat 40); Total Fat 4g (Saturated Fat 2.5g; Trans Fat 0g); Cholesterol 20mg; Sodium 820mg; Total Carbohydrate 43g (Dietary Fiber 3g); Protein 18g **% Daily Value:** Vitamin A 15%; Vitamin C 8%; Calcium 60%; Iron 6% **Exchanges:** 1½ Starch, 1 Other Carbohydrate, ½ Skim Milk, 1 Lean Meat **Carbohydrate Choices:** 3

posole

Prep Time: 30 Minutes   **Start to Finish:** 30 Minutes   **Makes:** 4 servings (1⅓ cups each)

1   pork tenderloin (1 lb), trimmed of fat, cut into bite-size pieces
2   teaspoons salt-free southwest chipotle seasoning blend
    Cooking spray
1   can (15.5 oz) white hominy, undrained

1   can (14.5 oz) Mexican-style stewed tomatoes with jalapeño peppers, garlic and onion, undrained
1   cup water
¼   cup chopped fresh cilantro

1. Spray 3-quart saucepan with cooking spray; heat over medium-high heat. Sprinkle pork with seasoning blend; spray with cooking spray. Add pork to saucepan; cook 4 minutes, stirring frequently, until browned.

2. Stir in hominy, tomatoes and water. Heat to boiling; reduce heat. Cover; simmer 20 minutes, stirring occasionally, or until pork is no longer pink in center. Stir in cilantro.

1 Serving: Calories 250 (Calories from Fat 70); Total Fat 8g (Saturated Fat 2.5g; Trans Fat 0g); Cholesterol 40mg; Sodium 480mg; Total Carbohydrate 20g (Dietary Fiber 3g); Protein 24g **% Daily Value:** Vitamin A 15%; Vitamin C 10%; Calcium 4%; Iron 15% **Exchanges:** 1½ Starch, 2½ Lean Meat **Carbohydrate Choices:** 1

ham and butternut squash soup

Prep Time: 15 Minutes   **Start to Finish:** 15 Minutes   **Makes:** 4 servings

2 packages (12 oz each) frozen butternut squash	½ teaspoon pepper
1 cup reduced-sodium chicken broth	2 teaspoons olive oil
2 tablespoons cinnamon sugar	1 cup diced cooked ham
	1 tablespoon chopped fresh rosemary leaves

1. Microwave squash on High 5 minutes or until thawed. In large microwavable bowl, mix squash, broth, cinnamon sugar and pepper. Microwave uncovered on High 3 to 5 minutes or until thoroughly heated.

2. Meanwhile, in 10-inch nonstick skillet, heat oil over medium-high heat. Pat ham dry with paper towels. Cook ham in oil 2 minutes, stirring occasionally, until lightly browned. Add rosemary; cook 1 minute longer.

3. Divide soup among 4 bowls; sprinkle each with about 2 tablespoons ham topping.

1 Serving: Calories 170 (Calories from Fat 50); Total Fat 5g (Saturated Fat 1.5g; Trans Fat 0g); Cholesterol 20mg; Sodium 650mg; Total Carbohydrate 21g (Dietary Fiber 3g); Protein 10g **% Daily Value:** Vitamin A 330%; Vitamin C 20%; Calcium 10%; Iron 10% **Exchanges:** 1 Starch, 1 Vegetable, ½ Lean Meat, ½ Fat **Carbohydrate Choices:** 1½

hearty seafood stew

Prep Time: 30 Minutes   **Start to Finish:** 1 Hour   **Makes:** 6 servings

300 Calories

2	tablespoons vegetable oil
2	medium carrots, thinly sliced (1 cup)
2	medium stalks celery, sliced (1 cup)
1	large onion, chopped (1 cup)
1	clove garlic, finely chopped
1	can (14.5 oz) stewed tomatoes, undrained
2	cups water
1	tablespoon beef bouillon granules
1	medium potato, cut into ½-inch pieces
1	lb cod or other medium-firm fish fillets, cut into 1-inch pieces

½	lb uncooked medium shrimp, thawed if frozen, peeled, deveined
1	can (15.5 oz) great northern beans, rinsed, drained
1	small zucchini, cut in half lengthwise, then cut crosswise into slices (1 cup)
1	teaspoon chopped fresh or ¼ teaspoon dried thyme leaves
½	teaspoon pepper
	Chopped fresh parsley, if desired

1. In 4-quart Dutch oven or saucepan, heat oil over medium-high heat. Add carrots, celery, onion and garlic; cook about 5 minutes, stirring frequently, until vegetables are tender. Stir in tomatoes, water, bouillon and potato. Heat to boiling; reduce heat. Cover; simmer 20 minutes.

2. Stir in cod, shrimp, beans, zucchini, thyme and pepper. Heat to boiling; reduce heat. Cover; simmer 6 to 10 minutes or until fish flakes easily with fork and shrimp are pink. Garnish with parsley.

1 Serving: Calories 300 (Calories from Fat 60); Total Fat 6g (Saturated Fat 1g; Trans Fat 0g); Cholesterol 90mg; Sodium 720mg; Total Carbohydrate 34g (Dietary Fiber 7g); Protein 27g **% Daily Value:** Vitamin A 80%; Vitamin C 15%; Calcium 15%; Iron 25% **Exchanges:** 2 Starch, 1 Vegetable, 1 Very Lean Meat, 1½ Lean Meat **Carbohydrate Choices:** 2

270 Calories

italian bean soup with greens

Prep Time: 25 Minutes   **Start to Finish:** 1 Hour 15 Minutes   **Makes:** 8 servings (about 1⅓ cups each)

2 tablespoons olive oil	2 teaspoons dried basil leaves
2 medium carrots, sliced (1 cup)	1 teaspoon dried oregano leaves
1 large onion, chopped (1 cup)	½ teaspoon salt
1 stalk celery, chopped (⅓ cup)	¼ teaspoon pepper
2 cloves garlic, finely chopped	4 cups vegetable broth
2 cans (15 to 15.5 oz each) great northern or cannellini beans, drained, rinsed	4 cups packed fresh spinach leaves
1 can (28 oz) diced tomatoes, undrained	½ cup shredded Parmesan cheese (2 oz)

1. In 5-quart Dutch oven or saucepan, heat oil over medium-high heat. Add carrots, onion, celery and garlic; cook about 5 minutes, stirring frequently, until onion is tender.

2. Stir in beans, tomatoes, basil, oregano, salt, pepper and broth. Cover; simmer 30 to 45 minutes or until vegetables are tender.

3. Increase heat to medium; stir in spinach. Cover; cook 3 to 5 minutes longer or until spinach is wilted. Sprinkle individual servings with cheese.

1 Serving: Calories 270 (Calories from Fat 50); Total Fat 6g (Saturated Fat 2g; Trans Fat 0g); Cholesterol 0mg; Sodium 990mg; Total Carbohydrate 39g (Dietary Fiber 9g); Protein 15g **% Daily Value:** Vitamin A 100%; Vitamin C 20%; Calcium 25%; Iron 30% **Exchanges:** 2 Starch, 1 Vegetable, 1 Medium-Fat Meat **Carbohydrate Choices:** 2½

Kitchen Tip Spinach will discolor if cooked in an aluminum saucepan and may also discolor the pan. For this recipe, use a Dutch oven that is made of stainless steel, is porcelain covered or made of other nonreactive material.

tomato-lentil soup

Prep Time: 15 Minutes   **Start to Finish:** 50 Minutes   **Makes:** 6 servings

1	tablespoon olive or vegetable oil	4	cups water
1	large onion, finely chopped (1 cup)	4	teaspoons chicken or vegetable bouillon granules
1	medium stalk celery, cut into ½-inch pieces	1	teaspoon dried thyme leaves
2	cloves garlic, finely chopped	¼	teaspoon pepper
2	medium carrots, cut into ½-inch pieces (1 cup)	1	dried bay leaf
1	cup dried lentils (8 oz), sorted, rinsed	1	can (28 oz) diced tomatoes, undrained

1. In 3-quart saucepan, heat oil over medium-high heat. Cook onion, celery and garlic in oil about 5 minutes, stirring occasionally, until softened.

2. Stir in all remaining ingredients except tomatoes. Heat to boiling; reduce heat. Cover; simmer 15 to 20 minutes or until lentils and vegetables are tender.

3. Stir in tomatoes. Simmer uncovered about 15 minutes longer or until thoroughly heated. Remove and discard bay leaf before serving.

1 Serving: Calories 180 (Calories from Fat 25); Total Fat 3g (Saturated Fat 0g; Trans Fat 0g); Cholesterol 0mg; Sodium 790mg; Total Carbohydrate 30g (Dietary Fiber 7g); Protein 10g **% Daily Value:** Vitamin A 80%; Vitamin C 6%; Calcium 6%; Iron 25% **Exchanges:** 1½ Starch, 1 Vegetable, ½ Lean Meat **Carbohydrate Choices:** 2

Health Smart Lentils are low in calories and are a good source of fiber. They also have no cholesterol and very little fat. Lentils are available in a variety of colors: grayish brown (the most widely available), yellow, red, and green. Use whatever color you like.

summer vegetable ratatouille soup

Prep Time: 25 Minutes   **Start to Finish:** 6 Hours 55 Minutes   **Makes:** 9 servings (1½ cups each)

6 mini pattypan squash, cut into quarters, or 1 yellow summer squash, sliced	¼ teaspoon pepper
4 medium tomatoes, chopped (3 cups)	7 cups chicken broth
1 orange bell pepper, cut into bite-size strips	1 zucchini, cut in half lengthwise, then cut crosswise into slices
1 medium onion, sliced	1 baby eggplant, cut lengthwise into quarters, then cut crosswise into slices
2 cloves garlic, finely chopped	Shredded Parmesan cheese, if desired
¼ cup chopped fresh parsley	Chopped fresh basil leaves, if desired
1 teaspoon salt	

1. Spray 5- to 6-quart slow cooker with cooking spray. In slow cooker, mix squash, tomatoes, bell pepper, onion, garlic, parsley, salt, pepper and broth.

2. Cover; cook on Low heat setting 6 to 8 hours (or on High heat setting 3 to 4 hours).

3. Stir in zucchini and eggplant. If cooking on Low, increase heat setting to High. Cover; cook about 30 minutes longer or until zucchini and eggplant are tender. Garnish individual servings with cheese and basil.

1 Serving: Calories 80 (Calories from Fat 15); Total Fat 1.5g (Saturated Fat 0g; Trans Fat 0g); Cholesterol 0mg; Sodium 1020mg; Total Carbohydrate 11g (Dietary Fiber 4g); Protein 6g **% Daily Value:** Vitamin A 15%; Vitamin C 45%; Calcium 4%; Iron 6% **Exchanges:** 2 Vegetable, ½ Fat **Carbohydrate Choices:** 1

Try This

This French-inspired soup is a great way to put your garden veggies to use. Made in a slow cooker, it won't heat up the kitchen!

tomato-basil soup

Prep Time: 30 Minutes   **Start to Finish:** 1 Hour   **Makes:** 4 servings

170 Calories

2 tablespoons olive or vegetable oil	1 can (8 oz) tomato sauce
1 medium carrot, finely chopped (½ cup)	¼ cup thinly sliced fresh or 2 teaspoons dried basil leaves
1 medium onion, finely chopped (½ cup)	½ teaspoon sugar
1 clove garlic, finely chopped	¼ teaspoon salt
6 large tomatoes, peeled, seeded and chopped (6 cups)	Dash pepper

1. In 3-quart saucepan, heat oil over medium heat. Cook carrot, onion and garlic in oil about 10 minutes, stirring occasionally, until tender but not browned.

2. Stir in tomatoes. Cook uncovered 10 minutes, stirring occasionally. Stir in all remaining ingredients. Cook uncovered about 10 minutes longer, stirring occasionally, until hot.

1 Serving: Calories 170 (Calories from Fat 70); Total Fat 8g (Saturated Fat 1g; Trans Fat 0g); Cholesterol 0mg; Sodium 550mg; Total Carbohydrate 22g (Dietary Fiber 6g); Protein 4g **% Daily Value:** Vitamin A 170%; Vitamin C 50%; Calcium 4%; Iron 10% **Exchanges:** 4 Vegetable, 1 Fat **Carbohydrate Choices:** 1½

Try This

Fully ripe, juicy tomatoes provide the best flavor for this soup. If your tomatoes aren't completely ripe, you may need to increase the salt and sugar just a bit. Or you may substitute 3 cans (14.5 oz each) diced tomatoes, undrained; omit salt and increase sugar to 1 teaspoon.

240
Calories

butternut squash soup

Prep Time: 30 Minutes   **Start to Finish:** 45 Minutes   **Makes:** 6 servings

2 tablespoons butter	½ teaspoon dried marjoram leaves
1 medium onion, chopped (½ cup)	¼ teaspoon black pepper
1 butternut squash (2 lb), peeled, seeded and cubed	⅛ teaspoon ground red pepper (cayenne)
2 cups chicken broth	1 package (8 oz) cream cheese, cubed
	Additional chicken broth or water, if desired

1. In 3-quart saucepan, melt butter over medium heat. Cook onion in butter, stirring occasionally, until crisp-tender.

2. Add squash, broth, marjoram, black pepper and red pepper. Heat to boiling; reduce heat. Cover; simmer 12 to 15 minutes or until squash is tender. Remove from heat; cool slightly.

3. In blender or food processor, place one-third each of the soup mixture and cream cheese. Cover; blend on high speed until smooth, scraping down sides of blender if needed. Repeat twice with remaining soup mixture and cream cheese. Return mixture to saucepan. Heat over medium heat, stirring with whisk, until blended and hot (do not boil). Add additional broth if thinner consistency is desired.

1 Serving: Calories 240 (Calories from Fat 160); Total Fat 17g (Saturated Fat 10g; Trans Fat 0.5g); Cholesterol 50mg; Sodium 490mg; Total Carbohydrate 15g (Dietary Fiber 2g); Protein 5g **% Daily Value:** Vitamin A 260%; Vitamin C 15%; Calcium 10%; Iron 6% **Exchanges:** 1 Starch, ½ Vegetable, 3½ Fat **Carbohydrate Choices:** 1

Slow Cooker Directions: In 10-inch skillet, melt butter over medium heat. Cook onion in butter, stirring occasionally, until crisp-tender. Spray 3½- to 4-quart slow cooker with cooking spray. In slow cooker, mix onion and remaining ingredients except cream cheese and additional broth. Cover; cook on Low heat setting 6 to 8 hours. In blender or food processor, place one-third to one-half of the soup mixture at a time. Cover; blend on high speed until smooth. Return mixture to slow cooker. Stir in cream cheese with wire whisk. Cover; cook on Low heat setting about 30 minutes, stirring occasionally with wire whisk, until cheese is melted and soup is smooth. Add additional broth if thinner consistency is desired.

Kitchen Tip Squash will be easier to peel if you microwave it first. Pierce whole squash with knife in several places to allow steam to escape. Place on paper towel and microwave on High 4 to 6 minutes or until squash is hot and peel is firm but easy to cut. Cool slightly before peeling.

Try This

Top bowls of this soup with a spoonful of Maple-Pecan-Apple Salsa. In small bowl, mix ½ cup diced unpeeled apple, ½ cup chopped toasted pecans, 2 tablespoons real maple syrup and ½ teaspoon ground cinnamon. Or simply sprinkle individual servings with pumpkin seeds or toasted chopped walnuts.

southwestern corn chowder

Prep Time: 20 Minutes   **Start to Finish:** 40 Minutes   **Makes:** 6 servings

1	large onion, chopped (1 cup)	1	medium red bell pepper, chopped
1	medium leek, cut in half lengthwise, rinsed and chopped	⅛	teaspoon black pepper
		⅛	teaspoon ground red pepper (cayenne)
2	bags (12 oz each) frozen corn	3	saffron threads, crushed, if desired
3½	cups reduced-sodium chicken broth		Fresh chives, if desired

1. Spray 4- to 5-quart Dutch oven or saucepan with cooking spray; heat over medium heat. Add onion and leek; cook about 5 minutes, stirring occasionally, until tender.

2. Add corn. Cook about 5 minutes, stirring occasionally, until corn softens. Add 1¾ cups of the broth. Heat to boiling; reduce heat. Cover; simmer about 20 minutes or until corn is very tender. Remove from heat; cool slightly.

3. Transfer half of the corn mixture to blender or food processor. Cover; blend or process until smooth. Return mixture to Dutch oven.

4. Add remaining 1¾ cups broth, the bell pepper, black pepper, red pepper and saffron; cook until thoroughly heated. Garnish individual servings with chives.

1 Serving: Calories 140 (Calories from Fat 10); Total Fat 1g (Saturated Fat 0g; Trans Fat 0g); Cholesterol 0mg; Sodium 330mg; Total Carbohydrate 28g (Dietary Fiber 3g); Protein 5g **% Daily Value:** Vitamin A 20%; Vitamin C 25%; Calcium 0%; Iron 6% **Exchanges:** ½ Starch, 1 Other Carbohydrate, 1½ Vegetable **Carbohydrate Choices:** 2

Try This

Stir in 1½ cups cubed cooked turkey ham with the remaining broth, and top each serving with 1 tablespoon shredded Cheddar cheese. It adds just 50 calories per serving.

290
Calories

ratatouille chili

Prep Time: 25 Minutes **Start to Finish:** 25 Minutes **Makes:** 4 servings

2 tablespoons olive or vegetable oil
1 large eggplant (1 lb), cut into ½-inch cubes (4 cups)
1 large onion, chopped (1 cup)
1 medium green bell pepper, chopped (1 cup)
1 clove garlic, finely chopped
½ cup sliced zucchini
3 teaspoons chili powder

1 teaspoon chopped fresh or ¼ teaspoon dried basil leaves
¼ teaspoon salt
1 can (15.5 oz) great northern beans, drained, rinsed
1 can (14.5 oz) whole peeled tomatoes, undrained
1 can (8 oz) tomato sauce

1. In 4-quart Dutch oven or saucepan, heat oil over medium-high heat. Add eggplant, onion, bell pepper and garlic; cook, stirring occasionally, until vegetables are crisp-tender.

2. Stir in all remaining ingredients, breaking up tomatoes. Cook about 10 minutes, stirring occasionally, until zucchini is tender.

1 Serving: Calories 290 (Calories from Fat 70); Total Fat 8g (Saturated Fat 1g; Trans Fat 0g); Cholesterol 0mg; Sodium 830mg; Total Carbohydrate 43g (Dietary Fiber 14g); Protein 12g **% Daily Value:** Vitamin A 20%; Vitamin C 40%; Calcium 15%; Iron 30% **Exchanges:** 1 Other Carbohydrate, 6 Vegetable, 1½ Fat **Carbohydrate Choices:** 3

Kitchen Tip From the Provence region of France, ratatouille is often served as a side dish or appetizer. The flavors typical of this dish include eggplant, zucchini, tomatoes, olive oil and garlic, all of which flavor this savory chili version.

roasted vegetable stew

230 Calories

Prep Time: 55 Minutes   **Start to Finish:** 55 Minutes   **Makes:** 6 servings

5 small red potatoes (¾ lb), cut into quarters	2 cloves garlic, finely chopped
1 large onion, cut into quarters	2 tablespoons olive or vegetable oil
1 medium red bell pepper, cut into quarters	1 can (14 oz) vegetable broth
1 medium green bell pepper, cut into quarters	2 cans (14.5 oz each) Italian-style stewed tomatoes, undrained
1 medium carrot, cut into ¼-inch diagonal slices (½ cup)	1¼ cups uncooked rotini pasta (4 oz)
1 small zucchini, cut into ½-inch slices	2 tablespoons chopped fresh parsley
4 oz medium whole mushrooms	Freshly ground pepper, if desired

1. Set oven control to broil. In large bowl, toss potatoes, onion, bell peppers, carrot, zucchini, mushrooms, garlic and oil. Spread vegetable mixture, skin sides up, in ungreased 15 x 10 x 1-inch pan.

2. Broil with tops 4 to 6 inches from heat 10 to 15 minutes or until roasted. Remove vegetables as they become soft; cool. Remove skins from peppers. Coarsely chop potatoes, onion and bell peppers.

3. In 4-quart Dutch oven or saucepan, mix roasted vegetables, broth, tomatoes and pasta. Heat to boiling; reduce heat to low. Cover; simmer about 15 minutes, stirring occasionally, until pasta is tender. Sprinkle individual servings with parsley and pepper.

1 Serving: Calories 230 (Calories from Fat 50); Total Fat 5g (Saturated Fat 1g; Trans Fat 0g); Cholesterol 0mg; Sodium 530mg; Total Carbohydrate 40g (Dietary Fiber 5g); Protein 6g **% Daily Value:** Vitamin A 70%; Vitamin C 60%; Calcium 6%; Iron 15% **Exchanges:** 2 Starch, ½ Other Carbohydrate, ½ Vegetable, 1 Fat **Carbohydrate Choices:** 2½

Quick Meal Idea Complete this substantial meatless meal with bread and a crisp green salad.

smashed potato stew

Prep Time: 30 Minutes   **Start to Finish:** 30 Minutes   **Makes:** 6 servings

3½ cups fat-free (skim) milk	¼ teaspoon black pepper
3 tablespoons all-purpose flour	⅛ teaspoon ground red pepper (cayenne)
1 tablespoon canola oil or butter	1½ cups shredded reduced-fat sharp Cheddar cheese (6 oz)
1 large onion, finely chopped (1 cup)	⅓ cup reduced-fat sour cream
4 medium unpeeled potatoes (1½ lb), cut into ¼-inch pieces	8 medium green onions, sliced (½ cup)
1 teaspoon salt	

1. In small bowl, beat ½ cup of the milk and the flour with whisk until smooth; set aside. In 4-quart Dutch oven or saucepan, heat oil over medium heat. Cook onion in oil about 2 minutes, stirring occasionally, until tender. Increase heat to high; stir in remaining 3 cups milk.

2. Stir in potatoes, salt, black pepper and red pepper. Heat to boiling; reduce heat. Simmer uncovered 15 to 16 minutes, stirring frequently, until potatoes are tender.

3. Beat in flour mixture with whisk. Cook about 2 minutes, stirring frequently, until thickened. Remove from heat. Beat potato mixture with whisk until potatoes are slightly mashed. Stir in cheese, sour cream and green onions.

1 Serving: Calories 250 (Calories from Fat 60); Total Fat 6g (Saturated Fat 2.5g; Trans Fat 0g); Cholesterol 15mg; Sodium 740mg; Total Carbohydrate 34g (Dietary Fiber 3g); Protein 15g **% Daily Value:** Vitamin A 10%; Vitamin C 10%; Calcium 40%; Iron 8% **Exchanges:** 2 Starch, 1 Vegetable, 1 Medium-Fat Meat **Carbohydrate Choices:** 2

Quick Meal Idea This stew is so thick and creamy that you'll want to make it the star of your meal. You could partner it with a slice of crusty French bread and a fresh garden salad for a stick-to-your-ribs dinner.

black bean-sweet potato chili

260 Calories

Prep Time: 35 Minutes   **Start to Finish:** 7 Hours 35 Minutes   **Makes:** 8 servings

- 2 large dark orange sweet potatoes (1½ lb), peeled, cut into ½-inch cubes (about 5 cups)
- 3 large onions, chopped (3 cups)
- 3 cloves garlic, finely chopped
- 2 tablespoons chili powder
- 1 tablespoon ground cumin
- 1 can (28 oz) diced tomatoes, undrained

- 1 can (16 oz) refried black beans
- 1 can (15 oz) black beans, drained, rinsed
- 2 cups vegetable or chicken broth
- 2 teaspoons red wine vinegar
  Shredded Cheddar or Monterey Jack cheese, if desired
  Reduced-fat sour cream, if desired

1. Spray 5- to 6-quart slow cooker with cooking spray. In slow cooker, mix sweet potatoes, onions, garlic, chili powder, cumin, tomatoes, refried beans, black beans and broth.

2. Cover; cook on Low heat setting 7 to 8 hours (or on High heat setting 3 hours 30 minutes to 4 hours).

3. Before serving, stir in vinegar. Serve chili with cheese and sour cream.

1 Serving: Calories 260 (Calories from Fat 20); Total Fat 2g (Saturated Fat 0.5g; Trans Fat 0g); Cholesterol 0mg; Sodium 900mg; Total Carbohydrate 48g (Dietary Fiber 13g); Protein 12g **% Daily Value:** Vitamin A 270%; Vitamin C 25%; Calcium 15%; Iron 25% **Exchanges:** 2½ Other Carbohydrate, 2 Vegetable, 1 Lean Meat **Carbohydrate Choices:** 3

Try This

Make quick work of chopping the garlic and onions by enlisting the help of your food processor. Start by chopping the garlic using the metal blade attachment, then add the onions and continue processing. Depending on the size of your food processor, you may need to do the onions in batches. Either way, you save time and tears!

260 Calories

black bean soup with avocado salsa

Prep Time: 20 Minutes   **Start to Finish:** 20 Minutes   **Makes:** 4 servings   (photo on page C10)

SOUP

1	can (15 oz) black beans, drained, rinsed
1	cup water
1	can (14.5 oz) fire-roasted diced tomatoes, undrained
½	cup chipotle salsa
1	teaspoon ground cumin

AVOCADO SALSA

1	cup peeled, diced ripe avocado
½	teaspoon grated lime peel
1	tablespoon fresh lime juice
2	tablespoons finely chopped fresh cilantro
⅛	teaspoon salt
	Reduced-fat sour cream, if desired

1. In 2-quart saucepan, mash beans slightly with potato masher. Stir in water, tomatoes, chipotle salsa and cumin. Heat to boiling over high heat; reduce heat. Cover; simmer 8 minutes, stirring occasionally. Uncover; simmer 2 minutes longer or until soup is slightly thickened.

2. Meanwhile, in small bowl, gently toss all avocado salsa ingredients.

3. Ladle 1 cup soup into each of 4 bowls. Top each serving with ¼ cup avocado salsa. Garnish with sour cream.

1 Serving: Calories 260 (Calories from Fat 60); Total Fat 7g (Saturated Fat 1g; Trans Fat 0g); Cholesterol 0mg; Sodium 430mg; Total Carbohydrate 38g (Dietary Fiber 15g); Protein 11g **% Daily Value:** Vitamin A 10%; Vitamin C 6%; Calcium 15%; Iron 20% **Exchanges:** 2 Starch, 1 Vegetable, ½ Lean Meat, 1 Fat **Carbohydrate Choices:** 2½

Kitchen Tip The rich avocado topping is the secret ingredient in this recipe. It soothes the slow burn from the smoky chipotle heat and adds a burst of fresh flavor.

spicy poblano and corn soup

220 Calories

Prep Time: 15 Minutes   **Start to Finish:** 15 Minutes   **Makes:** 4 servings

1   bag (16 oz) frozen baby gold and white corn, thawed
2   cups fat-free (skim) milk
4   poblano chiles (about 1 lb), seeded, chopped
1   cup refrigerated prechopped onion (from 8-oz container)

1   tablespoon water
¾   teaspoon salt
½   cup shredded reduced-fat sharp Cheddar cheese (2 oz)

1. In 3-quart saucepan, heat 1 cup of the corn and 1½ cups of the milk to boiling over medium heat.

2. In medium microwavable bowl, mix chiles, onion and water. Cover; microwave on High 4 minutes.

3. Meanwhile, in blender, place remaining corn and remaining ½ cup milk. Cover; blend on high speed until smooth. Add pureed mixture to corn mixture in saucepan. Stir in chile mixture and salt. Cook 6 minutes over medium heat, stirring occasionally, until hot.

4. Ladle about 1⅓ cups soup into each of 4 bowls. Top each serving with 2 tablespoons cheese.

1 Serving: Calories 220 (Calories from Fat 25); Total Fat 3g (Saturated Fat 1.5g; Trans Fat 0g); Cholesterol 10mg; Sodium 730mg; Total Carbohydrate 37g (Dietary Fiber 4g); Protein 11g **% Daily Value:** Vitamin A 20%; Vitamin C 100%; Calcium 25%; Iron 6% **Exchanges:** 1½ Starch, ½ Skim Milk, 1 Vegetable, ½ Fat **Carbohydrate Choices:** 2½

Quick Meal Idea Sliced tomatoes and warmed flour tortillas are nice accompaniments to bowls of this southwestern-inspired soup.

sweet potato-broccoli soup

Prep Time: 15 Minutes   **Start to Finish:** 45 Minutes   **Makes:** 6 servings

1 tablespoon olive oil	1 medium apple, peeled, cut into 1-inch pieces
1 large onion, chopped (1 cup)	
1 leek, cut in half lengthwise, rinsed and thinly sliced	2 cups chopped fresh broccoli florets
	1 tablespoon water
3½ cups vegetable broth or reduced-sodium chicken broth	6 tablespoons reduced-fat sour cream
	½ medium apple, cut into 12 thin slices
3 medium sweet potatoes, peeled, cut into 1-inch pieces (about 4 cups)	

1. In 4-quart saucepan, heat oil over medium heat. Cook onion and leek in oil 4 minutes, stirring frequently, until soft. Stir in broth, sweet potatoes and apple pieces. Heat to boiling; reduce heat. Cover; simmer about 20 minutes or until sweet potatoes are tender. Remove from heat; cool slightly.

2. Meanwhile, in small microwavable bowl, place broccoli and water; cover with microwavable plastic wrap. Microwave on High 1 minute 30 seconds or until crisp-tender.

3. In blender or food processor, place about one-third of soup mixture. Cover; blend on high speed until smooth, stopping blender to scrape side if necessary. Pour into large bowl. Repeat 2 times more with remaining soup mixture. Pour soup back into saucepan; stir in broccoli. Cover; cook over low heat about 10 minutes or until hot.

4. Divide soup evenly among 6 bowls, about 1⅓ cups each. Top each serving with 1 tablespoon sour cream and 2 apple slices.

1 Serving: Calories 170 (Calories from Fat 40); Total Fat 4.5g (Saturated Fat 1.5g; Trans Fat 0g); Cholesterol 5mg; Sodium 590mg; Total Carbohydrate 29g (Dietary Fiber 4g); Protein 3g **% Daily Value:** Vitamin A 280%; Vitamin C 40%; Calcium 8%; Iron 6% **Exchanges:** ½ Starch, 1 Other Carbohydrate, 1 Vegetable, 1 Fat **Carbohydrate Choices:** 2

Try This

Blending soups results in a wonderful consistency. Another way to puree soups is by using an immersion blender. The soup can be kept in its original pan; just make sure to keep the end of the blender fully immersed to prevent the soup from splattering.

roasted red pepper soup with mozzarella

200 Calories

Prep Time: 1 Hour 10 Minutes   **Start to Finish:** 1 Hour 10 Minutes   **Makes:** 4 servings
(photo on page C10)

4 red bell peppers	¼ teaspoon cracked black pepper
1 tablespoon olive oil	1 cup thinly sliced fresh basil leaves
2 large onions, chopped (2 cups)	½ yellow bell pepper, diced
3 cloves garlic, sliced	8 small fresh mozzarella cheese balls, cut into quarters
2 cups vegetable broth or reduced-sodium chicken broth	4 slices crusty multigrain or whole wheat bread
1 cup water	

1. Set oven control to broil. On rack in broiler pan, place red bell peppers. Broil with tops about 5 inches from heat, turning occasionally, until skin is blistered and evenly browned. Place roasted peppers in large bowl; cover with plastic wrap. Let stand 15 minutes.

2. Meanwhile, in 4-quart saucepan, heat oil over medium-low heat. Cook onions and garlic in oil 7 to 9 minutes, stirring occasionally, until onions begin to turn brown; remove from heat.

3. Remove skin, stems, seeds and membranes from roasted peppers; cut peppers into strips. Into onion mixture, stir bell pepper strips, broth, water and pepper. Heat to boiling; reduce heat. Simmer uncovered 10 minutes, stirring occasionally. Stir in ½ cup of the basil. Remove from the heat; cool slightly.

4. In blender or food processor, place about one-third of the soup mixture. Cover; blend on high speed until smooth, stopping blender to scrape side if necessary. Pour into large bowl. Repeat 2 times more with remaining soup mixture.

5. Divide soup among 4 bowls, about 1½ cups each. Top each serving with yellow bell pepper and mozzarella; sprinkle evenly with remaining ½ cup basil. Serve with bread.

1 Serving: Calories 200 (Calories from Fat 50); Total Fat 6g (Saturated Fat 1.5g; Trans Fat 0g); Cholesterol 0mg; Sodium 620mg; Total Carbohydrate 29g (Dietary Fiber 6g); Protein 7g **% Daily Value:** Vitamin A 90%; Vitamin C 160%; Calcium 10%; Iron 10% **Exchanges:** 1½ Starch, 1½ Vegetable, 1 Fat **Carbohydrate Choices:** 2

Kitchen Tip If too much hot soup is added to the blender at one time, steam can build up during blending and cause soup to pop out of the lid. It's easy to blend without problems if you do it in small batches with a towel held over the lid of blender. Take care when removing the lid, as the hot steam escapes.

Slow Cooker Suppers

260 Calories

chicken chow mein

Prep Time: 15 Minutes   **Start to Finish:** 6 Hours 30 Minutes   **Makes:** 5 servings

1 tablespoon vegetable oil	1 cup chicken broth
1½ lb boneless skinless chicken thighs, trimmed of excess fat, cut into 1-inch pieces	2 tablespoons soy sauce
2 medium carrots, sliced diagonally (1 cup)	½ teaspoon finely chopped gingerroot
2 medium stalks celery, coarsely chopped (1 cup)	2 tablespoons cornstarch
1 medium onion, chopped (½ cup)	3 tablespoons cold water
2 cloves garlic, finely chopped	1 cup sliced fresh mushrooms (3 oz)
1 can (8 oz) sliced water chestnuts, drained	1 cup fresh snow pea pods (4 oz)
	Chow mein noodles, if desired

1. In 10-inch skillet, heat oil over medium-high heat. Cook chicken in oil about 5 minutes, turning once, until brown.

2. Spray 3½- to 6-quart slow cooker with cooking spray. In slow cooker, place carrots, celery, onion, garlic and water chestnuts; top with chicken. In small bowl, mix broth, soy sauce and gingerroot; pour over chicken.

3. Cover; cook on Low heat setting 6 to 8 hours.

4. In small bowl, mix cornstarch and water until smooth; stir into chicken mixture. Stir in mushrooms and pea pods. Increase heat setting to High. Cover; cook 15 minutes longer. Serve with chow mein noodles.

1 Serving: Calories 260 (Calories from Fat 90); Total Fat 10g (Saturated Fat 2.5g; Trans Fat 0g); Cholesterol 55mg; Sodium 650mg; Total Carbohydrate 21g (Dietary Fiber 3g); Protein 21g **% Daily Value:** Vitamin A 90%; Vitamin C 10%; Calcium 6%; Iron 15% **Exchanges:** 1 Starch, 1 Vegetable, 2½ Very Lean Meat, 1½ Fat **Carbohydrate Choices:** 1½

Try This

Boneless skinless chicken breasts can be substituted for the chicken thighs.

chicken and barley risotto with edamame

250 Calories

Prep Time: 25 Minutes   **Start to Finish:** 4 Hours 50 Minutes   **Makes:** 9 servings (about 1 cup each)   (photo on page C11)

1¼ lb boneless skinless chicken breasts, cut into ¾-inch cubes	½ teaspoon salt
3 medium onions, chopped (1½ cups)	½ teaspoon dried thyme leaves
1¼ cups uncooked pearl barley	1 carton (32 oz) chicken broth (4 cups)
½ cup shredded carrot	1 cup frozen shelled edamame (from 10-oz bag), thawed
2 cloves garlic, finely chopped	½ cup shredded Parmesan cheese (2 oz)

1. Spray 4- to 5-quart slow cooker with cooking spray. In slow cooker, mix chicken, onions, barley, carrot, garlic, salt, thyme and 3 cups of the broth.

2. Cover; cook on Low heat setting 4 to 5 hours.

3. In 2-cup microwavable measuring cup, microwave remaining 1 cup broth uncovered on High 2 to 3 minutes or until boiling. Stir thawed edamame and boiling broth into chicken mixture in slow cooker.

4. Increase heat setting to High. Cover; cook 25 to 30 minutes longer or until edamame are tender. Stir in cheese.

1 Serving: Calories 250 (Calories from Fat 50); Total Fat 6g (Saturated Fat 2g; Trans Fat 0g); Cholesterol 45mg; Sodium 690mg; Total Carbohydrate 27g (Dietary Fiber 6g); Protein 23g **% Daily Value:** Vitamin A 20%; Vitamin C 4%; Calcium 10%; Iron 10% **Exchanges:** 1½ Starch, 1 Vegetable, 2 Lean Meat **Carbohydrate Choices:** 2

Quick Meal Idea Complete the meal with a colorful salad using a variety of greens of different colors and textures.

Try This

Omit the chicken and use vegetable broth instead of chicken broth in this recipe—it's delicious either way!

290 Calories

italian chicken-lentil soup

Prep Time: 15 Minutes   **Start to Finish:** 5 Hours 30 Minutes   **Makes:** 6 servings

4 medium carrots, sliced (2 cups)	1 lb boneless skinless chicken thighs, trimmed of excess fat
1 medium zucchini, chopped (2 cups)	
1 medium onion, chopped (½ cup)	1 can (28 oz) diced tomatoes, undrained
1 cup dried lentils (8 oz), sorted, rinsed	1 cup sliced fresh mushrooms (3 oz)
4½ cups chicken broth	¼ cup chopped fresh or 1 tablespoon dried basil leaves
½ teaspoon salt	
¼ teaspoon pepper	Shredded Parmesan cheese, if desired

1. Spray 3½- to 6-quart slow cooker with cooking spray. In slow cooker, mix carrots, zucchini, onion, lentils, broth, salt and pepper; top with chicken.

2. Cover; cook on Low heat setting 5 to 6 hours.

3. Transfer chicken from slow cooker to cutting board or plate. Shred chicken, using 2 forks; return chicken to slow cooker. Stir in tomatoes and mushrooms. Cover; cook about 15 minutes or until thoroughly heated. Sprinkle individual servings with basil and cheese.

1 Serving: Calories 290 (Calories from Fat 50); Total Fat 6g (Saturated Fat 1.5g; Trans Fat 0g); Cholesterol 30mg; Sodium 1220mg; Total Carbohydrate 35g (Dietary Fiber 9g); Protein 25g **% Daily Value:** Vitamin A 150%; Vitamin C 15%; Calcium 8%; Iron 30% **Exchanges:** 2 Starch, 1½ Vegetable, 2½ Very Lean Meat, ½ Fat **Carbohydrate Choices:** 2

garlic chicken with rice

280 Calories

Prep Time: 10 Minutes   **Start to Finish:** 5 Hours 10 Minutes   **Makes:** 6 servings

- 1 box (6 oz) original long-grain and wild rice mix
- 1 medium onion, chopped (½ cup)
- 1 small red bell pepper, chopped (½ cup)
- 2 tablespoons olive or vegetable oil
- 6 cloves garlic, peeled
- 1 can (14 oz) chicken broth
- 3½ lb bone-in chicken pieces, skin removed

1. Spray 3- to 4-quart slow cooker with cooking spray. In slow cooker, mix rice, contents of seasoning packet, onion, bell pepper, oil, garlic and broth. Arrange chicken on top.

2. Cover; cook on Low heat setting 5 to 6 hours.

1 Serving: Calories 280 (Calories from Fat 100); Total Fat 11g (Saturated Fat 3g; Trans Fat 0g); Cholesterol 95mg; Sodium 550mg; Total Carbohydrate 11g (Dietary Fiber 0g); Protein 35g **% Daily Value:** Vitamin A 10%; Vitamin C 15%; Calcium 6%; Iron 20% **Exchanges:** ½ Starch, 4½ Very Lean Meat, 1½ Fat **Carbohydrate Choices:** 1

Quick Meal Idea Serve the chicken and rice with cooked green beans.

Kitchen Tip Since the garlic in this recipe is left whole, it is milder than if it were chopped or crushed. The longer, slower cooking also mellows the garlic. If you like, just before serving, use a fork to crush the garlic cloves against the side of the slow cooker and stir into the rice.

white chicken chili

Prep Time: 15 Minutes   **Start to Finish:** 4 Hours 30 Minutes   **Makes:** 8 servings

1 large onion, chopped (1 cup)	6 bone-in chicken thighs (1½ lb)
2 cloves garlic, finely chopped	2 cans (15.5 oz each) great northern beans, drained, rinsed
1 can (14 oz) chicken broth	
1 teaspoon ground cumin	1 can (11 oz) vacuum packed white shoepeg corn, drained
1 teaspoon dried oregano leaves	
½ teaspoon salt	3 tablespoons lime juice
¼ teaspoon red pepper sauce	2 tablespoons chopped fresh cilantro

1. Spray 3½- to 4-quart slow cooker with cooking spray. In slow cooker, mix onion, garlic, broth, cumin, oregano, salt and pepper sauce. Remove skin and excess fat from chicken; add to slow cooker.

2. Cover; cook on Low heat setting 4 to 5 hours.

3. Remove chicken from slow cooker. Remove and discard bones. Shred chicken, using 2 forks; return chicken to slow cooker. Stir in beans, corn and lime juice.

4. Cover; cook 15 to 20 minutes longer or until beans and corn are hot. Sprinkle with cilantro.

1 Serving: Calories 290 (Calories from Fat 45); Total Fat 5g (Saturated Fat 1.5g; Trans Fat 0g); Cholesterol 35mg; Sodium 500mg; Total Carbohydrate 37g (Dietary Fiber 8g); Protein 24g **% Daily Value:** Vitamin A 0%; Vitamin C 6%; Calcium 10%; Iron 30% **Exchanges:** 2 Starch, 1 Vegetable, 2 Very Lean Meat, ½ Fat **Carbohydrate Choices:** 2½

chile-chicken tacos

Prep Time: 15 Minutes   **Start to Finish:** 6 Hours 30 Minutes   **Makes:** 12 tacos

1¼ lb boneless skinless chicken thighs
1   package (1 oz) taco seasoning mix
1   tablespoon packed brown sugar
1   can (4.5 oz) chopped green chiles
1   cup frozen corn (from 12-oz bag), thawed
1   can (10 oz) enchilada sauce

4   medium green onions, sliced (¼ cup)
1   box (4.6 oz) taco shells (12 shells), heated as directed on box
3   cups shredded lettuce
1   medium tomato, chopped (¾ cup)

1. Spray 3- to 4-quart slow cooker with cooking spray. Place chicken in slow cooker. Sprinkle with taco seasoning mix and brown sugar; toss to coat. Mix in green chiles, corn and ½ cup of the enchilada sauce. Refrigerate remaining enchilada sauce.

2. Cover; cook on Low heat setting 6 to 7 hours.

3. Transfer chicken from slow cooker to cutting board or plate. Shred chicken, using 2 forks; return chicken to slow cooker. Stir in onions. Cover; cook 15 minutes longer.

4. Heat remaining enchilada sauce. Serve chicken mixture in taco shells with lettuce, tomatoes and enchilada sauce.

1 Taco: Calories 160 (Calories from Fat 60); Total Fat 6g (Saturated Fat 2g; Trans Fat 0g); Cholesterol 30mg; Sodium 350mg; Total Carbohydrate 14g (Dietary Fiber 1g); Protein 11g **% Daily Value:** Vitamin A 10%; Vitamin C 6%; Calcium 4%; Iron 8% **Exchanges:** 1 Starch, ½ Vegetable, 1 Very Lean Meat, 1 Fat **Carbohydrate Choices:** 1

Try This

Mild, medium or hot enchilada sauce will vary the flavor—and the heat level—of these tacos.

healthified new orleans-style stuffed peppers

Prep Time: 25 Minutes   **Start to Finish:** 6 Hours 25 Minutes   **Makes:** 4 servings
(photo on page C11)

1 teaspoon olive oil	1 medium jalapeño chile, seeded, finely chopped
½ lb ground chicken breast	
½ cup thinly sliced celery	½ teaspoon Cajun seasoning
1 can (14.5 oz) diced tomatoes with garlic and onion	⅛ teaspoon salt
	4 large red bell peppers
1⅓ cups cooked brown rice	

1. In 12-inch skillet, heat oil over medium heat. Cook chicken and celery in oil, stirring occasionally, until chicken is no longer pink. Drain tomatoes, reserving liquid. Add half of the tomatoes to chicken mixture; stir in rice, chile, Cajun seasoning and salt. Remove from heat.

2. Remove tops of bell peppers. Remove seeds and membranes; rinse peppers. If necessary, cut thin slice from bottom of each pepper so it stands upright. Spoon chicken mixture into peppers.

3. Spray 5- to 6-quart slow cooker with cooking spray. Pour reserved tomato liquid and remaining tomatoes into slow cooker. Stand stuffed peppers in slow cooker.

4. Cover; cook on Low heat setting 6 to 7 hours (or on High heat setting 3 hours to 3 hours 30 minutes). Transfer stuffed peppers from slow cooker to serving plate; serve with tomatoes from slow cooker.

1 Serving: Calories 240 (Calories from Fat 25); Total Fat 3g (Saturated Fat 0.5g; Trans Fat 0g); Cholesterol 35mg; Sodium 590mg; Total Carbohydrate 34g (Dietary Fiber 6g); Protein 17g **% Daily Value:** Vitamin A 110%; Vitamin C 350%; Calcium 4%; Iron 10% **Exchanges:** 1½ Starch, 2 Vegetable, 1½ Very Lean Meat **Carbohydrate Choices:** 2

healthified spicy ginger chicken

Prep Time: 20 Minutes   **Start to Finish:** 6 Hours 20 Minutes   **Makes:** 6 servings

12	chicken drumsticks or thighs, or 6 of each (2½ to 3 lb)	4	cloves garlic, finely chopped
2	cans (14.5 oz each) no-salt-added diced tomatoes	2	teaspoons packed brown sugar
2	tablespoons quick-cooking tapioca	½	teaspoon salt
1	tablespoon grated gingerroot	½	teaspoon crushed red pepper flakes
1	tablespoon chopped fresh cilantro or parsley	3	cups hot cooked whole-grain couscous
		2	tablespoons chopped fresh parsley

1. Spray 3½- to 4-quart slow cooker with cooking spray. Remove skin from chicken; place in slow cooker.

2. Drain tomatoes, reserving juice from 1 can. In medium bowl, mix tomatoes, reserved juice, the tapioca, gingerroot, cilantro, garlic, brown sugar, salt and pepper flakes. Pour over chicken.

3. Cover; cook on Low heat setting 6 to 7 hours (or on High heat setting 3 hours to 3 hours 30 minutes).

4. Skim fat from sauce. Serve chicken and sauce with couscous in shallow bowls. Sprinkle with parsley.

1 Serving: Calories 300 (Calories from Fat 50); Total Fat 6g (Saturated Fat 2g; Trans Fat 0g); Cholesterol 70mg; Sodium 280mg; Total Carbohydrate 33g (Dietary Fiber 2g); Protein 28g **% Daily Value:** Vitamin A 15%; Vitamin C 10%; Calcium 6%; Iron 15% **Exchanges:** 1½ Starch, ½ Other Carbohydrate, 3½ Very Lean Meat, ½ Fat **Carbohydrate Choices:** 2

300 Calories

turkey, bacon and avocado wraps

Prep Time: 20 Minutes **Start to Finish:** 5 Hours 20 Minutes **Makes:** 8 wraps

4 slices bacon, cut into ½-inch pieces	8 flour tortillas (6 or 8 inch), heated as directed on package
2 lb turkey breast tenderloins, cut crosswise into 1-inch slices	1 medium ripe avocado, pitted, peeled and mashed
¾ cup barbecue sauce	2 cups shredded lettuce
2 tablespoons taco seasoning mix (from 1-oz package)	½ cup drained roasted red or yellow bell peppers (from 7-oz jar), large pieces cut up

1. In 12-inch nonstick skillet, cook bacon over medium heat 4 to 6 minutes, stirring occasionally, until almost crisp. Add turkey slices; cook 4 to 6 minutes, stirring occasionally, until brown on all sides.

2. Spray 3- to 4-quart slow cooker with cooking spray. In slow cooker, place bacon and turkey. Top with barbecue sauce and taco seasoning mix; mix well.

3. Cover; cook on Low heat setting 5 to 6 hours.

4. Transfer turkey from slow cooker to cutting board or plate. Break up turkey, using 2 forks; return to slow cooker. On each warmed tortilla, layer avocado, lettuce, turkey mixture and roasted peppers; roll up.

1 Wrap: Calories 300 (Calories from Fat 70); Total Fat 8g (Saturated Fat 1.5g; Trans Fat 1g); Cholesterol 80mg; Sodium 790mg; Total Carbohydrate 27g (Dietary Fiber 2g); Protein 30g **% Daily Value:** Vitamin A 10%; Vitamin C 20%; Calcium 6%; Iron 15% **Exchanges:** 2 Starch, 3 Lean Meat **Carbohydrate Choices:** 2

Quick Meal Idea Refried beans and a fruit salad with cantaloupe and pineapple chunks are perfect partners for these south-of-the-border sandwiches.

Kitchen Tip Tender, low-fat meats like the turkey tenderloins in this recipe will get dry and tough if overcooked, so follow the cooking times carefully.

turkey with wild rice, squash and cranberries

290 Calories

Prep Time: 15 Minutes   **Start to Finish:** 7 Hours 15 Minutes   **Makes:** 6 servings

¾ cup uncooked wild rice	½ teaspoon dried thyme leaves
1 medium butternut squash, peeled, seeded and cut into 1-inch pieces	½ teaspoon salt
1 medium onion, cut into wedges	½ teaspoon pepper
1¼ lb turkey breast tenderloins	3 cups chicken broth
	½ cup dried cranberries

1. Spray 3½- to 4-quart slow cooker with cooking spray. Add rice to slow cooker; top with squash, onion and turkey. Sprinkle with thyme, salt and pepper. Pour broth over all ingredients.

2. Cover; cook on Low heat setting 7 to 9 hours or until rice is tender.

3. Transfer turkey from slow cooker to cutting board; cut into slices. Stir cranberries into rice mixture; serve with turkey.

1 Serving: Calories 290 (Calories from Fat 20); Total Fat 2g (Saturated Fat 0.5g; Trans Fat 0g); Cholesterol 65mg; Sodium 760mg; Total Carbohydrate 39g (Dietary Fiber 4g); Protein 29g **% Daily Value:** Vitamin A 250%; Vitamin C 15%; Calcium 8%; Iron 15% **Exchanges:** 2 Starch, 1 Vegetable, 3 Very Lean Meat **Carbohydrate Choices:** 2½

Kitchen Tip Butternut squash resembles the shape of a peanut as it's wider at one end than the other. It usually weighs between 2 and 3 pounds and has a golden yellow to caramel-colored shell. You can also use about 2 pounds of other winter squash, such as Hubbard or buttercup.

280 Calories

salsa swiss steak with noodles

Prep Time: 10 Minutes   **Start to Finish:** 8 Hours 10 Minutes   **Makes:** 10 servings

1   boneless beef round steak (3 lb), cut into 10 serving pieces
1   jar (16 oz) chunky-style salsa

1   package (0.87 oz) brown gravy mix
1   bag (16 oz) frozen home-style egg noodles

1. Spray 3- to 4-quart slow cooker with cooking spray. Place beef in slow cooker. In small bowl, mix salsa and gravy mix; pour over beef.

2. Cover; cook on Low heat setting 8 to 10 hours.

3. About 15 minutes before serving, cook and drain noodles as directed on package. Serve beef and sauce over noodles.

1 Serving: Calories 280 (Calories from Fat 50); Total Fat 5g (Saturated Fat 1.5g; Trans Fat 0g); Cholesterol 120mg; Sodium 400mg; Total Carbohydrate 26g (Dietary Fiber 0g); Protein 32g **% Daily Value:** Vitamin A 6%; Vitamin C 0%; Calcium 0%; Iron 20% **Exchanges:** 1½ Starch, 4 Very Lean Meat, ½ Fat **Carbohydrate Choices:** 2

Try This

Mix it up by serving this southwestern steak dinner with long-grain brown rice instead of noodles.

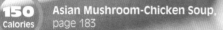
150 Calories

Asian Mushroom-Chicken Soup, page 183

Beefy Corn and Black Bean Chili, page 190

210 Calories

Black Bean Soup with Avocado Salsa, page 208

260 Calories

Roasted Red Pepper Soup with Mozzarella, page 211

200 Calories

250 Calories — Chicken and Barley Risotto with **Edamame,** page 215

240 Calories — Healthified New Orleans–Style **Stuffed Peppers,** page 220

300 Calories — Chunky Beef Ragù, page 227

290 Calories — Hearty Pork Stew, page 233

190 Calories — Maple–Butternut Squash Soup, page 237

180 Calories — Healthified Tandoori Turkey Tenderloins, page 251

**Healthified Lamb Chops With
Blackberry–Red Wine Sauce**, page 252

170 Calories

180 Calories

**Southwestern Pork Chops
with Peach Salsa**, page 257

Garlic Steak Salad,
page 265

240 Calories

C-13

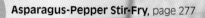

Broccoli with Roasted Red Peppers and Hazelnuts, page 279

70 Calories

90 Calories

Roasted Beets, page 289

Chipotle Twice-Baked
Sweet Potatoes, page 291

140 Calories

50 Calories

Cucumber-Mango
Salad, page 304

C-15

Raspberry Yogurt Celebration
Dessert, page 311

140
Calories

Cantaloupe Granita,
page 326

50
Calories

C-16

colombian beef and sweet potato stew

260 Calories

Prep Time: 15 Minutes   **Start to Finish:** 8 Hours 30 Minutes   **Makes:** 6 servings

1 teaspoons olive or vegetable oil	1 dried bay leaf
1 lb boneless beef chuck flatiron steak, trimmed of excess fat, cut into 1-inch pieces	1 cinnamon stick
½ teaspoon salt	1 large onion, cut into eighths
¼ teaspoon pepper	2 cans (14.5 oz each) Italian-style stewed tomatoes, undrained
3 cups 1-inch pieces peeled sweet potatoes	8 dried apricots, cut in half
2 teaspoons finely chopped garlic	Chopped fresh parsley, if desired
2 whole cloves	

1. In 10-inch skillet, heat oil over medium-high heat. Add beef to skillet; sprinkle with salt and pepper. Cook about 5 minutes, stirring occasionally, until brown.

2. Spray 4- to 5-quart slow cooker with cooking spray. In slow cooker, mix beef and all remaining ingredients except apricots and parsley.

3. Cover; cook on Low heat setting 8 hours or until beef is tender.

4. Stir in apricots. Cover; cook about 15 minutes longer or until apricots are softened. Remove and discard cloves, bay leaf and cinnamon stick. Sprinkle stew with parsley.

1 Serving: Calories 260 (Calories from Fat 80); Total Fat 9g (Saturated Fat 3.5g; Trans Fat 0g); Cholesterol 40mg; Sodium 630mg; Total Carbohydrate 27g (Dietary Fiber 5g); Protein 17g **% Daily Value:** Vitamin A 220%; Vitamin C 25%; Calcium 4%; Iron 10% **Exchanges:** ½ Starch, 1 Other Carbohydrate, 1 Vegetable, 2 Lean Meat, ½ Fat **Carbohydrate Choices:** 2

Quick Meal Idea Enjoy this chunky stew over hot cooked couscous.

burgundy stew with herb dumplings

Prep Time: 25 Minutes **Start to Finish:** 8 Hours 50 Minutes **Makes:** 8 servings

STEW

2	lb boneless beef bottom or top round, tip or chuck steak, cut into 1-inch pieces
4	medium carrots, cut into ¼-inch slices (2 cups)
2	medium stalks celery, sliced (1 cup)
2	medium onions, sliced
1	can (14.5 oz) diced tomatoes, undrained
2	cans (4 oz each) sliced mushrooms, drained
¾	cup dry red wine or beef broth
1½	teaspoons salt
1	teaspoon dried thyme leaves
1	teaspoon ground mustard
¼	teaspoon pepper
¼	cup water
3	tablespoons all-purpose flour

DUMPLINGS

1½	cups Original Bisquick mix
½	teaspoon dried thyme leaves
¼	teaspoon dried sage leaves, crumbled
½	cup milk

1. Spray 3½- to 6-quart slow cooker with cooking spray. In slow cooker, mix all stew ingredients except water and flour.

2. Cover; cook on Low heat setting 8 to 10 hours (or on High heat setting 4 to 5 hours) or until beef is tender.

3. In small bowl, mix water and flour until well blended; gradually stir into beef mixture. Cover.

4. In medium bowl, mix all dumpling ingredients just until moistened. Drop dough by 8 spoonfuls onto hot beef mixture. If using Low heat setting, increase to High. Cover; cook 25 to 35 minutes or until toothpick inserted in center of dumplings comes out clean.

1 Serving: Calories 280 (Calories from Fat 60); Total Fat 6g (Saturated Fat 2g; Trans Fat 1g); Cholesterol 65mg; Sodium 830mg; Total Carbohydrate 22g (Dietary Fiber 2g); Protein 29g **% Daily Value:** Vitamin A 90%; Vitamin C 8%; Calcium 6%; Iron 20% **Exchanges:** 1½ Starch, ½ Vegetable, 3½ Very Lean Meat, ½ Fat **Carbohydrate Choices:** 1½

chunky beef ragù

Prep Time: 35 Minutes   **Start to Finish:** 8 Hours 35 Minutes   **Makes:** 6 servings
(photo on page C11)

300 Calories

3 oz thinly sliced prosciutto or pancetta, chopped	2 cloves garlic, finely chopped
1½ lb beef stew meat, cut into 1-inch pieces	1 can (14.5 oz) diced tomatoes, undrained
2 jars (7 oz each) sun-dried tomatoes in oil, drained, chopped (1¼ cups)	½ cup dry red wine
	1½ teaspoons dried basil leaves
2 medium carrots, sliced (1 cup)	1½ teaspoons dried oregano leaves
1 cup chopped celery	½ teaspoon salt
1 medium onion, chopped (½ cup)	¼ teaspoon crushed red pepper flakes

1. In 8-inch nonstick skillet, cook prosciutto over medium-high heat about 5 minutes, stirring frequently, until crisp. Drain on paper towels.

2. Spray 5- to 6-quart slow cooker with cooking spray. In slow cooker, mix prosciutto and all remaining ingredients.

3. Cover; cook on Low heat setting 8 to 9 hours (or on High heat setting 4 hours to 4 hours 30 minutes).

1 Serving: Calories 300 (Calories from Fat 150); Total Fat 16g (Saturated Fat 6g; Trans Fat 0.5g); Cholesterol 70mg; Sodium 640mg; Total Carbohydrate 13g (Dietary Fiber 3g); Protein 26g **% Daily Value:** Vitamin A 80%; Vitamin C 30%; Calcium 8%; Iron 15% **Exchanges:** ½ Other Carbohydrate, 1 Vegetable, 3½ Lean Meat, 1 Fat **Carbohydrate Choices:** 1

Quick Meal Idea Serve your favorite pasta with this hearty meat sauce.

300 Calories

caramelized onion pot roast

Prep Time: 25 Minutes **Start to Finish:** 8 Hours 25 Minutes **Makes:** 12 servings

1	tablespoon olive or vegetable oil	1½	cups beef broth
1	boneless beef chuck roast (4 lb), trimmed of excess fat	¾	cup regular or nonalcoholic beer
1	teaspoon salt	2	tablespoons packed brown sugar
½	teaspoon pepper	3	tablespoons Dijon mustard
6	medium onions, sliced	2	tablespoons cider vinegar

1. In 10-inch skillet, heat oil over medium-high heat. Cook beef in oil about 10 minutes, turning occasionally, until brown on all sides. Sprinkle with salt and pepper.

2. Spray 3½- to 6-quart slow cooker with cooking spray. In slow cooker, place onions and beef. In medium bowl, mix all remaining ingredients; pour over beef and onions.

3. Cover; cook on Low heat setting 8 to 10 hours or until beef is tender.

4. Using slotted spoon, remove beef and onions from slow cooker. Slice beef across the grain. Skim fat from beef juices, if desired; serve juices with beef and onions.

1 Serving: Calories 300 (Calories from Fat 160); Total Fat 17g (Saturated Fat 6g; Trans Fat 0.5g); Cholesterol 80mg; Sodium 480mg; Total Carbohydrate 8g (Dietary Fiber 1g); Protein 29g **% Daily Value:** Vitamin A 0%; Vitamin C 4%; Calcium 4%; Iron 10% **Exchanges:** ½ Other Carbohydrate, 4 Lean Meat, 1 Fat **Carbohydrate Choices:** ½

chipotle beef stew

Prep Time: 15 Minutes   **Start to Finish:** 8 Hours 15 Minutes   **Makes:** 6 servings

STEW
- 1   bag (12 oz) frozen corn
- 1   lb boneless beef top sirloin, trimmed of fat, cut into 1-inch cubes
- 1   chipotle chile in adobo sauce (from 7-oz can), finely chopped
- 2   large onions, chopped (2 cups)
- 2   poblano chiles, seeded, chopped
- 3   cloves garlic, finely chopped
- 2   cans (14.5 oz each) diced tomatoes, undrained

- 1½   teaspoons ground cumin
- ½   teaspoon salt
- ¼   teaspoon cracked black pepper

TOPPINGS
- 1   ripe avocado, pitted, peeled and cut into 12 wedges
- 12   baked tortilla chips, crushed
- 6   small sprigs fresh cilantro, coarsely chopped
- 6   tablespoons reduced-fat sour cream

1. In medium microwavable bowl, microwave corn uncovered on High 2 minutes or until thawed. Spray 4- to 5-quart slow cooker with cooking spray. In slow cooker, mix corn and all remaining stew ingredients.

2. Cover; cook on Low heat setting 8 to 10 hours (or on High heat setting 4 to 5 hours).

3. Divide stew evenly among 6 bowls, about 1⅓ cups each. Top with avocado, tortilla chips, cilantro and sour cream.

1 Serving: Calories 300 (Calories from Fat 80); Total Fat 9g (Saturated Fat 3g; Trans Fat 0g); Cholesterol 60mg; Sodium 590mg; Total Carbohydrate 29g (Dietary Fiber 5g); Protein 25g **% Daily Value:** Vitamin A 25%; Vitamin C 25%; Calcium 6%; Iron 20% **Exchanges:** 1½ Starch, 1 Vegetable, 2½ Lean Meat **Carbohydrate Choices:** 2

Quick Meal Idea Chips and salsa are a crunchy and flavorful side to serve with this stew. One ounce of baked tortilla chips and 2 tablespoons salsa add 130 calories per serving.

280 Calories

cheeseburger joes

Prep Time: 20 Minutes   **Start to Finish:** 6 Hours 20 Minutes   **Makes:** 12 sandwiches

1½ lb lean (at least 80%) ground beef*	1 medium green bell pepper, chopped (1 cup)
½ teaspoon garlic-pepper blend	1 small onion, chopped (⅓ cup)
1 loaf (8 oz) prepared cheese product, cut into small cubes (2 cups)	2 cloves garlic, finely chopped
2 tablespoons milk	12 burger buns, split
	Sliced dill pickles, if desired

1. In 12-inch skillet, place beef; sprinkle with garlic-pepper blend. Cook over medium heat 8 to 10 minutes, stirring occasionally, until beef is thoroughly cooked; drain.

2. Spray 3- to 4-quart slow cooker with cooking spray. In slow cooker, mix beef, cheese, milk, bell pepper, onion and garlic.

3. Cover; cook on Low heat setting 6 to 7 hours. Stir beef mixture; serve in buns with pickles.

*Ground turkey or pork can be substituted.

1 Sandwich: Calories 280 (Calories from Fat 120); Total Fat 13g (Saturated Fat 6g; Trans Fat 0.5g); Cholesterol 50mg; Sodium 520mg; Total Carbohydrate 21g (Dietary Fiber 1g); Protein 17g **% Daily Value:** Vitamin A 4%; Vitamin C 8%; Calcium 20%; Iron 15% **Exchanges:** 1½ Starch, 2 Medium-Fat Meat **Carbohydrate Choices:** 1½

maple-sage pork roast

Prep Time: 30 Minutes   **Start to Finish:** 8 Hours 30 Minutes   **Makes:** 8 servings

1   boneless pork shoulder roast (2 to 3 lb)
2   tablespoons real maple or maple-flavored syrup
1   clove garlic, finely chopped
2   teaspoons dried sage leaves
½   teaspoon beef bouillon granules
1   cup water

2   cups cubed (1½ inch) peeled butternut squash
2   cups ready-to-eat baby-cut carrots, cut in half lengthwise
2   small onions, cut into wedges
3   tablespoons cornstarch

1. Spray 4- to 5-quart slow cooker with cooking spray. If pork roast comes in netting or is tied, remove netting or strings. Place pork in slow cooker. In small bowl, mix syrup, garlic, sage, bouillon granules and ½ cup of the water; spoon over pork. Arrange squash, carrots and onions around pork.

2. Cover; cook on Low heat setting 8 to 9 hours.

3. Using slotted spoon, transfer pork and vegetables from slow cooker to serving plate; cover to keep warm. If desired, skim fat from cooking liquid. Pour liquid into 4-cup microwavable measuring cup. In small bowl, mix cornstarch and remaining ½ cup water until smooth; stir into liquid. Microwave uncovered on High 2 to 3 minutes, stirring every minute, until mixture thickens. Serve with pork and vegetables.

1 Serving: Calories 280 (Calories from Fat 120); Total Fat 14g (Saturated Fat 5g; Trans Fat 0g); Cholesterol 75mg; Sodium 120mg; Total Carbohydrate 14g (Dietary Fiber 1g); Protein 25g **% Daily Value:** Vitamin A 170%; Vitamin C 6%; Calcium 4%; Iron 6% **Exchanges:** 1 Starch, ½ Vegetable, ½ Very Lean Meat, 2½ Lean Meat, 1 Fat **Carbohydrate Choices:** 1

Try This

Whole carrots, quartered lengthwise and then cut crosswise into 2-inch sections, can be substituted for the baby carrots.

260 Calories

orange pork tenderloin with butternut squash

Prep Time: 20 Minutes   **Start to Finish:** 7 Hours 20 Minutes   **Makes:** 6 servings

1 butternut squash (3 lb), peeled, cut into 2-inch pieces (6 cups)	¼ cup orange marmalade
½ teaspoon salt	2 cloves garlic, finely chopped
2 pork tenderloins (¾ to 1 lb each)	

1. Spray 3- to 4-quart slow cooker with cooking spray. Arrange squash around edge of slow cooker; sprinkle with salt. Top with pork (it will overlap squash slightly). In small bowl, mix marmalade and garlic; spread evenly over pork.

2. Cover; cook on Low heat setting 7 hours or until meat thermometer inserted in center of pork reads 145°F.

3. Remove pork from slow cooker to cutting board. Cut pork into slices; serve with squash.

1 Serving: Calories 260 (Calories from Fat 60); Total Fat 6g (Saturated Fat 2g; Trans Fat 0g); Cholesterol 65mg; Sodium 490mg; Total Carbohydrate 20g (Dietary Fiber 3g); Protein 30g **% Daily Value:** Vitamin A 130%; Vitamin C 10%; Calcium 4%; Iron 6% **Exchanges:** 1 Starch, ½ Other Carbohydrate, 4 Very Lean Meat, ½ Fat **Carbohydrate Choices:** 1

Health Smart If you are watching your salt intake, omit the salt, and season with ¼ teaspoon pepper instead.

Kitchen Tip This is a great recipe for entertaining. Fan pork slices in a circular pattern on a platter, and spoon squash in the center. Drizzle cooking juices over pork, and garnish with orange slices and parsley sprigs.

hearty pork stew

Prep Time: 25 Minutes   **Start to Finish:** 6 Hours 55 Minutes   **Makes:** 6 servings
(photo on page C12)

290 Calories

1½ lb boneless pork loin, cut into 1-inch cubes	1 medium onion, chopped (½ cup)
2 cups diced (½ inch) peeled parsnips (3 medium)	1 carton (32 oz) chicken broth (4 cups)
1½ cups cubed (1 inch) peeled butternut squash	½ teaspoon salt
3 medium carrots, cut into ¼-inch slices (1½ cups)	½ teaspoon pepper
	3 tablespoons all-purpose flour
	3 tablespoons butter, softened

1. Spray 3½- to 6-quart slow cooker with cooking spray. In slow cooker, mix all ingredients except flour and butter.

2. Cover; cook on Low heat setting 6 to 7 hours (or on High heat setting 3 to 4 hours) or until pork is no longer pink and vegetables are tender.

3. In small bowl, mix flour and butter; gently stir into pork mixture, one spoonful at a time, until blended. If using Low heat setting, increase to High. Cover; cook 30 to 45 minutes longer, stirring occasionally, until thickened.

1 Serving: Calories 290 (Calories from Fat 100); Total Fat 11g (Saturated Fat 5g; Trans Fat 0g); Cholesterol 65mg; Sodium 960mg; Total Carbohydrate 19g (Dietary Fiber 4g); Protein 27g **% Daily Value:** Vitamin A 170%; Vitamin C 10%; Calcium 6%; Iron 8% **Exchanges:** 1 Starch, 1 Vegetable, 3 Lean Meat, ½ Fat **Carbohydrate Choices:** 1

270 Calories

pork roast with creamy mustard sauce

Prep Time: 20 Minutes   **Start to Finish:** 7 Hours 35 Minutes   **Makes:** 8 servings

1	tablespoon vegetable oil
1	boneless pork loin roast (2½ to 3 lb), trimmed of excess fat
¾	cup dry white wine or nonalcoholic white wine
2	tablespoons all-purpose flour
1	teaspoon salt
½	teaspoon pepper

2	medium carrots, finely chopped or shredded (1 cup)
1	medium onion, finely chopped (½ cup)
1	small shallot, finely chopped (2 tablespoons)
¼	cup half-and-half
2	to 3 tablespoons country-style Dijon mustard

1. In 10-inch skillet, heat oil over medium-high heat. Cook pork in oil about 10 minutes, turning occasionally, until brown on all sides.

2. Spray 3½- to 6-quart slow cooker with cooking spray. Place pork in slow cooker. In medium bowl, mix all remaining ingredients except half-and-half and mustard; pour over pork.

3. Cover; cook on Low heat setting 7 to 9 hours or until pork is tender.

4. Transfer pork from slow cooker to serving plate; cover to keep warm. Skim fat from cooking juices, if desired. Stir half-and-half and mustard into juices. Increase heat setting to High. Cover; cook about 15 minutes or until slightly thickened. Serve sauce with pork.

1 Serving: Calories 270 (Calories from Fat 120); Total Fat 13g (Saturated Fat 4.5g; Trans Fat 0g); Cholesterol 90mg; Sodium 460mg; Total Carbohydrate 5g (Dietary Fiber 0g); Protein 31g **% Daily Value:** Vitamin A 50%; Vitamin C 2%; Calcium 2%; Iron 8% **Exchanges:** 1 Vegetable, 4 Lean Meat, ½ Fat **Carbohydrate Choices:** ½

lentil and canadian bacon soup

260 Calories

Prep Time: 20 Minutes **Start to Finish:** 8 Hours 20 Minutes **Makes:** 8 servings

1 bag (16 oz) dried lentils (2 cups), sorted, rinsed

3½ cups vegetable broth

1 package (6 oz) sliced Canadian bacon, coarsely chopped

2 medium carrots, cut into ½-inch pieces (1 cup)

1 medium potato, peeled, cut into ½-inch pieces (1 cup)

1 medium onion, chopped (½ cup)

1 medium stalk celery, cut into ½-inch pieces (½ cup)

4 cups water

1 teaspoon dried thyme leaves

½ teaspoon salt

¼ teaspoon pepper

1. Spray 3½- to 6-quart slow cooker with cooking spray. In slow cooker, mix all ingredients.

2. Cover; cook on Low heat setting 8 to 9 hours (or High heat setting 3 to 5 hours) or until lentils are tender. Stir well before serving.

1 Serving: Calories 260 (Calories from Fat 20); Total Fat 2.5g (Saturated Fat 0.5g; Trans Fat 0g); Cholesterol 10mg; Sodium 910mg; Total Carbohydrate 39g (Dietary Fiber 10g); Protein 20g **% Daily Value:** Vitamin A 60%; Vitamin C 4%; Calcium 6%; Iron 30% **Exchanges:** 2 Starch, 2 Vegetable, 1 Lean Meat **Carbohydrate Choices:** 2½

Kitchen Tip Canadian bacon is a closer relative to ham than to regular bacon. It's lean and fully cooked. If you prefer ham, use 1½ cups chopped cooked ham instead of the Canadian bacon.

smoky chipotle soft tacos

Prep Time: 20 Minutes   **Start to Finish:** 4 Hours 20 Minutes   **Makes:** 18 tacos

Cooking spray
1 large onion, chopped (1 cup)
1 Anaheim chile, chopped (⅓ cup)
6 cups frozen soy-protein burger crumbles
¾ cup chili sauce
1½ cups water
½ cup mole sauce (from 8.25-oz jar)

1 tablespoon chopped chipotle chiles in adobo sauce (from 7-oz can)
1 teaspoon ground cumin
¾ teaspoon salt
18 flour tortillas (6 inch), heated as directed on package
2 cups shredded Cheddar cheese (8 oz)
3 medium tomatoes, chopped (2¼ cups)

1. Generously spray 8-inch skillet with cooking spray. Add onion and Anaheim chile to skillet; spray onion and chile with cooking spray. Cook over medium heat 4 to 5 minutes, stirring occasionally, until onion is crisp-tender.

2. Spray 3½- to 4-quart slow cooker with cooking spray. In slow cooker, mix onion mixture and all remaining ingredients except tortillas, cheese and tomatoes.

3. Cover; cook on Low heat setting 4 to 5 hours.

4. To serve, spoon ⅓ cup mixture down center of each warmed tortilla; top with 1 heaping tablespoon cheese and 2 tablespoons tomatoes. Roll up.

1 Taco: Calories 170 (Calories from Fat 40); Total Fat 4g (Saturated Fat 1.5g; Trans Fat 1g); Cholesterol 0mg; Sodium 660mg; Total Carbohydrate 22g (Dietary Fiber 4g); Protein 12g **% Daily Value:** Vitamin A 8%; Vitamin C 10%; Calcium 10%; Iron 10% **Exchanges:** 1½ Starch, 1 Lean Meat **Carbohydrate Choices:** 1½

Kitchen Tip Very smoky flavored, chipotle chiles are dried, smoked jalapeño chiles. Look for them dried or in cans with very spicy adobo sauce. Often, some of the sauce is also used to flavor recipes.

maple-butternut squash soup

190 Calories

Prep Time: 25 Minutes   **Start to Finish:** 7 Hours 40 Minutes   **Makes:** 8 servings (1⅓ cups each)   (photo on page C12)

8 cups cubed peeled seeded butternut squash (about 3 lb)	⅛ teaspoon pepper
1 large apple, peeled, chopped	1 carton (32 oz) chicken broth (4 cups)
1 large onion, cut into 1-inch pieces	½ cup half-and-half or milk
1 teaspoon ground cinnamon	½ real maple syrup
½ teaspoon ground nutmeg	¾ cup plain yogurt or sour cream
½ teaspoon salt	2 tablespoons chopped fresh chives

1. Spray 4- to 5-quart slow cooker with cooking spray. In slow cooker, mix squash, apple, onion, cinnamon, nutmeg, salt and pepper. Pour broth over vegetable mixture.

2. Cover; cook on Low heat setting 7 to 8 hours (or on High heat setting 3 hours 30 minutes to 4 hours).

3. Pour about 3 cups of the soup mixture into blender. Cover; blend until smooth. Pour into 8-cup measuring cup or heatproof pitcher. Blend remaining soup mixture in 2 more batches; pour into measuring cup. Pour pureed soup back into slow cooker. Stir in half-and-half and syrup.

4. If using Low heat setting, increase to High. Cover; cook about 15 minutes longer or unto hot. Top individual servings with yogurt and chives.

1 Serving: Calories 190 (Calories from Fat 25); Total Fat 3g (Saturated Fat 1.5g; Trans Fat 0g); Cholesterol 5mg; Sodium 660mg; Total Carbohydrate 34g (Dietary Fiber 2g); Protein 5g **% Daily Value:** Vitamin A 270%; Vitamin C 20%; Calcium 15%; Iron 8% **Exchanges:** ½ Starch, 1½ Other Carbohydrate, 1 Vegetable, ½ Fat **Carbohydrate Choices:** 2

Kitchen Tip Sometimes in the fall you can find butternut squash already peeled and cut up at your local supermarket. If you're cutting it yourself, a sturdy, swivel-headed vegetable peeler is the tool of choice to make quick work of peeling the squash.

CHAPTER 8

Grilled Entrées

chicken with chipotle-peach glaze

Prep Time: 30 Minutes **Start to Finish:** 30 Minutes **Makes:** 8 servings

½ cup peach preserves

¼ cup lime juice
1 chipotle chile in adobo sauce (from 7-oz can), seeded, chopped
1 teaspoon adobo sauce (from can of chipotle chiles)
2 tablespoons chopped fresh cilantro

8 boneless skinless chicken breasts (about 2½ lb)
1 teaspoon garlic-pepper blend
½ teaspoon salt
½ teaspoon ground cumin
4 peaches, cut into quarters, if desired

1. Heat gas or charcoal grill. In 1-quart saucepan, mix preserves, lime juice, chile and adobo sauce. Heat over low heat, stirring occasionally, until preserves are melted. Stir in chopped cilantro; set aside.

2. Sprinkle chicken with garlic-pepper blend, salt and cumin. Place chicken on grill over medium heat. Cover grill; cook 15 to 20 minutes, turning once or twice and brushing with preserves mixture during last 2 minutes of grilling, until juice of chicken is clear when center of thickest part is cut (at least 165°F). Add peach quarters to grill for last 2 to 3 minutes of grilling; heat just until hot.

3. Heat any remaining preserves mixture to boiling; boil and stir 1 minute. Serve with chicken and peaches.

1 Serving: Calories 230 (Calories from Fat 45); Total Fat 5g (Saturated Fat 1.5g; Trans Fat 0g); Cholesterol 90mg; Sodium 340mg; Total Carbohydrate 15g (Dietary Fiber 0g); Protein 32g **% Daily Value:** Vitamin A 4%; Vitamin C 4%; Calcium 2%; Iron 8% **Exchanges:** 1 Other Carbohydrate, 4½ Very Lean Meat, ½ Fat **Carbohydrate Choices:** 1

Try This

Serve this special dish in a large heated cast-iron skillet to keep the food warm. Wrap a colorful southwestern-patterned napkin around the handle.

moroccan chicken kabobs

Prep Time: 15 Minutes   **Start to Finish:** 15 Minutes   **Makes:** 4 servings

½ cup apricot preserves
1 teaspoon ground cumin
1 teaspoon ground cinnamon
½ teaspoon ground coriander

½ teaspoon salt
4 boneless skinless chicken breasts (1½ lb), cut into 1½-inch pieces
   Cooking spray

1. Heat gas or charcoal grill. In large bowl, mix preserves, cumin, cinnamon, coriander and salt. Add chicken pieces; turn to coat. On each of 4 (10- to 12-inch) metal skewers, thread chicken.

2. Spray chicken with cooking spray. Carefully brush oil on grill rack. Place skewers on grill over medium-high heat. Cover grill; cook 10 minutes, turning once, until chicken is no longer pink in center.

1 Serving: Calories 260 (Calories from Fat 40); Total Fat 4g (Saturated Fat 1g; Trans Fat 0g); Cholesterol 75mg; Sodium 380mg; Total Carbohydrate 28g (Dietary Fiber 1g); Protein 28g **% Daily Value:** Vitamin A 0%; Vitamin C 4%; Calcium 4%; Iron 8% **Exchanges:** 2 Starch, 3 Very Lean Meat **Carbohydrate Choices:** 2

chicken citrus teriyaki

260 Calories

Prep Time: 30 Minutes   **Start to Finish:** 1 Hour   **Makes:** 2 servings

¼ cup teriyaki baste and glaze (from 12-oz bottle)

¼ cup frozen (thawed) orange juice concentrate

2 teaspoons grated orange peel

½ lb uncooked chicken breast tenders (not breaded)

1 cup fresh sugar snap pea pods

1 cup sliced fresh mushrooms (3 oz)

1 medium zucchini, cut into ½-inch slices (2 cups)

½ medium red bell pepper, cut into 1-inch pieces (¾ cup)

1. In medium bowl, mix teriyaki glaze, orange juice concentrate and orange peel. Reserve 2 tablespoons marinade. Add chicken to remaining marinade; toss to coat. Cover; refrigerate 30 minutes to marinate.

2. Heat gas or charcoal grill. Place grill basket (grill "wok") over medium heat. Remove chicken from marinade; discard marinade. Place chicken in grill basket. Cover grill; cook 6 to 8 minutes, shaking basket or stirring chicken occasionally, until chicken is brown.

3. Add pea pods, mushrooms, zucchini and bell pepper to grill basket. Cover grill; cook 6 to 8 minutes, shaking basket or stirring occasionally, until vegetables are crisp-tender and chicken is no longer pink in center.

4. Add 2 tablespoons reserved marinade; stir to coat vegetables and chicken. Cover grill; cook 2 to 3 minutes longer or until thoroughly heated.

1 Serving: Calories 260 (Calories from Fat 10); Total Fat 1g (Saturated Fat 0g; Trans Fat 0g); Cholesterol 50mg; Sodium 960mg; Total Carbohydrate 34g (Dietary Fiber 3g); Protein 29g **% Daily Value:** Vitamin A 30%; Vitamin C 110%; Calcium 8%; Iron 15% **Exchanges:** 1 Fruit, ½ Other Carbohydrate, 2 Vegetable, 3½ Very Lean Meat **Carbohydrate Choices:** 2

Quick Meal Idea Complete this meal by serving the chicken and vegetables over hot, cooked rice.

Try This

For a different citrus flavor, try using grated lime or lemon peel instead of orange.

chicken with oregano-peach sauce

280 Calories

Prep Time: 30 Minutes   **Start to Finish:** 30 Minutes   **Makes:** 4 servings

½	cup peach preserves		4	boneless skinless chicken breasts (1¼ lb)
¼	cup raspberry vinegar		½	teaspoon garlic-pepper blend
2	tablespoons chopped fresh oregano leaves		½	teaspoon seasoned salt

1. Heat gas or charcoal grill. In 1-quart saucepan, heat preserves and vinegar to boiling, stirring constantly, until preserves are melted. Spoon about ¼ cup mixture into small bowl for brushing on chicken. Stir oregano into remaining mixture; reserve for serving.

2. Sprinkle chicken with garlic-pepper blend and seasoned salt. Place chicken on grill over medium heat. Cover grill; cook 15 to 20 minutes, turning once and brushing with preserves mixture during last 10 minutes of grilling, until juice of chicken is clear when center of thickest part is cut (at least 165°F).

3. Discard any remaining preserves mixture used for brushing. Serve chicken with reserved preserves mixture.

1 Serving: Calories 280 (Calories from Fat 40); Total Fat 4.5g (Saturated Fat 1.5g; Trans Fat 0g); Cholesterol 90mg; Sodium 390mg; Total Carbohydrate 28g (Dietary Fiber 0g); Protein 32g **% Daily Value:** Vitamin A 0%; Vitamin C 4%; Calcium 4%; Iron 8% **Exchanges:** 2 Starch, 3½ Very Lean Meat **Carbohydrate Choices:** 2

Quick Meal Idea This elegant chicken dish makes an easy special-occasion meal when served with cooked orzo and grilled fresh asparagus. For dessert, serve vanilla frozen yogurt or ice cream topped with fresh blueberries.

Kitchen Tip When buying fresh oregano, look for bright green bunches with no sign of wilting or yellowing. Store it in the refrigerator in a plastic bag up to 3 days.

270 Calories

chicken with lemon, rosemary and garlic

Prep Time: 20 Minutes   **Start to Finish:** 50 Minutes   **Makes:** 4 servings

3 tablespoons olive oil	½ teaspoon salt
¼ cup lemon juice	¼ teaspoon pepper
3 cloves garlic, finely chopped	4 boneless skinless chicken breasts (1¼ lb)
2 tablespoons chopped fresh rosemary leaves	

1. In shallow glass or plastic dish or resealable food-storage plastic bag, mix oil, lemon juice, garlic, rosemary, salt and pepper. Add chicken, turning to coat with marinade. Cover dish or seal bag; refrigerate 30 minutes to marinate.

2. Heat gas or charcoal grill. Remove chicken from marinade; discard marinade. Place chicken on grill over medium heat. Cover grill; cook 12 to 15 minutes, turning once, until juice of chicken is clear when center of thickest part is cut (at least 165°F).

1 Serving: Calories 270 (Calories from Fat 130); Total Fat 15g (Saturated Fat 2.5g; Trans Fat 0g); Cholesterol 90mg; Sodium 380mg; Total Carbohydrate 2g (Dietary Fiber 0g); Protein 32g **% Daily Value:** Vitamin A 0%; Vitamin C 6%; Calcium 2%; Iron 8% **Exchanges:** 4½ Very Lean Meat, 2½ Fat **Carbohydrate Choices:** 0

Try This

Fresh thyme can be substituted for rosemary and lime juice for the lemon juice.

mediterranean chicken packets

Prep Time: 20 Minutes **Start to Finish:** 45 Minutes **Makes:** 4 servings

290 Calories

1 package (4 oz) crumbled tomato-basil feta cheese

2 tablespoons grated lemon peel

1 teaspoon dried oregano leaves

4 boneless skinless chicken breasts (about 1¼ lb)

4 plum (Roma) tomatoes, each cut into 3 slices

1 small red onion, finely chopped (¼ cup)

20 pitted kalamata olives

1. Heat gas or charcoal grill. In small bowl, mix cheese, lemon peel and oregano.

2. Cut 4 (18 x 12-inch) sheets of heavy-duty foil. On one side of each sheet of foil, place 1 chicken breast, 3 tomato slices, 1 tablespoon onion and 5 olives. Spoon one-quarter of cheese mixture over chicken and vegetables on each sheet.

3. Bring 2 sides of foil up over chicken and vegetables so edges meet. Seal edges, making tight ½-inch fold; fold again, allowing space for heat circulation and expansion. Fold other sides to seal.

4. Place foil packets on grill over medium heat. Cover grill; cook 20 to 25 minutes or until juice of chicken is clear when center of thickest part is cut (at least 165°F). To serve, cut large x across top of each packet; carefully fold back foil to allow steam to escape.

1 Serving: Calories 290 (Calories from Fat 120); Total Fat 13g (Saturated Fat 6g; Trans Fat 0g); Cholesterol 115mg; Sodium 570mg; Total Carbohydrate 6g (Dietary Fiber 2g); Protein 36g **% Daily Value:** Vitamin A 15%; Vitamin C 10%; Calcium 20%; Iron 10% **Exchanges:** ½ Vegetable, 5 Lean Meat **Carbohydrate Choices:** ½

Try This

One package (4 ounces) regular crumbled feta cheese can be substituted for the flavored feta cheese.

240 Calories

chicken fajitas

Prep Time: 35 Minutes **Start to Finish:** 1 Hour 5 Minutes **Makes:** 8 servings

3 tablespoons chopped fresh cilantro	2 cloves garlic, finely chopped
1 tablespoon chopped fresh or 1 teaspoon dried oregano leaves	4 boneless skinless chicken breasts (1 lb)
2 tablespoons lime juice	2 medium bell peppers (any color), cut into quarters
1 tablespoon vegetable oil	2 large onions, cut into ½-inch slices
2 teaspoons chili powder	8 flour tortillas (8 to 10 inch), heated as directed on package

1. In shallow glass or plastic dish or resealable food-storage plastic bag, mix cilantro, oregano, lime juice, oil, chili powder and garlic. Add chicken, turning to coat with marinade. Cover dish or seal bag; refrigerate 30 minutes to marinate.

2. Heat gas or charcoal grill. Remove chicken from marinade; reserve marinade. Place chicken on grill over medium heat. Cover grill; cook 15 to 20 minutes, brushing with reserved marinade and turning occasionally, until juice of chicken is clear when center of thickest part is cut (at least 165°F). Grill bell peppers and onions 10 to 15 minutes, turning frequently, until crisp-tender. Discard any remaining marinade.

3. Cut chicken and bell peppers into strips; divide chicken, peppers and onions evenly among warmed tortillas. Fold tortillas over filling; serve immediately.

1 Serving: Calories 240 (Calories from Fat 60); Total Fat 7g (Saturated Fat 1.5g; Trans Fat 0.5g); Cholesterol 25mg; Sodium 320mg; Total Carbohydrate 30g (Dietary Fiber 2g); Protein 14g **% Daily Value:** Vitamin A 6%; Vitamin C 25%; Calcium 8%; Iron 15% **Exchanges:** 2 Starch, ½ Vegetable, 1 Very Lean Meat, 1 Fat **Carbohydrate Choices:** 2

Quick Meal Idea Create a build-your-own-fajita buffet. Set out colorful bowls filled with a variety of toppings such as shredded cheese, guacamole, salsa, chopped tomatoes, torn lettuce, sliced ripe olives and chopped fresh cilantro.

Try This

To make Steak Fajitas, substitute 1 pound of beef boneless top round steak, about 1 inch thick, for the chicken. Marinate as directed, and grill 12 to 16 minutes for medium doneness.

asian chicken kabobs

Prep Time: 20 Minutes   **Start to Finish:** 20 Minutes   **Makes:** 4 servings

180 Calories

1	lb boneless skinless chicken breasts, cut into 24 (1-inch) cubes	8	whole fresh mushrooms
1	red bell pepper, cut into 8 (1-inch) pieces	½	cup teriyaki baste and glaze (from 12-oz bottle)
½	red onion, cut into 8 wedges, separated into layers		Chopped fresh cilantro, if desired
			Lime wedges, if desired

1. Heat gas or charcoal grill. On 4 (12-inch) skewers, alternately thread chicken and vegetables.

2. Place skewers on grill over medium heat. Cover grill; cook 10 to 11 minutes, turning occasionally, until chicken is no longer pink in center and vegetables are done as desired. During last 2 to 3 minutes of grilling, brush kabobs generously with teriyaki glaze and turn frequently. Sprinkle with cilantro; serve with lime wedges.

1 Serving: Calories 180 (Calories from Fat 35); Total Fat 3.5g (Saturated Fat 1g; Trans Fat 0g); Cholesterol 65mg; Sodium 1440mg; Total Carbohydrate 10g (Dietary Fiber 1g); Protein 27g **% Daily Value:** Vitamin A 20%; Vitamin C 35%; Calcium 2%; Iron 10% **Exchanges:** 1½ Vegetable, 3½ Very Lean Meat, ½ Fat **Carbohydrate Choices:** ½

Quick Meal Idea Serve the kabobs with additional teriyaki baste and glaze, if desired.

Try This

Substitute your favorite vegetables in these kabobs. For example, use 1 small zucchini, sliced about ¾ inch thick, instead of the onion.

140 Calories

sesame-ginger chicken

Prep Time: 25 Minutes **Start to Finish:** 25 Minutes **Makes:** 4 servings

2 tablespoons teriyaki sauce	1 teaspoon ground ginger
1 tablespoon sesame seed, toasted*	4 boneless skinless chicken breasts (about 1¼ lb)

1. Heat gas or charcoal grill. In small bowl, mix teriyaki sauce, sesame seed and ginger.

2. Carefully brush oil on grill rack. Place chicken on grill over medium heat. Cover grill; cook 15 to 20 minutes, brushing frequently with sauce mixture and turning after 10 minutes, until juice of chicken is clear when center of thickest part is cut (at least 165°F). Discard any remaining sauce mixture.

*To toast sesame seed, cook in an ungreased heavy skillet over medium-low heat 5 to 7 minutes, stirring frequently until browning begins, then stirring constantly until golden brown.

1 Serving: Calories 140 (Calories from Fat 40); Total Fat 4.5g (Saturated Fat 1g; Trans Fat 0g); Cholesterol 65mg; Sodium 410mg; Total Carbohydrate 2g (Dietary Fiber 0g); Protein 24g **% Daily Value:** Vitamin A 0%; Vitamin C 0%; Calcium 0%; Iron 6% **Exchanges:** 3½ Very Lean Meat, ½ Fat **Carbohydrate Choices:** 0

tex-mex chicken with corn salsa

Prep Time: 45 Minutes   **Start to Finish:** 45 Minutes   **Makes:** 4 servings

270
Calories

2	teaspoons chili powder	¼	cup chopped red onion
1	teaspoon ground cumin	2	plum (Roma) tomatoes, seeded, diced
½	teaspoon salt	⅓	cup diced green bell pepper
½	teaspoon garlic powder	2	tablespoons chopped fresh cilantro
4	boneless skinless chicken breasts (1¼ lb)	2	tablespoons lime juice
	Cooking spray	½	jalapeño chile, finely chopped, if desired
1	bag (12 oz) frozen corn, thawed		

1. Heat gas or charcoal grill. In small bowl, mix 1½ teaspoons of the chili powder, the cumin, salt and garlic powder. Spray chicken with cooking spray; sprinkle seasoning mixture evenly over both sides of chicken. Set aside.

2. Spray sheet of heavy-duty foil with cooking spray; place corn in center of foil. Turn up edges of foil; place on grill over medium heat. Cover grill; cook 10 minutes, stirring once, until corn begins to brown. Transfer corn from grill to medium bowl; set aside.

3. Place chicken on grill. Cover grill; cook 12 to 15 minutes, turning once, until juice of chicken is clear when center of thickest part is cut (at least 165°F). Transfer chicken to plate; cover to keep warm.

4. Add onion, tomatoes, bell pepper, cilantro, lime juice, chile and remaining ½ teaspoon chili powder to corn; toss to combine. Serve with chicken.

1 Serving: Calories 270 (Calories from Fat 50); Total Fat 6g (Saturated Fat 1.5g; Trans Fat 0g); Cholesterol 90mg; Sodium 390mg; Total Carbohydrate 20g (Dietary Fiber 3g); Protein 35g **% Daily Value:** Vitamin A 15%; Vitamin C 15%; Calcium 4%; Iron 10% **Exchanges:** 1 Starch, 1½ Vegetable, 4 Very Lean Meat, ½ Fat **Carbohydrate Choices:** 1

Kitchen Tip Substitute 2 green onions, chopped, for the red onion and ⅓ cup drained roasted red bell peppers (look for them in jars) for the green bell pepper.

Try This

The corn salsa would also be good served with baked tortilla chips.

140 Calories

peppered sage turkey mignons

Prep Time: 25 Minutes   **Start to Finish:** 25 Minutes   **Makes:** 4 servings

4 slices bacon	1 teaspoon dried sage leaves
1 turkey breast tenderloin (¾ to 1 lb)	½ teaspoon garlic-pepper blend
1 tablespoon olive or canola oil	¼ teaspoon salt

1. Heat closed medium-size contact grill 5 to 10 minutes. Place bacon in grill. Close grill; cook 2 to 3 minutes or until brown but not crisp. Drain bacon on paper towels just until cool enough to handle.

2. Cut turkey tenderloin crosswise into 4 pieces. Brush both sides of each piece with oil; sprinkle with sage, garlic-pepper blend and salt. Wrap 1 bacon slice around each turkey piece; secure with toothpick. (Fold or press together end of turkey to look like round piece.)

3. Place turkey on grill. Close grill; cook 7 to 9 minutes or until turkey is no longer pink in center.

1 Serving: Calories 140 (Calories from Fat 50); Total Fat 6g (Saturated Fat 1.5g; Trans Fat 0g); Cholesterol 60mg; Sodium 420mg; Total Carbohydrate 0g (Dietary Fiber 0g); Protein 21g **% Daily Value:** Vitamin A 0%; Vitamin C 0%; Calcium 0%; Iron 6% **Exchanges:** 1 Very Lean Meat, 2 Lean Meat **Carbohydrate Choices:** 0

Health Smart Turkey and other poultry should be stored in the coldest part of your refrigerator as soon as you get it home from the grocery store. Be sure to use it by the "sell-by" date, as poultry tends to lose its freshness fast.

healthified tandoori turkey tenderloins

180 Calories

Prep Time: 20 Minutes   **Start to Finish:** 6 Hours 20 Minutes   **Makes:** 4 servings
(photo on page C12)

4 cloves garlic, finely chopped	¼ teaspoon salt
1 tablespoon grated gingerroot	2 turkey breast tenderloins (8 oz each), cut lengthwise in half
1 tablespoon curry powder	¾ cup fat-free plain yogurt
2 teaspoons olive or canola oil	
1 teaspoon ground cumin	

1. In small bowl, mix garlic, ginger, curry powder, oil, cumin and salt. Rub mixture evenly on all sides of turkey. (Wear disposable gloves so the spices don't stain your hands.) Place turkey in shallow glass dish. Cover; refrigerate at least 6 hours to marinate but no longer than 24 hours.

2. Heat gas or charcoal grill. Place turkey on grill over medium heat. Cover grill; cook 12 to 15 minutes, turning once, until juice of turkey is clear when center of thickest part is cut (at least 165°F). Serve turkey with yogurt.

1 Serving: Calories 180 (Calories from Fat 35); Total Fat 4g (Saturated Fat 1g; Trans Fat 0g); Cholesterol 75mg; Sodium 230mg; Total Carbohydrate 5g (Dietary Fiber 1g); Protein 31g **% Daily Value:** Vitamin A 2%; Vitamin C 4%; Calcium 10%; Iron 10% **Exchanges:** 4½ Very Lean Meat **Carbohydrate Choices:** 0

healthified lamb chops with blackberry-red wine sauce

170 Calories

Prep Time: 40 Minutes   **Start to Finish:** 40 Minutes   **Makes:** 4 servings   (photo on page C13)

2 teaspoons canola or olive oil	½ teaspoon ground allspice
1 large pear, peeled, coarsely chopped (about 1⅓ cups)	¼ teaspoon salt
	¼ teaspoon coarse ground black pepper
4 medium green onions, sliced (¼ cup)	4 lamb rib chops (1 inch thick and 4 to 5 oz each) or 8 lamb loin chops (1 inch thick and 3 oz each)
⅛ teaspoon ground cloves	
1 cup fresh or frozen (thawed) blackberries	
1 tablespoon red wine vinegar	

1. Heat gas or charcoal grill. In 10-inch skillet, heat oil over medium heat. Add pear, onions and cloves; cook about 3 minutes, stirring occasionally, just until pear is tender. Add blackberries; reduce heat. Cook 3 minutes, stirring often. Remove from heat; stir in vinegar. Set aside to cool.

2. In small bowl, mix allspice, salt and pepper. Rub mixture on both sides of lamb chops.

3. Place lamb chops on grill over medium heat. Cover grill; cook 12 to 17 minutes, turning once, until desired doneness (145°F for medium-rare, 160°F for medium). Serve lamb chops with sauce.

1 Serving: Calories 170 (Calories from Fat 70); Total Fat 8g (Saturated Fat 2.5g; Trans Fat 0g); Cholesterol 40mg; Sodium 200mg; Total Carbohydrate 13g (Dietary Fiber 4g); Protein 13g **% Daily Value:** Vitamin A 4%; Vitamin C 20%; Calcium 4%; Iron 8% **Exchanges:** ½ Fruit, ½ Other Carbohydrate, 2 Lean Meat, ½ Fat **Carbohydrate Choices:** 1

pork tenderloin with raspberry-chipotle glaze

260 Calories

Prep Time: 15 Minutes   **Start to Finish:** 15 Minutes   **Makes:** 4 servings

1 pork tenderloin (about 1 lb)	⅓ cup seedless red raspberry jam
2 teaspoons olive or vegetable oil	1 to 2 teaspoons finely chopped chipotle chiles in adobo sauce (from 7-oz can)
½ teaspoon salt	
½ teaspoon chili powder	1 teaspoon water
¼ teaspoon pepper	

1. Heat closed medium-size contact grill 5 minutes. Position drip tray to catch drippings.

2. Cut pork lengthwise in half, then cut crosswise to make 4 equal pieces. Brush all sides with oil; sprinkle with salt, chili powder and pepper.

3. Place pork on grill. Close grill; cook 7 to 9 minutes or until no longer pink in center.

4. Meanwhile, in small microwavable bowl, mix jam, chiles and water. Microwave uncovered on High 20 to 30 seconds or until jam is melted and mixture is warm; stir well. Drizzle raspberry glaze over pork.

1 Serving: Calories 260 (Calories from Fat 80); Total Fat 9g (Saturated Fat 2.5g; Trans Fat 0g); Cholesterol 50mg; Sodium 410mg; Total Carbohydrate 22g (Dietary Fiber 1g); Protein 23g **% Daily Value:** Vitamin A 6%; Vitamin C 30%; Calcium 0%; Iron 6% **Exchanges:** 1½ Other Carbohydrate, 3 Lean Meat **Carbohydrate Choices:** 1½

Quick Meal Idea Serve the pork with your favorite rice pilaf.

Kitchen Tip One end of a pork tenderloin is usually thinner than the other end. Cut those pieces a little larger than the thicker end, and they will be about the same weight.

210 Calories

peach- and mustard-glazed pork tenderloin

Prep Time: 35 Minutes   **Start to Finish:** 1 Hour 35 Minutes   **Makes:** 6 servings

½ cup peach preserves	¼ teaspoon dried thyme leaves
2 tablespoons Dijon mustard	¼ teaspoon salt
2 teaspoons olive or vegetable oil	2 pork tenderloins (about ¾ lb each)

1. In shallow glass or plastic dish or resealable plastic food-storage bag, mix preserves, mustard, oil, thyme and salt. Add pork; turn to coat. Cover dish or seal bag; refrigerate at least 1 hour to marinate but no longer than 8 hours, turning pork occasionally.

2. Heat gas or charcoal grill. Remove pork from marinade; reserve marinade. Place pork on grill over medium-low heat. Cover grill; cook 15 to 20 minutes, brushing with marinade and turning occasionally, until meat thermometer inserted in center of pork reads 145°F.

3. Transfer pork from grill to cutting board or plate; cover with foil. Let stand at least 3 minutes before slicing. Meanwhile, in 1-quart saucepan, heat remaining marinade to boiling; boil and stir 1 minute. Cut pork into slices; serve with warm marinade.

1 Serving: Calories 210 (Calories from Fat 50); Total Fat 6g (Saturated Fat 1.5g; Trans Fat 0g); Cholesterol 45mg; Sodium 280mg; Total Carbohydrate 19g (Dietary Fiber 0g); Protein 21g **% Daily Value:** Vitamin A 0%; Vitamin C 2%; Calcium 0%; Iron 4% **Exchanges:** 1½ Starch, 2 Lean Meat **Carbohydrate Choices:** 1

Kitchen Tip Zippered food-storage plastic bags are great for mess-free marinating. Place the meat in the bag with the marinade, fold over the top of the bag and squeeze out all the air, allowing marinade to completely coat the food. When it's time to grill, take the bag outside and transfer the marinated meat to the grill.

Try This

Apricot preserves can be used instead of the peach preserves.

lemon-pepper pork tenderloin

Prep Time: 30 Minutes **Start to Finish:** 35 Minutes **Makes:** 6 servings

140 Calories

1 teaspoon grated lemon peel	¼ teaspoon dried thyme or marjoram leaves
½ teaspoon seasoned salt	2 teaspoons olive or vegetable oil
½ teaspoon coarse ground black pepper	2 pork tenderloins (about ¾ lb each)
½ teaspoon paprika	

1. Heat gas or charcoal grill. In small bowl, mix all ingredients except oil and pork. Brush oil over all sides of pork. Rub lemon peel mixture over pork.

2. Place pork on grill over medium-low heat. Cover grill; cook 15 to 20 minutes, turning occasionally, until meat thermometer inserted in center of pork reads 145°F.

3. Transfer pork from grill to cutting board or plate; cover with foil. Let stand at least 3 minutes before slicing.

1 Serving: Calories 140 (Calories from Fat 50); Total Fat 6g (Saturated Fat 1.5g; Trans Fat 0g); Cholesterol 45mg; Sodium 160mg; Total Carbohydrate 0g (Dietary Fiber 0g); Protein 21g **% Daily Value:** Vitamin A 2%; Vitamin C 0%; Calcium 0%; Iron 4% **Exchanges:** 1 Very Lean Meat, 2 Lean Meat **Carbohydrate Choices:** 0

Kitchen Tip To remove the silverskin from pork tenderloin, slide a long, narrow knife under silverskin; hold silverskin tightly with one hand while slicing under membrane.

260
Calories

pork chops with maple-apple glaze

Prep Time: 20 Minutes **Start to Finish:** 20 Minutes **Makes:** 4 servings

¼ cup real maple or maple-flavored syrup

¼ cup apple butter
½ teaspoon ground mustard
4 bone-in pork loin chops (½ to ¾ inch thick), trimmed of fat

½ teaspoon garlic-pepper blend
¼ teaspoon salt

1. Heat gas or charcoal grill. In 1-quart saucepan, mix syrup, apple butter and mustard. Cook over low heat about 1 minute, stirring occasionally, until well blended.

2. Sprinkle pork with garlic-pepper blend and salt; place on grill over medium heat. Brush with maple mixture. Cover grill; cook 10 to 12 minutes, turning and brushing with maple mixture 2 or 3 times, until meat thermometer inserted in center of pork reads 145°F. Discard any remaining maple mixture.

1 Serving: Calories 260 (Calories from Fat 70); Total Fat 8g (Saturated Fat 3g; Trans Fat 0g); Cholesterol 65mg; Sodium 190mg; Total Carbohydrate 23g (Dietary Fiber 0g); Protein 23g **% Daily Value:** Vitamin A 0%; Vitamin C 0%; Calcium 2%; Iron 6% **Exchanges:** 1 Starch, ½ Other Carbohydrate, 2½ Lean Meat **Carbohydrate Choices:** 1½

southwestern pork chops with peach salsa

180 Calories

Prep Time: 25 Minutes **Start to Finish:** 25 Minutes **Makes:** 4 servings (photo on page C13)

SALSA
- 3 ripe medium peaches, peeled, chopped (about 1½ cups)
- ¼ cup finely chopped red bell pepper
- 2 tablespoons finely chopped red onion
- 1 tablespoon chopped fresh cilantro
- 2 teaspoons packed brown sugar
- 2 teaspoons lime juice
- ¼ teaspoon finely chopped serrano or jalapeño chile

PORK CHOPS
- 1 tablespoon chili powder
- 4 bone-in pork loin chops, ½ inch thick (4 oz each)

1. Heat gas or charcoal grill. In medium bowl, mix all salsa ingredients; set aside.

2. Rub chili powder on both sides of pork chops. Place pork on grill over medium heat. Cover grill; cook 6 to 9 minutes, turning once, until meat thermometer inserted in center of pork reads 145°F.

3. Serve pork chops topped with salsa, or serve salsa on the side.

1 Serving: Calories 180 (Calories from Fat 60); Total Fat 7g (Saturated Fat 2g; Trans Fat 0g); Cholesterol 50mg; Sodium 50mg; Total Carbohydrate 11g (Dietary Fiber 2g); Protein 19g **% Daily Value:** Vitamin A 20%; Vitamin C 40%; Calcium 0%; Iron 6% **Exchanges:** 1 Other Carbohydrate, 2½ Lean Meat **Carbohydrate Choices:** 1

Kitchen Tip If you don't have the peaches, you can use about 1½ cups chopped mango or pineapple instead.

Try This
Boneless pork chops can be used instead of bone-in chops.

jamaican jerk pork chops with mango salsa

240 Calories

Prep Time: 35 Minutes   **Start to Finish:** 1 Hour 5 Minutes   **Makes:** 4 servings

JERK SEASONING

2	teaspoons dried thyme leaves
1	teaspoon ground allspice
1	teaspoon packed brown sugar
½	teaspoon salt
½	teaspoon cracked black pepper
¼	to ½ teaspoon ground red pepper (cayenne)
¼	teaspoon crushed dried sage leaves
4	cloves garlic, finely chopped

PORK

4	pork loin or rib chops, about ½ inch thick (about 1½ lb), trimmed of fat

SALSA

1	medium mango, cut lengthwise in half, seed removed and chopped (1 cup)
¼	cup finely chopped red onion
1	tablespoon finely chopped fresh mint leaves or 1 teaspoon mint flakes
1	small jalapeño chile, finely chopped (2 to 3 teaspoons)
2	tablespoons lime juice
⅛	teaspoon salt

1. In small bowl, mix all jerk seasoning ingredients. Rub seasoning into pork chops. Cover; refrigerate at least 30 minutes but no longer than 1 hour.

2. Meanwhile, in small glass or plastic bowl, mix all salsa ingredients. Cover; refrigerate until serving time.

3. Heat gas or charcoal grill. Place pork on grill over medium heat. Cover grill; cook 9 to 12 minutes, turning once, until meat thermometer inserted in center of pork reads 145°F. Serve pork chops with salsa.

1 Serving: Calories 240 (Calories from Fat 90); Total Fat 10g (Saturated Fat 3.5g; Trans Fat 0g); Cholesterol 75mg; Sodium 420mg; Total Carbohydrate 12g (Dietary Fiber 1g); Protein 27g **% Daily Value:** Vitamin A 8%; Vitamin C 15%; Calcium 4%; Iron 10% **Exchanges:** 1 Starch, 3 Lean Meat **Carbohydrate Choices:** 1

Kitchen Tip Mango adds a tropical flavor that particularly enhances pork and chicken. If fresh mangoes aren't available, use fresh or frozen peaches, thawed.

Try This

Instead of making your own jerk seasoning, use 2 tablespoons of purchased Jamaican jerk blend seasoning. You'll find it in the spice aisle of your supermarket.

ham steak with mustard sauce

240 Calories

Prep Time: 15 Minutes   **Start to Finish:** 15 Minutes   **Makes:** 4 servings

1 tablespoon Dijon mustard	1 tablespoon apricot preserves
1 tablespoon honey	1 cooked ham steak, ½ inch thick (1 lb)

1. Heat gas or charcoal grill. In small bowl, mix mustard, honey and preserves.

2. Place ham on grill over medium-high heat. Cover grill; cook 4 minutes. Turn ham; brush with half of the mustard mixture. Cover grill; cook 4 minutes. Turn ham again; brush with remaining mustard mixture. Cover grill; cook about 2 minutes longer or until ham is thoroughly heated.

1 Serving: Calories 240 (Calories from Fat 130); Total Fat 15g (Saturated Fat 5g; Trans Fat 0g); Cholesterol 60mg; Sodium 980mg; Total Carbohydrate 8g (Dietary Fiber 0g); Protein 19g **% Daily Value:** Vitamin A 0%; Vitamin C 0%; Calcium 0%; Iron 8% **Exchanges:** ½ Other Carbohydrate, 2½ Lean Meat, 1½ Fat **Carbohydrate Choices:** ½

Kitchen Tip Ham steak, sometimes labeled "ham slice," is a center-cut piece of ham that's usually fairly lean. Look for it with the other ham in the meat department.

Quick Meal Idea Add a crisp salad and fresh steamed veggies to complete the meal.

280 Calories

herbed beef kabobs

Prep Time: 25 Minutes   **Start to Finish:** 4 Hours 25 Minutes   **Makes:** 4 servings

MARINADE
2   tablespoons olive or vegetable oil
¼   cup red wine vinegar
2   cloves garlic, finely chopped
1   tablespoon chopped fresh or 1 teaspoon dried rosemary leaves, crushed

1   tablespoon chopped fresh or 1 teaspoon dried oregano leaves
½   teaspoon salt

KABOBS
1   lb boneless beef cubes for kabobs
½   red bell pepper, cut into 8 pieces
½   yellow bell pepper, cut into 8 pieces8 small fresh portabella mushrooms

1. In shallow glass or plastic dish or resealable food-storage plastic bag, mix all marinade ingredients. Add beef, bell peppers and mushrooms; stir to coat. Cover dish or seal bag; refrigerate at least 4 hours to marinate but no longer than 24 hours.

2. Heat gas or charcoal grill. Remove beef and vegetables from marinade; discard marinade. On each of 4 (10- to 12-inch) metal skewers, alternately thread beef and vegetables.

3. Place kabobs on grill over medium heat. Cover grill; cook 7 to 12 minutes, turning once, until vegetables are tender and beef is desired doneness.

1 Serving: Calories 280 (Calories from Fat 160); Total Fat 18g (Saturated Fat 5g; Trans Fat 0g); Cholesterol 55mg; Sodium 350mg; Total Carbohydrate 9g (Dietary Fiber 3g); Protein 22g **% Daily Value:** Vitamin A 10%; Vitamin C 40%; Calcium 4%; Iron 10% **Exchanges:** ½ Starch, 3 Lean Meat, 1½ Fat **Carbohydrate Choices:** ½

Kitchen Tips The kabob cubes can usually be purchased at the fresh meat counter. If they are not available, substitute 1 pound boneless beef top sirloin, cut into 1- to 1½-inch cubes.

Skewers with flat sides (rather than round) hold ingredients more securely and keep food pieces in place when you turn the kabobs. For even cooking, all food pieces on kabobs should be cut into the same size.

cilantro-orange marinated flank steak

250 Calories

Prep Time: 40 Minutes   **Start to Finish:** 4 Hours 40 Minutes   **Makes:** 4 servings (3 ounces cooked meat and ¾ cup vegetables each)

1	lb beef flank steak, trimmed of fat	2	teaspoons ground cumin
⅓	cup orange juice	1	teaspoon ground coriander
¼	cup chopped fresh cilantro	¼	teaspoon salt
2	tablespoons red wine vinegar	¼	teaspoon crushed red pepper flakes
1	tablespoon olive oil	2	bell peppers (any color), cut in half, seeded
4	cloves garlic, finely chopped	1	red onion, cut into ½-inch-thick slices

1. On both sides of steak, make cuts about 1 inch apart and ¼ inch deep in crisscross pattern. Place steak in resealable food-storage plastic bag. In small bowl, stir orange juice, cilantro, vinegar, oil, garlic, cumin, coriander, salt and pepper flakes. Pour over steak. Seal bag; turn to coat. Refrigerate 4 to 6 hours to marinate, turning bag occasionally.

2. Heat gas or charcoal grill. Drain steak, reserving marinade. Brush bell pepper halves and onion slices with reserved marinade. Discard any remaining marinade.

3. Place steak on grill over medium heat. Cover grill; cook 8 minutes. Turn steak. Place vegetables, cut sides down, on grill. Cover grill; cook 9 to 13 minutes, turning vegetables occasionally, until steak is of desired doneness (145°F for medium-rare, 160°F for medium) and vegetables are crisp-tender.

4. Thinly slice steak across grain; cut bell peppers into strips. Serve with grilled onion.

1 Serving: Calories 250 (Calories from Fat 80); Total Fat 8g (Saturated Fat 2g; Trans Fat 0g); Cholesterol 85mg; Sodium 200mg; Total Carbohydrate 9g (Dietary Fiber 1g); Protein 34g **% Daily Value:** Vitamin A 8%; Vitamin C 50%; Calcium 4%; Iron 25% **Exchanges:** ½ Starch, ½ Vegetable, 2½ Very Lean Meat, 2 Lean Meat **Carbohydrate Choices:** ½

230 Calories

balsamic-garlic marinated steak

Prep Time: 30 Minutes   **Start to Finish:** 8 Hours 30 Minutes   **Makes:** 6 servings

4 cloves garlic, finely chopped, or ½ teaspoon garlic powder	½ teaspoon Italian seasoning
½ cup balsamic vinegar	¼ teaspoon salt
¼ cup chili sauce or ketchup	¼ teaspoon coarse ground black pepper
2 tablespoons packed brown sugar	1 boneless beef top round steak, 1 to 1½ inches thick (1½ lb)
2 tablespoons olive or vegetable oil	

1. In shallow glass dish or resealable food-storage plastic bag, mix all ingredients except beef. Add beef; turn to coat. Cover dish or seal bag; refrigerate at least 8 hours to marinate but no longer than 12 hours, turning beef occasionally.

2. Heat gas or charcoal grill. Remove beef from marinade; reserve marinade. Place beef on grill over medium heat. Cover grill; cook 15 to 20 minutes, turning and brushing with marinade once or twice, until steak is of desired doneness (145°F for medium-rare, 160°F for medium).

3. Discard any remaining marinade. To serve, cut beef across grain into thin slices.

1 Serving: Calories 230 (Calories from Fat 80); Total Fat 8g (Saturated Fat 2g; Trans Fat 0g); Cholesterol 70mg; Sodium 290mg; Total Carbohydrate 11g (Dietary Fiber 0g); Protein 28g **% Daily Value:** Vitamin A 0%; Vitamin C 2%; Calcium 2%; Iron 15% **Exchanges:** ½ Starch, 3½ Lean Meat **Carbohydrate Choices:** 1

Kitchen Tip Always marinate food in a nonmetal dish. Acid-based marinades—such as those made with vinegar, lemon juice, tomato or wine—can react with some metals and cause an off flavor in the food.

sirloin steaks with cilantro chimichurri

270 Calories

Prep Time: 25 Minutes **Start to Finish:** 25 Minutes **Makes:** 4 servings

1 cup loosely packed fresh cilantro	2 teaspoons vegetable oil
1 small onion, cut into quarters	½ teaspoon salt
2 cloves garlic, cut in half	2 teaspoons ground cumin
1 jalapeño chile, cut in half, seeded	½ teaspoon pepper
2 teaspoons lime juice	4 beef sirloin steaks, 1 inch thick (about 1½ lb)

1. Heat gas or charcoal grill. In food processor, place cilantro, onion, garlic, chile, lime juice, oil and ¼ teaspoon of the salt. Cover; process until finely chopped. Blend in 2 to 3 teaspoons water to make sauce thinner, if desired. Transfer to small bowl; set aside until serving time.

2. In small bowl, mix cumin, pepper and remaining ¼ teaspoon salt; rub evenly over steaks. Place steaks on grill over medium heat. Cover grill; cook 10 to 16 minutes, turning once, until of desired doneness (145°F for medium-rare, 160°F for medium).

3. Serve 2 tablespoons chimichurri over each steak.

1 Serving: Calories 270 (Calories from Fat 80); Total Fat 9g (Saturated Fat 2.5g; Trans Fat 0g); Cholesterol 110mg; Sodium 350mg; Total Carbohydrate 3g (Dietary Fiber 0g); Protein 45g **% Daily Value:** Vitamin A 6%; Vitamin C 4%; Calcium 2%; Iron 30% **Exchanges:** ½ Vegetable, 6½ Very Lean Meat, 1 Fat **Carbohydrate Choices:** 0

Try This

For the freshest flavor, purchase whole cumin seed, and grind in a mortar and pestle or spice grinder just before using.

290 Calories

peppercorn t-bones

Prep Time: 25 Minutes   **Start to Finish:** 25 Minutes   **Makes:** 6 servings

6 beef T-bone steaks, 1 inch thick (about 1½ lb)	4½ teaspoons Dijon mustard
3 cloves garlic, cut in half	¾ teaspoon Worcestershire sauce
4½ teaspoons black peppercorns, crushed*	¼ teaspoon lime juice
⅓ cup butter, softened	Salt and pepper, if desired

1. Heat gas or charcoal grill. Trim fat on steaks to ¼-inch thickness. Rub garlic on beef. Press crushed peppercorns into beef.

2. In small bowl, mix butter, mustard, Worcestershire sauce and lime juice.

3. Place steaks on grill over medium heat. Cover grill; cook 10 to 16 minutes, turning once, until of desired doneness (145°F for medium-rare, 160°F for medium). Sprinkle steaks with salt and pepper. Serve with butter mixture.

*To crush peppercorns, place in a heavy-duty resealable freezer plastic bag and use a rolling pin or meat mallet to crush into smaller pieces.

1 Serving: Calories 290 (Calories from Fat 170); Total Fat 19g (Saturated Fat 10g; Trans Fat 1g); Cholesterol 80mg; Sodium 210mg; Total Carbohydrate 2g (Dietary Fiber 0g); Protein 28g **% Daily Value:** Vitamin A 8%; Vitamin C 0%; Calcium 2%; Iron 15% **Exchanges:** 4 Medium-Fat Meat **Carbohydrate Choices:** 0

garlic steak salad

Prep Time: 30 Minutes **Start to Finish:** 30 Minutes **Makes:** 6 servings (photo on page C13)

240 Calories

SPICY GARLIC DRESSING
- ⅓ cup olive or vegetable oil
- 2 tablespoons chopped fresh parsley
- 3 tablespoons red wine vinegar
- 1 tablespoon lemon juice
- 1½ teaspoons chopped fresh or ½ teaspoon dried oregano leaves
- ½ teaspoon crushed red pepper flakes
- 2 cloves garlic, finely chopped

SALAD
- 1 large red or yellow bell pepper, cut into strips
- 1 cup sliced fresh mushrooms (3 oz)
- 1 boneless beef sirloin steak, 1 to 1½ inches thick (1 lb)
- ¼ teaspoon salt
- ⅛ teaspoon pepper
- 6 cups bite-size pieces salad greens

1. Heat gas or charcoal grill. In tightly covered container, shake all dressing ingredients; reserve ¼ cup.

2. Toss bell pepper and mushrooms with 2 tablespoons of the dressing; place in grill basket (grill "wok"). Place beef on grill over medium heat. Cover grill; cook 15 to 20 minutes, turning once, until of desired doneness (145°F for medium-rare, 160°F for medium). Add grill basket to grill for last 5 minutes of cooking time, shaking basket or stirring vegetables occasionally, until bell pepper is crisp-tender.

3. Transfer beef from grill to cutting board. Sprinkle with salt and pepper; cut into ¼-inch slices. In large bowl, toss beef with reserved ¼ cup dressing. Add salad greens, grilled vegetables and remaining dressing; toss.

1 Serving: Calories 240 (Calories from Fat 130); Total Fat 15g (Saturated Fat 2.5g; Trans Fat 0g); Cholesterol 50mg; Sodium 140mg; Total Carbohydrate 5g (Dietary Fiber 2g); Protein 21g **% Daily Value:** Vitamin A 80%; Vitamin C 40%; Calcium 4%; Iron 15% **Exchanges:** 1 Vegetable, 2½ Lean Meat, 1½ Fat **Carbohydrate Choices:** ½

Quick Meal Idea Enjoy this sizzling salad with a crusty French baguette and tall glasses of iced tea.

Kitchen Tip Bell peppers are available in a rainbow of colors, such as red, yellow, green, orange, purple and chocolate brown. Pick whatever color you like, or use a variety!

tuna with avocado-kiwi salsa

Prep Time: 40 Minutes   **Start to Finish:** 1 Hour 10 Minutes   **Makes:** 6 servings

TUNA

1½	lb tuna steaks, ¾ to 1 inch thick
¼	cup lime juice
2	teaspoons chili oil
2	tablespoons finely chopped fresh cilantro
1	clove garlic, finely chopped
½	teaspoon salt

SALSA

1	small ripe avocado, pitted, peeled and coarsely chopped (1 cup)
1	kiwifruit, peeled, chopped (½ cup)
3	medium green onions, chopped (3 tablespoons)
1	small jalapeño chile, seeded, finely chopped (1 tablespoon)
2	tablespoons lime juice
2	tablespoons chopped fresh cilantro
¼	teaspoon salt

1. If tuna steaks are large, cut into 6 serving pieces. In shallow glass or plastic dish, mix all remaining tuna ingredients. Add tuna; turn to coat with marinade. Cover; refrigerate to marinate, turning once, at least 30 minutes but no longer than 2 hours.

2. Meanwhile, in medium bowl, mix all salsa ingredients; refrigerate until serving time.

3. Heat gas or charcoal grill. Remove tuna from marinade; reserve marinade. Carefully brush oil on grill rack. Place tuna on grill over medium heat. Cover grill; cook 11 to 16 minutes, brushing 2 or 3 times with marinade and turning once, until fish flakes easily with fork and is slightly pink in center.

4. Discard any remaining marinade. Serve tuna topped with salsa.

1 Serving: Calories 220 (Calories from Fat 100); Total Fat 11g (Saturated Fat 2.5g; Trans Fat 0g); Cholesterol 65mg; Sodium 360mg; Total Carbohydrate 6g (Dietary Fiber 2g); Protein 23g **% Daily Value:** Vitamin A 4%; Vitamin C 40%; Calcium 2%; Iron 6% **Exchanges:** ½ Other Carbohydrate, 3½ Lean Meat **Carbohydrate Choices:** ½

sea bass with citrus-olive butter

180 Calories

Prep Time: 25 Minutes **Start to Finish:** 55 Minutes **Makes:** 4 servings

CITRUS-OLIVE BUTTER

2	tablespoons butter, softened
1	tablespoon finely chopped kalamata olives
2	teaspoons chopped fresh parsley
½	teaspoon balsamic vinegar
¼	teaspoon grated orange peel

SEA BASS

1	lb sea bass, salmon or snapper fillets, about 1 inch thick
1	tablespoon olive or vegetable oil
¼	teaspoon salt
⅛	teaspoon pepper

1. In small bowl, mix all citrus-olive butter ingredients. Refrigerate 30 minutes or until firm.

2. Heat gas or charcoal grill. Brush all surfaces of fish with oil; sprinkle with salt and pepper.

3. Place fish on grill over medium heat. Cover grill; cook 10 to 13 minutes, turning once, until fish flakes easily with fork. Serve with citrus-olive butter.

1 Serving: Calories 180 (Calories from Fat 100); Total Fat 11g (Saturated Fat 4.5g; Trans Fat 0g); Cholesterol 75mg; Sodium 300mg; Total Carbohydrate 0g (Dietary Fiber 0g); Protein 21g **% Daily Value:** Vitamin A 6%; Vitamin C 0%; Calcium 2%; Iron 2% **Exchanges:** 3 Lean Meat, ½ Fat **Carbohydrate Choices:** 0

Kitchen Tip Sea bass isn't just one fish, but rather several varieties of saltwater fish of the drum or grouper family. It has firm, lean to moderately fat flesh. You can grill it, bake it, poach it or even fry it.

salmon with cowboy marinade

Prep Time: 25 Minutes   **Start to Finish:** 55 Minutes   **Makes:** 8 servings

1   salmon fillet (about 2 lb), cut into
    8 serving pieces
1   tablespoon packed brown sugar
1   tablespoon butter, melted

1   tablespoon olive or vegetable oil
1   tablespoon honey
1   tablespoon soy sauce
1   clove garlic, finely chopped

1. Place salmon in shallow glass or plastic dish. In small bowl, mix all remaining ingredients. Pour over salmon. Cover; refrigerate to marinate at least 30 minutes but no longer than 1 hour.

2. Heat gas or charcoal grill. Remove salmon from marinade; reserve marinade. Place salmon, skin side down, on grill over medium heat. Cover grill; cook 10 to 20 minutes, brushing 2 or 3 times with marinade, until fish flakes easily with fork. Discard any remaining marinade.

1 Serving: Calories 200 (Calories from Fat 90); Total Fat 10g (Saturated Fat 2.5g; Trans Fat 0g); Cholesterol 75mg; Sodium 190mg; Total Carbohydrate 4g (Dietary Fiber 0g); Protein 24g **% Daily Value:** Vitamin A 4%; Vitamin C 0%; Calcium 0%; Iron 4% **Exchanges:** 3½ Lean Meat **Carbohydrate Choices:** 0

lemon-garlic halibut steaks

200 Calories

Prep Time: 20 Minutes   **Start to Finish:** 30 Minutes   **Makes:** 4 servings

¼ cup fresh lemon juice
1 tablespoon olive or vegetable oil
¼ teaspoon salt
¼ teaspoon pepper
2 cloves garlic, finely chopped

4 halibut or tuna steaks, about 1 inch thick (about 2 lb)
¼ cup chopped fresh parsley
1 tablespoon grated lemon peel

1. In shallow glass or plastic dish or resealable food-storage plastic bag, mix lemon juice, oil, salt, pepper and garlic. Add fish; turn several times to coat. Cover dish or seal bag; refrigerate 10 minutes.

2. Heat gas or charcoal grill. Remove fish from marinade; reserve marinade. Carefully brush oil on grill rack. Place fish on grill over medium heat. Cover grill; cook 10 to 15 minutes, turning once and brushing with marinade, until fish flakes easily with fork.

3. Discard any remaining marinade. Sprinkle fish with parsley and lemon peel.

1 Serving: Calories 200 (Calories from Fat 50); Total Fat 6g (Saturated Fat 1g; Trans Fat 0g); Cholesterol 100mg; Sodium 300mg; Total Carbohydrate 2g (Dietary Fiber 0g); Protein 35g **% Daily Value:** Vitamin A 8%; Vitamin C 10%; Calcium 4%; Iron 4% **Exchanges:** 4 Very Lean Meat, 1 Lean Meat **Carbohydrate Choices:** 0

CHAPTER 9

Side Dishes

100 Calories

green beans with bacon, onion and tomato

Prep Time: 30 Minutes   **Start to Finish:** 30 Minutes   **Makes:** 4 servings

1 lb fresh green beans, cut into 1-inch pieces*	1 teaspoon chopped fresh or ½ teaspoon dried oregano leaves
4 slices bacon, cut up	½ teaspoon salt
1 medium onion, chopped (½ cup)	Dash pepper
1 medium tomato, chopped (¾ cup)	2 tablespoons lemon or lime juice
1 clove garlic, finely chopped	

1. In 2-quart saucepan, place beans in 1 inch water. Heat to boiling; reduce heat. Simmer uncovered 6 to 8 minutes or until crisp-tender; drain. Immediately rinse with cold water; drain.

2. Meanwhile, in 10-inch skillet, cook bacon over medium heat 8 to 10 minutes, stirring occasionally, until crisp. Remove bacon with slotted spoon; drain on paper towels. Drain all but 1 tablespoon drippings in skillet.

3. Cook onion in bacon drippings over medium heat 3 to 4 minutes, stirring occasionally, until tender. Stir in tomato, garlic, oregano, salt and pepper. Simmer uncovered 5 minutes. Stir in beans; heat through. Drizzle with lemon juice. Sprinkle with bacon.

1 Serving: Calories 100 (Calories from Fat 35); Total Fat 3.5g (Saturated Fat 1g; Trans Fat 0g); Cholesterol 10mg; Sodium 490mg; Total Carbohydrate 11g (Dietary Fiber 3g); Protein 5g **% Daily Value:** Vitamin A 20%; Vitamin C 20%; Calcium 6%; Iron 8% **Exchanges:** ½ Starch, 1 Vegetable, ½ Fat **Carbohydrate Choices:** 1

Try This

You can substitute 1 bag (1 pound) frozen cut green beans for the fresh green beans. Cook them as you would the fresh green beans, as directed in step 1.

lemony beans with toasted garlic

50 Calories

Prep Time: 10 Minutes   **Start to Finish:** 10 Minutes   **Makes:** 10 servings (½ cup each)

¼ cup butter
4 cloves garlic, slivered
½ teaspoon salt
½ teaspoon freshly ground pepper

6¼ cups frozen whole green beans (from two 12-oz bags)
1 teaspoon grated lemon peel

1. In 3-quart saucepan, melt butter over medium heat. Add garlic, salt and pepper; cook 1 minute, stirring constantly.

2. Add green beans; cook 5 to 6 minutes, stirring occasionally, until tender. Stir in lemon peel.

1 Serving: Calories 50 (Calories from Fat 40); Total Fat 4.5g (Saturated Fat 3g; Trans Fat 0g); Cholesterol 10mg; Sodium 150mg; Total Carbohydrate 2g (Dietary Fiber 1g); Protein 0g **% Daily Value:** Vitamin A 6%; Vitamin C 0%; Calcium 0%; Iron 0% **Exchanges:** 1 Fat **Carbohydrate Choices:** 0

Try This

Substitute orange peel for the lemon peel.

130 Calories

baby peas with bacon and almonds

Prep Time: 15 Minutes   **Start to Finish:** 15 Minutes   **Makes:** 6 servings (½ cup each)

4   cups frozen baby sweet peas (from two 12-oz bags)
2   slices bacon, chopped
2   tablespoons finely chopped onion

¼   cup slivered almonds
2   tablespoons butter
½   teaspoon salt
Dash pepper

1. Cook peas as directed on bag; drain.

2. Meanwhile, in 10-inch nonstick skillet, cook bacon over medium-high heat 4 to 5 minutes, stirring occasionally, until crisp. Remove bacon with slotted spoon; drain on paper towels. Reserve drippings in skillet.

3. Cook onion and almonds in bacon drippings over medium-high heat 3 to 4 minutes, stirring frequently, until onion is tender and almonds are lightly browned. Remove from skillet.

4. In same skillet, melt butter over medium-high heat. Add peas, bacon, onion, almonds, salt and pepper; toss. Heat until hot.

1 Serving: Calories 130 (Calories from Fat 70); Total Fat 8g (Saturated Fat 2.5g; Trans Fat 0g); Cholesterol 10mg; Sodium 310mg; Total Carbohydrate 11g (Dietary Fiber 3g); Protein 5g **% Daily Value:** Vitamin A 10%; Vitamin C 6%; Calcium 2%; Iron 8% **Exchanges:** 1 Starch, 1½ Fat **Carbohydrate Choices:** 1

balsamic green beans and fennel

80 Calories

Prep Time: 20 Minutes   **Start to Finish:** 20 Minutes   **Makes:** 4 servings (about ¾ cup each)

2	teaspoons olive or canola oil	2	teaspoons packed brown sugar
1	medium bulb fennel, cut into thin wedges	¼	teaspoon salt
1	small onion, cut into thin wedges	¼	teaspoon freshly ground pepper
2	cups frozen whole green beans	1	tablespoon balsamic vinegar
¼	cup water		

1. In 12-inch nonstick skillet, heat oil over medium heat. Add fennel and onion; cook 7 to 8 minutes, stirring frequently, until fennel is light golden brown.

2. Add beans and water; heat to boiling. Stir; reduce heat to low. Cover; simmer 6 to 8 minutes or until beans are crisp-tender.

3. Stir in all remaining ingredients; cook and stir 15 to 30 seconds or until vegetables are coated.

1 Serving: Calories 80 (Calories from Fat 20); Total Fat 2.5g (Saturated Fat 0g; Trans Fat 0g); Cholesterol 0mg; Sodium 180mg; Total Carbohydrate 13g (Dietary Fiber 4g); Protein 1g **% Daily Value:** Vitamin A 8%; Vitamin C 8%; Calcium 6%; Iron 6% **Exchanges:** ½ Other Carbohydrate, 1 Vegetable, ½ Fat **Carbohydrate Choices:** 1

Kitchen Tip Fennel is cultivated in the Mediterranean and in the United States. Both the bulb and the stems can be eaten raw or cooked. The flavor is a little bit like anise but is sweeter and more delicate. The feathery greenery can be used as a garnish or snipped like dill weed and used for a last-minute flavor enhancer.

asparagus and corn with honey-mustard glaze

Prep Time: 20 Minutes   **Start to Finish:** 20 Minutes   **Makes:** 5 servings (½ cup each)

1	lb fresh asparagus spears	2	teaspoons Dijon mustard
½	cup water	2	teaspoons honey
1	cup frozen corn	¼	teaspoon lemon-pepper seasoning

1. Snap off tough ends of asparagus and discard. Cut asparagus into 1-inch pieces.

2. In 2-quart saucepan, heat water to boiling. Gently stir in asparagus and corn. Reduce heat. Simmer uncovered 5 to 8 minutes or until asparagus is crisp-tender; drain.

3. In small bowl, mix mustard, honey and lemon-pepper seasoning. Stir into hot vegetables.

1 Serving: Calories 60 (Calories from Fat 0); Total Fat 0g (Saturated Fat 0g; Trans Fat 0g); Cholesterol 0mg; Sodium 70mg; Total Carbohydrate 12g (Dietary Fiber 2g); Protein 3g **% Daily Value:** Vitamin A 15%; Vitamin C 6%; Calcium 2%; Iron 10% **Exchanges:** ½ Other Carbohydrate, 1 Vegetable **Carbohydrate Choices:** 1

Kitchen Tip Look for asparagus spears that are firm and uniform in size. When you "snap" off the ends, the spears will break where the most tender part of the asparagus starts—so you really don't need to use a knife.

asparagus-pepper stir-fry

40 Calories

Prep Time: 20 Minutes   **Start to Finish:** 20 Minutes   **Makes:** 4 servings   (photo on page C14)

1	lb fresh asparagus spears	2	cloves garlic, finely chopped
1	teaspoon canola oil	1	tablespoon orange juice
1	medium red, yellow or orange bell pepper, cut into ¾-inch pieces	1	tablespoon reduced-sodium soy sauce
		½	teaspoon ground ginger

1. Snap off and discard tough ends of asparagus. Cut asparagus into 1-inch pieces.

2. In 10-inch nonstick skillet or wok, heat oil over medium heat. Add asparagus, bell pepper and garlic; cook 3 to 4 minutes or until crisp-tender, stirring constantly.

3. In small bowl, mix orange juice, soy sauce and ginger until blended; stir into asparagus mixture. Cook and stir 15 to 30 seconds or until vegetables are coated.

1 Serving: Calories 40 (Calories from Fat 10); Total Fat 1.5g (Saturated Fat 0g; Trans Fat 0g); Cholesterol 0mg; Sodium 135mg; Total Carbohydrate 6g (Dietary Fiber 2g); Protein 2g **% Daily Value:** Vitamin A 30%; Vitamin C 35%; Calcium 2%; Iron 8% **Exchanges:** 1 Vegetable, ½ Fat **Carbohydrate Choices:** ½

Kitchen Tip Choose fresh asparagus that is firm and straight. It should be bright green (or creamy white), with no signs of decay, and the tips should be firm and closed. Thinner spears will cook more quickly than larger ones.

150 Calories

roasted candied carrots

Prep Time: 15 Minutes   **Start to Finish:** 45 Minutes   **Makes:** 8 servings

2   tablespoons olive oil
¼   cup honey
1   teaspoon ground cumin
½   teaspoon smoked paprika

½   teaspoon seasoned salt
1   bag (2 lb) fresh carrots, cut into
     2½-inch pieces

1. Heat oven to 450°F. Place 15x10x1-inch pan in oven 10 minutes to heat. Meanwhile, in large bowl, mix all ingredients except carrots until blended. Add carrots; toss to coat.

2. Spray hot pan with cooking spray. Spread carrots in single layer in pan.

3. Roast uncovered 30 minutes, stirring once, until golden brown. Immediately remove carrots from pan.

1 Serving: Calories 150 (Calories from Fat 45); Total Fat 5g (Saturated Fat 0.5g; Trans Fat 0g); Cholesterol 0mg; Sodium 210mg; Total Carbohydrate 25g (Dietary Fiber 4g); Protein 1g **% Daily Value:** Vitamin A 450%; Vitamin C 6%; Calcium 4%; Iron 4% **Exchanges:** 1½ Other Carbohydrate, 1 Vegetable, 1 Fat **Carbohydrate Choices:** 1½

Try This

Preheating the pan while you're mixing the other ingredients gives the carrots a jump-start on roasting.

broccoli with roasted red peppers and hazelnuts

70 Calories

Prep Time: 25 Minutes   **Start to Finish:** 25 Minutes   **Makes:** 8 servings (½ cup each)
(photo on page C15)

1 cup water	¼ cup chopped hazelnuts (filberts)
5 cups fresh broccoli florets	½ cup chopped drained roasted red bell peppers (from a jar)
1 tablespoon olive or vegetable oil	¼ teaspoon salt
1 clove garlic, finely chopped	

1. In 2-quart saucepan, heat water to boiling. Add broccoli. Cover; cook about 1 minute or just until crisp. Drain; immediately place broccoli in ice water.

2. In 12-inch skillet, heat oil over medium heat. Add garlic and hazelnuts; cook 1 to 2 minutes, stirring frequently, until nuts are lightly toasted.

3. Drain broccoli. Stir broccoli, roasted peppers and salt into nut mixture. Cook about 3 minutes, stirring occasionally, until broccoli is crisp-tender.

1 Serving: Calories 70 (Calories from Fat 35); Total Fat 4g (Saturated Fat 0g; Trans Fat 0g); Cholesterol 0mg; Sodium 90mg; Total Carbohydrate 5g (Dietary Fiber 2g); Protein 2g **% Daily Value:** Vitamin A 20%; Vitamin C 60%; Calcium 4%; Iron 4% **Exchanges:** 1 Vegetable, 1 Fat **Carbohydrate Choices:** ½

120 Calories

roasted cauliflower with asiago

Prep Time: 10 Minutes   **Start to Finish:** 40 Minutes   **Makes:** 10 servings

3 tablespoons olive oil	1 medium head cauliflower (2 lb), separated into florets
½ teaspoon grated orange peel	
½ teaspoon salt	1 cup shredded Asiago cheese (4 oz)
¼ teaspoon pepper	

1. Heat oven to 450°F. In large bowl, mix oil, orange peel, salt and pepper. Add cauliflower; toss until evenly coated. Spread in ungreased 15x10x1-inch pan.

2. Roast uncovered 20 to 25 minutes; stir. Sprinkle with cheese. Roast 1 to 2 minutes longer or until cheese is melted.

1 Serving: Calories 120 (Calories from Fat 80); Total Fat 9g (Saturated Fat 3.5g; Trans Fat 0g); Cholesterol 10mg; Sodium 270mg; Total Carbohydrate 5g (Dietary Fiber 2g); Protein 4g **% Daily Value:** Vitamin A 2%; Vitamin C 35%; Calcium 10%; Iron 2% **Exchanges:** 1 Vegetable, 2 Fat **Carbohydrate Choices:** ½

Quick Meal Idea This vegetable dish would go great with seafood entrées such as salmon, shrimp or halibut. You can garnish with additional orange peel if you like.

Try This

Shredded Parmesan can be used instead of the Asiago.

zucchini with edamame and tomatoes

60 Calories

Prep Time: 15 Minutes   **Start to Finish:** 15 Minutes   **Makes:** 4 servings (½ cup each)

¼ cup water
1 small zucchini, cut lengthwise into quarters, then cut crosswise into ½-inch slices
1 cup refrigerated fully cooked ready-to-eat shelled edamame or frozen (thawed) shelled edamame

1 medium tomato, coarsely chopped (½ cup)
2 teaspoons chopped fresh basil leaves
¼ teaspoon garlic salt
⅛ teaspoon pepper
1 tablespoon shredded Parmesan cheese

1. In 2-quart saucepan, heat water to boiling over medium heat. Add zucchini and edamame; simmer uncovered 3 to 5 minutes or until vegetables are crisp-tender. Drain well; return to saucepan.

2. Stir in tomato, basil, garlic salt and pepper. Cook about 1 minute, stirring constantly, until heated. Sprinkle with cheese.

1 Serving: Calories 60 (Calories from Fat 20); Total Fat 2.5g (Saturated Fat 0.5g; Trans Fat 0g); Cholesterol 0mg; Sodium 95mg; Total Carbohydrate 5g (Dietary Fiber 2g); Protein 5g **% Daily Value:** Vitamin A 6%; Vitamin C 10%; Calcium 6%; Iron 4% **Exchanges:** 1 Vegetable, ½ Very Lean Meat, ½ Fat **Carbohydrate Choices:** ½

70 Calories

dilled carrots and pea pods

Prep Time: 15 Minutes   **Start to Finish:** 15 Minutes   **Makes:** 4 servings

1½ cups ready-to-eat baby-cut carrots	2 teaspoons chopped fresh or ½ teaspoon dried dill weed
1½ cups fresh snow pea pods, strings removed	⅛ teaspoon salt
1 tablespoon butter	

1. In 2-quart saucepan, heat 1 inch water to boiling. Add carrots; cover. Return to boiling; reduce heat. Cover; cook about 4 minutes or until carrots are crisp-tender. Do not drain.

2. Add pea pods to carrots in saucepan. Heat to boiling. Boil uncovered 2 to 3 minutes, stirring occasionally, until pea pods are crisp-tender. Drain; return vegetables to saucepan.

3. Add butter, dill weed and salt; stir until butter is melted.

1 Serving: Calories 70 (Calories from Fat 30); Total Fat 3g (Saturated Fat 2g; Trans Fat 0g); Cholesterol 10mg; Sodium 135mg; Total Carbohydrate 8g (Dietary Fiber 2g); Protein 1g **% Daily Value:** Vitamin A 200%; Vitamin C 20%; Calcium 4%; Iron 6% **Exchanges:** 1½ Vegetable, ½ Fat **Carbohydrate Choices:** ½

Try This

Here's the easy way to remove the strings from pea pods. Simply snap off the stem end from each one, then pull the string across the pea pod.

butternut squash sauté

60 Calories

Prep Time: 40 Minutes   **Start to Finish:** 40 Minutes   **Makes:** 8 servings

2 slices bacon, cut into 1-inch pieces	½ teaspoon chopped fresh or ⅛ teaspoon dried thyme leaves
1 medium onion, chopped (½ cup)	⅛ teaspoon pepper
6 cups ½-inch pieces peeled butternut squash (2 small)	3 cups firmly packed baby spinach leaves

1. In 12-inch skillet, cook bacon over medium-low heat about 10 minutes, stirring occasionally, until crisp. Add onion. Cook about 2 minutes, stirring occasionally, until onion is crisp-tender.

2. Stir in squash, thyme and pepper. Cover; cook 8 to 10 minutes, stirring occasionally, until squash is tender. Add spinach; cook and stir just until spinach is wilted.

1 Serving: Calories 60 (Calories from Fat 10); Total Fat 1g (Saturated Fat 0g; Trans Fat 0g); Cholesterol 0mg; Sodium 60mg; Total Carbohydrate 11g (Dietary Fiber 2g); Protein 2g **% Daily Value:** Vitamin A 220%; Vitamin C 15%; Calcium 6%; Iron 6% **Exchanges:** ½ Other Carbohydrate, 1 Vegetable **Carbohydrate Choices:** 1

Health Smart That distinctive yellow-orange color of butternut squash comes from beta-carotene, a form of vitamin A. Winter squash, like butternut, is rich in vitamin A. When selecting butternut squash, look for those that have hard, tough rinds and are heavy for their size.

Try This

To save time, instead of washing spinach, purchase a bag of triple-washed baby spinach leaves from the produce section of the supermarket.

90 Calories

gourmet spinach

Prep Time: 25 Minutes   **Start to Finish:** 25 Minutes   **Makes:** 4 servings

1 lb fresh spinach	⅛ teaspoon pepper
1 jar (4.5 oz) whole mushrooms, drained	⅓ cup sour cream
1 small clove garlic, finely chopped	1 tablespoon fat-free half-and-half or fat-free (skim) milk
1 teaspoon dried minced onion	
½ teaspoon salt	

1. Remove imperfect leaves and root ends from spinach. Wash spinach several times in water, lifting spinach out of water each time so sand sinks to bottom; drain.

2. In 3-quart saucepan, place spinach with just the water that clings to leaves. Cover; cook over medium heat about 5 minutes or until wilted. Drain; chop.

3. In same saucepan, mix spinach, mushrooms, garlic, dried minced onion, salt and pepper. In small bowl, mix sour cream and half-and-half; pour over spinach mixture. Heat just to boiling, stirring occasionally.

1 Serving: Calories 90 (Calories from Fat 40); Total Fat 4.5g (Saturated Fat 2.5g; Trans Fat 0g); Cholesterol 10mg; Sodium 540mg; Total Carbohydrate 7g (Dietary Fiber 3g); Protein 4g **% Daily Value:** Vitamin A 210%; Vitamin C 25%; Calcium 15%; Iron 20% **Exchanges:** 2 Vegetable, 1 Fat **Carbohydrate Choices:** ½

Try This

To make the recipe in the oven, thaw and drain 1 bag (12 to 16 ounces frozen cut leaf spinach (omit steps 1 and 2). In ungreased 1-quart casserole, mix the spinach, 2 tablespoons butter and remaining ingredients. Cover and bake 1 hour.

easy grilled vegetables

Prep Time: 25 Minutes   **Start to Finish:** 1 Hour 25 Minutes   **Makes:** 6 servings

110 Calories

12	baby pattypan squash	1	large red onion, cut into ½-inch slices
2	medium red or green bell peppers, or 1 of each, cut into 6 pieces	⅓	cup Italian dressing
			Freshly ground pepper, if desired

1. In shallow glass dish, place squash, bell peppers and onion. Pour dressing over vegetables. Cover; let stand 1 hour to blend flavors.

2. Heat gas or charcoal grill. Remove vegetables from marinade; reserve marinade. Place squash and bell peppers in grill basket (grill "wok"). Place grill basket on grill over medium heat. Cover grill; cook 5 minutes.

3. Add onion to grill basket. Cover grill; cook 5 to 10 minutes longer, turning and brushing vegetables with marinade 2 or 3 times, until tender. Sprinkle with pepper.

1 Serving: Calories 110 (Calories from Fat 50); Total Fat 6g (Saturated Fat 0.5g; Trans Fat 0g); Cholesterol 0mg; Sodium 120mg; Total Carbohydrate 11g (Dietary Fiber 3g); Protein 2g **% Daily Value:** Vitamin A 50%; Vitamin C 80%; Calcium 6%; Iron 4% **Exchanges:** ½ Other Carbohydrate, 1 Vegetable, 1 Fat **Carbohydrate Choices:** 1

Kitchen Tip Look for baby pattypan squash about 1 inch in diameter. If they are larger, cut in half. Or 2 medium zucchini, cut into 1-inch pieces, can be substituted.

grilled summer squash stir-fry

Prep Time: 30 Minutes   **Start to Finish:** 30 Minutes   **Makes:** 4 servings

2 small zucchini, cut into ¼-inch slices
2 small yellow summer squash, cut into ¼-inch slices
6 baby pattypan squash, cut in half

¼ cup citrus vinaigrette dressing
2 medium plum (Roma) tomatoes, sliced
2 tablespoons chopped fresh cilantro

1. Heat gas or charcoal grill. In large bowl, mix zucchini, yellow squash, pattypan squash and dressing. Place mixture in grill basket (grill "wok"). Reserve dressing in bowl.

2. Place grill basket on grill over medium heat. Cover grill; cook 10 to 13 minutes, shaking basket or stirring squash occasionally, until crisp-tender. Return squash to bowl with dressing. Add tomatoes and cilantro; toss to coat.

1 Serving: Calories 80 (Calories from Fat 45); Total Fat 5g (Saturated Fat 0g; Trans Fat 0g); Cholesterol 0mg; Sodium 105mg; Total Carbohydrate 7g (Dietary Fiber 1g); Protein 1g **% Daily Value:** Vitamin A 10%; Vitamin C 20%; Calcium 2%; Iron 2% **Exchanges:** 1 Vegetable, 1 Fat **Carbohydrate Choices:** ½

Kitchen Tips Look for the citrus vinaigrette dressing with the salad dressings and sauces. If it's not available, balsamic and Asian vinaigrettes work well in this recipe.

Pattypan squash is a variety of summer squash. Round and slightly flattened, this small squash has a scalloped edge. Find it in grocery stores and farmers' markets.

herb-roasted root vegetables

70 Calories

Prep Time: 15 Minutes   **Start to Finish:** 1 Hour 10 Minutes   **Makes:** 6 servings (½ cup each)

2	medium turnips, peeled, cut into 1-inch pieces (3 cups)	1	cup ready-to-eat baby-cut carrots Cooking spray
2	medium parsnips, peeled, cut into ½-inch pieces (1½ cups)	2	teaspoons Italian seasoning
1	medium red onion, cut into 1-inch wedges (1 cup)	½	teaspoon coarse (kosher or sea) salt

1. Heat oven to 425°F. Spray 15x10x1-inch pan with cooking spray. Arrange vegetables in single layer in pan. Spray with cooking spray (2 or 3 seconds). Sprinkle with Italian seasoning and salt.

2. Roast uncovered 45 to 55 minutes, stirring once, until vegetables are tender.

1 Serving: Calories 70 (Calories from Fat 0); Total Fat 0g (Saturated Fat 0g; Trans Fat 0g); Cholesterol 0mg; Sodium 260mg; Total Carbohydrate 15g (Dietary Fiber 4g); Protein 1g **% Daily Value:** Vitamin A 70%; Vitamin C 20%; Calcium 6%; Iron 4% **Exchanges:** ½ Other Carbohydrate, 1 Vegetable **Carbohydrate Choices:** 1

Health Smart Roasting brings out the natural sweetness of vegetables and is a low-fat cooking option. As some of the moisture is evaporated in the high heat, the sugar is concentrated, so the food tastes sweeter.

60 Calories

roasted butternut squash combo

Prep Time: 15 Minutes   **Start to Finish:** 45 Minutes   **Makes:** 8 servings (½ cup each)

1 medium butternut squash, peeled, seeded and cut into 1-inch chunks (about 4 cups)	½ teaspoon seasoned salt
1 medium red or green bell pepper, cut into 16 pieces	½ teaspoon dried basil leaves
2 tablespoons olive or canola oil	¼ teaspoon garlic powder
	¼ teaspoon coarse ground black pepper

1. Heat oven to 425°F. Spray 13x9-inch pan with cooking spray. In large bowl, mix all ingredients until squash and bell pepper are coated with oil and seasonings. Spread in pan.

2. Roast uncovered 25 to 30 minutes, stirring once, until squash is tender.

1 Serving: Calories 60 (Calories from Fat 30); Total Fat 3.5g (Saturated Fat 0g; Trans Fat 0g); Cholesterol 0mg; Sodium 90mg; Total Carbohydrate 7g (Dietary Fiber 1g); Protein 0g **% Daily Value:** Vitamin A 140%; Vitamin C 30%; Calcium 2%; Iron 2% **Exchanges:** ½ Starch, ½ Fat **Carbohydrate Choices:** ½

Health Smart Butternut squash, the variety of winter squash that's shaped like a peanut, is a great source of vitamins A and C.

roasted beets

Prep Time: 10 Minutes **Start to Finish:** 1 Hour 20 Minutes **Makes:** 6 servings
(photo on page C15)

90 Calories

2	lb small beets (1½ to 2 inch)	2	tablespoons olive oil
½	teaspoon salt	2	tablespoons chopped fresh basil leaves
¼	teaspoon coarse ground black pepper	1	tablespoon balsamic vinegar

1. Heat oven to 425°F. Cut off all but 2 inches of beet tops. Wash beets; leave whole with root ends attached. Place beets in ungreased 13x9-inch pan. Sprinkle with salt and pepper. Drizzle with oil.

2. Roast uncovered about 40 minutes or until beets are tender. Let beets cool until easy to handle, about 30 minutes. Peel beets and cut off root ends; cut beets into ½-inch slices.

3. In medium bowl, toss beets, basil and vinegar. Serve warm or at room temperature.

1 Serving: Calories 90 (Calories from Fat 40); Total Fat 4.5g (Saturated Fat 0.5g; Trans Fat 0g); Cholesterol 0mg; Sodium 270mg; Total Carbohydrate 10g (Dietary Fiber 2g); Protein 2g **% Daily Value:** Vitamin A 0%; Vitamin C 4%; Calcium 0%; Iron 4% **Exchanges:** 2 Vegetable, 1 Fat **Carbohydrate Choices:** ½

Try This

If you have fresh beet greens, they are easy to cook. Wash thoroughly, cut the greens and stems from the beets and then cut them into pieces. Heat 1 tablespoon olive oil in a skillet over medium heat. Add the greens and stems; cook uncovered 5 to 10 minutes, stirring frequently, until greens are wilted and stems are crisp-tender. Season to taste with salt and pepper.

130 Calories

mashed sweet potatoes with bacon

Prep Time: 25 Minutes   **Start to Finish:** 1 Hour 45 Minutes   **Makes:** 10 servings (½ cup each)

3 lb dark orange sweet potatoes (about 4 potatoes)	1 teaspoon chopped fresh thyme leaves
8 slices bacon	½ teaspoon salt
1 large onion, chopped (¾ cup)	¼ teaspoon pepper
¼ cup half-and-half, warmed	Fresh thyme sprigs, if desired

1. Heat oven to 350°F. Pierce sweet potatoes all over with fork; place on cookie sheet with sides. Bake about 1 hour 15 minutes or until tender when pierced with fork. Let stand 15 minutes or until cool enough to handle.

2. Meanwhile, in 10-inch skillet, cook bacon over medium-high heat about 4 minutes, turning occasionally, until crisp. Remove bacon from skillet with slotted spoon; drain on paper towels. Drain all but 1 tablespoon drippings. Cook onion in bacon drippings over medium heat 5 to 8 minutes, stirring occasionally, until softened.

3. Peel sweet potatoes; place in large bowl. Mash until no lumps remain. Add warm half-and-half, thyme, salt and pepper; mash until very smooth.

4. Add onion to sweet potatoes. Crumble bacon; reserve 2 tablespoons for garnish. Add remaining bacon to potatoes; stir until blended. Garnish with reserved bacon and thyme sprigs.

1 Serving: Calories 130 (Calories from Fat 30); Total Fat 3.5g (Saturated Fat 1.5g; Trans Fat 0g); Cholesterol 10mg; Sodium 300mg; Total Carbohydrate 19g (Dietary Fiber 3g); Protein 4g **% Daily Value:** Vitamin A 320%; Vitamin C 15%; Calcium 4%; Iron 4% **Exchanges:** 1 Starch, ½ Other Carbohydrate, ½ Fat **Carbohydrate Choices:** 1

Kitchen Tip Two varieties of sweet potatoes are commercially grown in the United States—one with light yellow skin and pale yellow flesh, and a darker-skinned variety with dark orange flesh. The darker of the two is often confused with yams of Africa and Central and South America.

chipotle twice-baked sweet potatoes

140 Calories

Prep Time: 20 Minutes   **Start to Finish:** 1 Hour 25 Minutes   **Makes:** 4 servings   (photo on page C15)

4 small sweet potatoes (about 1¾ lb)	½ teaspoon salt
¼ cup fat-free half-and-half	8 teaspoons reduced-fat sour cream
1 chipotle chile in adobo sauce (from 7-oz can), finely chopped	4 teaspoons chopped fresh cilantro
1 teaspoon adobo sauce (from can of chipotle chiles)	

1. Heat oven to 375°F. Gently scrub sweet potatoes, but do not peel. Pierce potatoes several times with fork to allow steam to escape. Bake about 45 minutes or until potatoes are tender when pierced in center with fork.

2. When potatoes are cool enough to handle, cut lengthwise down through center of each potato to within ½ inch of ends and bottom. Carefully scoop out inside, leaving thin shell. In medium bowl, mash potatoes, half-and-half, chipotle chile, adobo sauce and salt with potato masher or electric mixer on low speed until light and fluffy.

3. Increase oven temperature to 400°F. In 13x9-inch pan, place potato shells. Divide potato mixture evenly among shells. Bake uncovered 20 minutes or until potato mixture is golden brown and hot.

4. Just before serving, top each potato with 2 teaspoons sour cream and 1 teaspoon cilantro.

1 Serving: Calories 140 (Calories from Fat 15); Total Fat 1.5g (Saturated Fat 1g; Trans Fat 0g); Cholesterol 0mg; Sodium 400mg; Total Carbohydrate 27g (Dietary Fiber 4g); Protein 3g **% Daily Value:** Vitamin A 470%; Vitamin C 20%; Calcium 8%; Iron 6% **Exchanges:** ½ Starch, 1 Other Carbohydrate, 1 Vegetable, ½ Fat **Carbohydrate Choices:** 2

Try This

If the potato shells look a bit uneven after filling with the mashed mixture, gently pinch both ends at the same time; pull in opposite directions to pull back into shape.

80 Calories

grilled seasoned potato packet

Prep Time: 15 Minutes   **Start to Finish:** 1 Hour 5 Minutes   **Makes:** 8 servings

4	small unpeeled red potatoes, cut into quarters (about 1½ cups)	½	teaspoon dried sage leaves
2	medium unpeeled russet potatoes, cut into 1-inch chunks (about 2 cups)	½	teaspoon paprika
		½	teaspoon seasoned salt
2	tablespoons cold butter, cut into small pieces	2	tablespoons chopped fresh chives

1. Heat gas or charcoal grill. Cut 18x12-inch sheet of heavy-duty foil; spray foil with cooking spray. Place potatoes on foil. Dot with butter; sprinkle with sage, paprika and seasoned salt.

2. Bring up 2 sides of foil over potatoes so edges meet. Seal edges, making tight ½-inch fold; fold again, allowing space for heat circulation and expansion. Fold other sides to seal.

3. Place packet on grill over medium heat. Cover grill; cook 40 to 50 minutes, rotating packet ½ turn after about 20 minutes, until potatoes are tender. Cut large x across top of packet; carefully fold back foil to allow steam to escape. Sprinkle with chives.

1 Serving: Calories 80 (Calories from Fat 25); Total Fat 3g (Saturated Fat 2g; Trans Fat 0g); Cholesterol 10mg; Sodium 110mg; Total Carbohydrate 12g (Dietary Fiber 1g); Protein 1g **% Daily Value:** Vitamin A 4%; Vitamin C 4%; Calcium 0%; Iron 4% **Exchanges:** 1 Other Carbohydrate, ½ Fat **Carbohydrate Choices:** 1

Try This

For a change of flavor, try dried thyme, marjoram or basil instead of the sage.

oven-fried potato wedges

Prep Time: 10 Minutes   **Start to Finish:** 40 Minutes   **Makes:** 4 servings

¾	teaspoon salt	¼	teaspoon garlic powder
½	teaspoon sugar	3	medium Idaho or russet baking potatoes
½	teaspoon paprika		(8 to 10 oz each)
¼	teaspoon ground mustard		Cooking spray

1. Heat oven to 425°F. In small bowl, mix salt, sugar, paprika, mustard and garlic powder.

2. Gently scrub potatoes, but do not peel. Cut each potato lengthwise in half; cut each half lengthwise into 4 wedges. Place potato wedges, skin sides down, in ungreased 13x9-inch pan. Spray potatoes with cooking spray until lightly coated. Sprinkle with seasoning mixture.

3. Bake uncovered 25 to 30 minutes or until potatoes are tender when pierced in center with fork. (Baking time will vary depending on the size and type of potato used.)

1 Serving: Calories 140 (Calories from Fat 0); Total Fat 0g (Saturated Fat 0g; Trans Fat 0g); Cholesterol 0mg; Sodium 460mg; Total Carbohydrate 30g (Dietary Fiber 3g); Protein 3g **% Daily Value:** Vitamin A 4%; Vitamin C 10%; Calcium 2%; Iron 8% **Exchanges:** 1 Starch, 1 Other Carbohydrate **Carbohydrate Choices:** 2

Health Smart If you love seasoned French fries but not the fat, then you'll love this recipe, especially since it's so easy! Simply spray potato wedges with cooking spray, sprinkle with seasonings and bake in the oven instead of deep-frying.

sweet potato fries

Prep Time: 10 Minutes   **Start to Finish:** 40 Minutes   **Makes:** 5 servings

4 medium unpeeled sweet potatoes (1½ lb), cut into ½-inch wedges	½ teaspoon salt
1 tablespoon vegetable oil	¼ teaspoon pepper

1. Heat oven to 450°F. Spray 15x10x1-inch pan with cooking spray.

2. In large bowl, toss sweet potatoes and oil. Sprinkle with salt and pepper. Spread potatoes in single layer in pan.

3. Bake uncovered 25 to 30 minutes, turning occasionally, until potatoes are golden brown and tender when pierced with fork.

1 Serving: Calories 100 (Calories from Fat 25); Total Fat 3g (Saturated Fat 0g; Trans Fat 0g); Cholesterol 0mg; Sodium 270mg; Total Carbohydrate 17g (Dietary Fiber 3g); Protein 1g **% Daily Value:** Vitamin A 320%; Vitamin C 15%; Calcium 4%; Iron 4% **Exchanges:** 1 Other Carbohydrate, ½ Vegetable, ½ Fat **Carbohydrate Choices:** 1

Try This

Instead of using salt and pepper, try your favorite seasoned salt or herb blend on these low-fat, oven-baked wedges.

confetti brown rice

Prep Time: 10 Minutes   **Start to Finish:** 2 Hours 55 Minutes   **Makes:** 6 servings

80 Calories

1½ cups sliced fresh mushrooms (4 oz)	1 cup water
½ cup chopped carrot	½ teaspoon salt
½ cup chopped red bell pepper	¼ teaspoon pepper
½ cup uncooked regular brown rice	1 cup chopped fresh broccoli

1. Spray 3- to 4-quart slow cooker with cooking spray. In slow cooker, mix all ingredients except broccoli.

2. Cover; cook on High heat setting 2 hours 30 minutes to 3 hours 30 minutes.

3. Stir in broccoli. Cover; cook 15 to 20 minutes longer or until broccoli is crisp-tender.

1 Serving: Calories 80 (Calories from Fat 5); Total Fat 0.5g (Saturated Fat 0g; Trans Fat 0g); Cholesterol 0mg; Sodium 410mg; Total Carbohydrate 15g (Dietary Fiber 3g); Protein 2g **% Daily Value:** Vitamin A 45%; Vitamin C 25%; Calcium 0%; Iron 2% **Exchanges:** ½ Starch, 1 Vegetable **Carbohydrate Choices:** 1

Try This

If you like the earthy flavor and meaty texture of baby portabella mushrooms, they'd make a great substitution for the regular white ones in this colorful side dish. Substitute orange or yellow bell pepper for the red bell pepper if you have one on hand.

140 Calories

brown rice pilaf with pea pods

Prep Time: 10 Minutes **Start to Finish:** 1 Hour **Makes:** 6 servings (²/₃ cup each)

1 can (14 oz) chicken broth	½ cup finely chopped red bell pepper
½ cup water	½ cup fresh sugar snap pea pods, cut into
1 teaspoon dried thyme leaves	¾-inch pieces
1 cup uncooked regular brown rice	⅓ cup sliced green onions (about 5 medium)
1 teaspoon vegetable oil	

1. In 2-quart saucepan, heat broth, water and thyme to boiling. Stir in rice. Cover; simmer 45 to 50 minutes or until rice is tender.

2. In 8-inch skillet, heat oil over medium-high heat. Cook bell pepper, pea pods and onions in oil 3 to 4 minutes, stirring frequently, until tender. Stir into cooked rice.

1 Serving: Calories 140 (Calories from Fat 20); Total Fat 2g (Saturated Fat 0g; Trans Fat 0g); Cholesterol 0mg; Sodium 290mg; Total Carbohydrate 26g (Dietary Fiber 4g); Protein 4g **% Daily Value:** Vitamin A 10%; Vitamin C 25%; Calcium 2%; Iron 6% **Exchanges:** 1½ Starch, ½ Fat **Carbohydrate Choices:** 2

Health Smart Brown rice is a whole grain with only the inedible outer husk removed. Light tan in color, it has a nutlike flavor and slightly chewy texture. Because it still has the bran, it can become rancid, so we recommend storing brown rice in the refrigerator or freezer.

toasted barley with mixed vegetables

Prep Time: 10 Minutes   **Start to Finish:** 1 Hour 20 Minutes   **Makes:** 6 servings

½   cup uncooked hulled barley
1   can (14 oz) chicken broth
2   large onions, chopped (2 cups)
2   packages (8 oz each) sliced fresh mushrooms (6 cups)
4   medium carrots, cut into julienne strips (2 cups)

1   large red bell pepper, coarsely chopped (1½ cups)
2   tablespoons chopped fresh or 1 tablespoon dried dill weed
½   teaspoon pepper
4   medium green onions, chopped (¼ cup)

1. Spray 12-inch skillet with cooking spray. Add barley; cook over medium heat 6 to 8 minutes, stirring frequently until barley begins to brown, then stirring constantly until golden brown. Reduce heat to low; add broth. Cover; simmer 40 minutes.

2. Stir in all remaining ingredients except green onions. Heat to boiling over high heat; reduce heat to low. Cover; simmer 20 minutes longer or until vegetables are tender. Sprinkle with green onions.

1 Serving: Calories 140 (Calories from Fat 10); Total Fat 1g (Saturated Fat 0g; Trans Fat 0g); Cholesterol 0mg; Sodium 320mg; Total Carbohydrate 26g (Dietary Fiber 6g); Protein 6g **% Daily Value:** Vitamin A 100%; Vitamin C 25%; Calcium 4%; Iron 8% **Exchanges:** 1 Starch, ½ Other Carbohydrate, 1 Vegetable **Carbohydrate Choices:** 2

Health Smart Barley is a good source of protein, and it can be used in many ways. Great in sides, soups or main dishes, it's often mixed with other grains and adds lots of texture. Toasting barley helps to bring out the wonderful flavor of this hearty grain.

couscous with vegetables

Prep Time: 15 Minutes **Start to Finish:** 20 Minutes **Makes:** 8 servings

⅓ cup chopped green onions (about 5 medium)

1 clove garlic, finely chopped

2 teaspoons butter

1½ cups water

½ teaspoon reduced-sodium chicken bouillon granules

1 cup uncooked couscous

¼ cup chopped fresh parsley

1 tablespoon chopped fresh or ½ teaspoon dried basil leaves

¼ teaspoon pepper

1 medium yellow summer squash, chopped (1 cup)

1 medium tomato, chopped (¾ cup)

1. In 2-quart saucepan, cook onions and garlic in butter, stirring frequently, until onions are tender.

2. Stir in water and bouillon granules. Heat to boiling; remove from heat. Stir in all remaining ingredients.

3. Cover; let stand 5 minutes or until liquid is absorbed. Fluff lightly with fork.

1 Serving: Calories 100 (Calories from Fat 10); Total Fat 1g (Saturated Fat 0.5g; Trans Fat 0g); Cholesterol 0mg; Sodium 15mg; Total Carbohydrate 19g (Dietary Fiber 1g); Protein 3g **% Daily Value:** Vitamin A 6%; Vitamin C 4%; Calcium 0%; Iron 2% **Exchanges:** 1 Starch, ½ Other Carbohydrate **Carbohydrate Choices:** 1

Quick Meal Idea Make a main dish out of this couscous side by stirring in leftover cut-up chicken, turkey or beef. Or go meatless by adding a 16-ounce can of garbanzo beans, drained and rinsed.

veggies and kasha with balsamic vinaigrette

120 Calories

Prep Time: 15 Minutes **Start to Finish:** 1 Hour 15 Minutes **Makes:** 4 servings (1 cup each)

SALAD

1	cup water
½	cup uncooked buckwheat kernels (kasha)
4	medium green onions, thinly sliced (¼ cup)
2	medium tomatoes, seeded, coarsely chopped (1½ cups)
1	medium unpeeled cucumber, seeded, chopped (1¼ cups)

VINAIGRETTE

2	tablespoons balsamic or red wine vinegar
1	tablespoon olive oil
2	teaspoons sugar
½	teaspoon salt
¼	teaspoon pepper
1	clove garlic, finely chopped

1. In 8-inch skillet, heat water to boiling. Add kasha; cook over medium-high heat 7 to 8 minutes, stirring occasionally, until tender. Drain if necessary.

2. In large bowl, mix kasha and all remaining salad ingredients.

3. In tightly covered container, shake all vinaigrette ingredients until blended. Pour vinaigrette over kasha mixture; toss. Cover; refrigerate 1 to 2 hours to blend flavors.

1 Serving: Calories 120 (Calories from Fat 35); Total Fat 4g (Saturated Fat 0.5g; Trans Fat 0g); Cholesterol 0mg; Sodium 300mg; Total Carbohydrate 18g (Dietary Fiber 3g); Protein 3g **% Daily Value:** Vitamin A 15%; Vitamin C 20%; Calcium 2%; Iron 4% **Exchanges:** ½ Starch, ½ Other Carbohydrate, 1 Vegetable, ½ Fat **Carbohydrate Choices:** 1

Kitchen Tip Kasha refers to crushed buckwheat kernels, or groats, that have been roasted to bring out their delicious nutlike flavor and aroma. In this recipe, the color and crunch of the vegetables along with the chewiness of the kasha create a salad that looks as good as it tastes.

50 Calories

thai broccoli slaw

Prep Time: 20 Minutes   **Start to Finish:** 1 Hour 20 Minutes   **Makes:** 8 servings (½ cup each)

DRESSING

- 2 tablespoons reduced-fat creamy peanut butter
- 1 tablespoon grated gingerroot
- 1 tablespoon rice vinegar
- 1 tablespoon orange marmalade
- 1½ teaspoons reduced-sodium soy sauce
- ¼ to ½ teaspoon chili-garlic sauce

SLAW

- 3 cups broccoli slaw mix (from 10-oz bag)
- ½ cup thin bite-size strips red bell pepper
- ½ cup julienne carrots (from 10-oz bag)
- ½ cup shredded red cabbage
- 2 tablespoons chopped fresh cilantro

1. In small bowl, gently beat all dressing ingredients with whisk until blended.

2. In large bowl, toss all slaw ingredients. Pour dressing over slaw; toss until coated. Cover; refrigerate at least 1 hour to blend flavors but no longer than 6 hours, tossing occasionally to blend dressing from bottom of bowl back into slaw mixture.

1 Serving: Calories 50 (Calories from Fat 15); Total Fat 1.5g (Saturated Fat 0g; Trans Fat 0g); Cholesterol 0mg; Sodium 75mg; Total Carbohydrate 7g (Dietary Fiber 1g); Protein 2g **% Daily Value:** Vitamin A 50%; Vitamin C 60%; Calcium 2%; Iron 2% **Exchanges:** ½ Starch **Carbohydrate Choices:** ½

Try This

For a less spicy version of this dish, use a little less ginger and stick to the ¼ teaspoon chili-garlic sauce. Look for chili-garlic sauce among the other Asian condiments at your grocery store.

blt potato salad

Prep Time: 20 Minutes **Start to Finish:** 45 Minutes **Makes:** 6 servings

4	small unpeeled red potatoes (about ¾ lb), cut into ½-inch cubes	¼	teaspoon salt
¼	cup reduced-fat mayonnaise or salad dressing	⅛	teaspoon pepper
1	teaspoon Dijon mustard	½	cup grape tomatoes or halved cherry tomatoes
2	teaspoons chopped fresh or ½ teaspoon dried dill weed	1½	cups bite-size pieces romaine lettuce
		2	slices turkey bacon, crisply cooked, crumbled

1. In 2-quart saucepan, place potatoes and enough water to cover. Heat to boiling; reduce heat to low. Cover; cook 10 to 15 minutes or until potatoes are tender. Drain; cool about 10 minutes.

2. Meanwhile, in medium bowl, mix mayonnaise, mustard, dill weed, salt and pepper. Add potatoes, tomatoes and lettuce; stir until coated. Sprinkle with bacon.

1 Serving: Calories 100 (Calories from Fat 45); Total Fat 5g (Saturated Fat 1g; Trans Fat 0g); Cholesterol 10mg; Sodium 300mg; Total Carbohydrate 12g (Dietary Fiber 1g); Protein 3g **% Daily Value:** Vitamin A 25%; Vitamin C 8%; Calcium 0%; Iron 4% **Exchanges:** ½ Starch, ½ Vegetable, 1 Fat **Carbohydrate Choices:** 1

Health Smart Leaving the peel on the potatoes adds extra nutrients, flavor and texture. Be sure to wash the potatoes well before cooking.

fennel and three-bean salad

Prep Time: 25 Minutes   **Start to Finish:** 1 Hour 25 Minutes   **Makes:** 12 servings (½ cup each)

SALAD

5	oz fresh green beans, trimmed
1	can (15 oz) cannellini beans, drained, rinsed
1	can (15 oz) dark red kidney beans, drained, rinsed
½	medium sweet onion, very thinly sliced (½ cup)
1	medium bulb fennel, very thinly sliced (1 cup)

DRESSING

¼	cup olive oil
2	tablespoons red wine vinegar
2	tablespoons Dijon mustard
1	tablespoon finely chopped fresh basil leaves
1	clove garlic, finely chopped
¼	teaspoon pepper
⅛	teaspoon salt

1. In 2-quart saucepan, place steamer basket; add ½ inch water (water should not touch bottom of basket). Place green beans in basket; cover tightly. Heat to boiling; reduce heat. Steam covered 10 to 12 minutes or until crisp-tender.

2. In large bowl, stir together green beans and all remaining salad ingredients.

3. In tightly covered container, shake all dressing ingredients. Pour dressing over salad; toss gently. Refrigerate 1 hour to blend flavors. Serve at room temperature.

1 Serving: Calories 120 (Calories from Fat 45); Total Fat 5g (Saturated Fat 0.5g; Trans Fat 0g); Cholesterol 0mg; Sodium 90mg; Total Carbohydrate 14g (Dietary Fiber 4g); Protein 5g **% Daily Value:** Vitamin A 2%; Vitamin C 6%; Calcium 2%; Iron 8% **Exchanges:** 1 Starch, 1 Fat **Carbohydrate Choices:** 1

strawberry-blueberry-orange salad

120 Calories

Prep Time: 15 Minutes   **Start to Finish:** 15 Minutes   **Makes:** 8 servings (½ cup each)

¼ cup mayonnaise	2 cups fresh strawberry halves
3 tablespoons sugar	2 cups fresh blueberries
1 tablespoon white vinegar	1 orange, peeled, chopped
2 teaspoons poppy seed	Toasted sliced almonds, if desired

1. In small bowl, mix mayonnaise, sugar, vinegar and poppy seed with whisk until well blended.

2. In medium bowl, mix strawberries, blueberries and orange. Just before serving, pour dressing over fruit; toss to combine. Sprinkle with almonds.

1 Serving: Calories 120 (Calories from Fat 50); Total Fat 6g (Saturated Fat 1g; Trans Fat 0g); Cholesterol 0mg; Sodium 40mg; Total Carbohydrate 15g (Dietary Fiber 2g); Protein 1g **% Daily Value:** Vitamin A 0%; Vitamin C 60%; Calcium 2%; Iron 2% **Exchanges:** 1 Fruit, 1 Fat **Carbohydrate Choices:** 1

Try This

Other favorite summer fruits, such as peaches and raspberries or kiwis and blackberries, can be used in this recipe.

50 Calories

cucumber-mango salad

Prep Time: 15 Minutes **Start to Finish:** 15 Minutes **Makes:** 4 servings (photo on page C15)

¼ teaspoon grated lime peel
1 tablespoon fresh lime juice
1 teaspoon honey
¼ teaspoon ground cumin
Dash salt

1 small cucumber, seeded, chopped (about 1 cup)
1 medium mango, seed removed, peeled and cut into ½-inch cubes
4 leaves Bibb lettuce

1. In small bowl, mix lime peel, lime juice, honey, cumin and salt. Stir in cucumber and mango.

2. Place lettuce leaves on serving plates. Divide mango mixture among lettuce leaves, about ½ cup each.

1 Serving: Calories 50 (Calories from Fat 0); Total Fat 0g (Saturated Fat 0g; Trans Fat 0g); Cholesterol 0mg; Sodium 40mg; Total Carbohydrate 12g (Dietary Fiber 1g); Protein 0g **% Daily Value:** Vitamin A 15%; Vitamin C 15%; Calcium 0%; Iron 2% **Exchanges:** ½ Other Carbohydrate, ½ Vegetable **Carbohydrate Choices:** 1

Try This

Mango is a great fresh fruit, but you could use peaches instead. Or for real convenience, look for jars of sliced mango in the produce department.

roasted asparagus-berry salad with pecans

Prep Time: 10 Minutes   **Start to Finish:** 35 Minutes   **Makes:** 4 servings

1 lb fresh asparagus spears	4 cups mixed salad greens
Cooking spray	¼ cup fat-free balsamic vinaigrette dressing
2 tablespoons chopped pecans	Cracked pepper, if desired
1 cup sliced fresh strawberries	

1. Heat oven to 400°F. Line 15x10x1-inch pan with foil; spray foil with cooking spray. Snap off and discard tough ends of asparagus. Cut asparagus into 1-inch pieces.

2. Place asparagus in single layer in pan; spray with cooking spray. Place pecans in another shallow pan.

3. Bake pecans 5 to 6 minutes, stirring occasionally, or until golden brown. Roast asparagus 10 to 12 minutes or until crisp-tender. Cool pecans and asparagus 8 to 10 minutes or until room temperature.

4. In medium bowl, mix asparagus, pecans, strawberries, greens and dressing. Sprinkle with pepper.

1 Serving: Calories 90 (Calories from Fat 25); Total Fat 3g (Saturated Fat 0g; Trans Fat 0g); Cholesterol 0mg; Sodium 180mg; Total Carbohydrate 11g (Dietary Fiber 4g); Protein 4g **% Daily Value:** Vitamin A 80%; Vitamin C 35%; Calcium 6%; Iron 20% **Exchanges:** 2 Vegetable, ½ Fat **Carbohydrate Choices:** 1

Try This

You can vary the fruit to suit your taste. Why not add a few raspberries or blueberries, or even slice a peach for a change?

CHAPTER 10

Desserts & Snacks

healthified honey-lemon fruit parfaits

Prep Time: 30 Minutes   **Start to Finish:** 1 Hour 30 Minutes   **Makes:** 6 servings

¾   cup fat-free milk

Dash salt
⅓   cup uncooked whole wheat couscous
½   cup lemon fat-free yogurt
½   cup fat-free sour cream
1   tablespoon honey
¼   teaspoon finely shredded lemon peel

3   cups assorted fresh fruit, sliced as needed (such as blueberries, raspberries, and/or strawberries, kiwifruit, nectarines or star fruit)
Chopped crystallized ginger, if desired
Fresh mint leaves, if desired

1. In 1-quart saucepan, heat milk and salt to boiling. Stir in couscous; reduce heat. Cover; simmer 1 minute. Remove from heat; let stand 5 minutes. Fluff with fork. Cool completely, about 1 hour.

2. In small bowl, mix yogurt, sour cream, honey and lemon peel. In medium bowl, mix desired fruit.

3. To serve, divide half of the fruit among 6 parfait glasses or dessert dishes. Layer with couscous, half of the yogurt mixture, remaining fruit and remaining yogurt mixture. Garnish with ginger and mint.

1 Serving: Calories 130 (Calories from Fat 10); Total Fat 1g (Saturated Fat 0g; Trans Fat 0g); Cholesterol 5mg; Sodium 65mg; Total Carbohydrate 27g (Dietary Fiber 3g); Protein 5g **% Daily Value:** Vitamin A 4%; Vitamin C 70%; Calcium 10%; Iron 4% **Exchanges:** 1½ Starch, ½ Fruit **Carbohydrate Choices:** 2

peach-berry cobbler

Prep Time: 25 Minutes **Start to Finish:** 55 Minutes **Makes:** 9 servings (²/₃ cup each)

150 Calories

BISCUIT TOPPING

1	cup all-purpose flour
2	tablespoons sugar
¾	teaspoon baking powder
¼	teaspoon baking soda
¼	teaspoon ground allspice, cardamom or cinnamon
⅛	teaspoon salt
⅓	cup plain fat-free yogurt
¼	cup fat-free egg product
2	tablespoons butter, melted

FILLING

4	cups sliced peeled fresh or frozen (thawed) peaches
¼	cup cold water
2	tablespoons sugar
4	teaspoons cornstarch
1	tablespoon lemon juice
¼	teaspoon ground allspice, cardamom or cinnamon
2	cups fresh or frozen (thawed) raspberries

1. Heat oven to 400°F. In medium bowl, mix flour, 2 tablespoons sugar, the baking powder, baking soda, ¼ teaspoon allspice and the salt. In small bowl, stir together yogurt, egg and melted butter; add to flour mixture, stirring just until moistened. Set aside.

2. In 3-quart saucepan, stir all filling ingredients except raspberries. Let stand 10 minutes. Cook and stir over medium heat until thickened and bubbly. Stir in raspberries; cook until hot, stirring gently.

3. Spoon hot filling into 2-quart round or square glass baking dish. Immediately drop biscuit topping into small mounds on hot filling.

4. Bake about 20 minutes or until browned and toothpick inserted into biscuit topping comes out clean. Serve warm.

1 Serving: Calories 150 (Calories from Fat 30); Total Fat 3g (Saturated Fat 1.5g; Trans Fat 0g); Cholesterol 5mg; Sodium 150mg; Total Carbohydrate 28g (Dietary Fiber 3g); Protein 3g **% Daily Value:** Vitamin A 8%; Vitamin C 10%; Calcium 6%; Iron 6% **Exchanges:** 1 Starch, ½ Fruit, ½ Other Carbohydrate, ½ Fat **Carbohydrate Choices:** 2

creamy pineapple-pecan dessert squares

Prep Time: 40 Minutes   **Start to Finish:** 4 Hours 40 Minutes   **Makes:** 18 servings

¾ cup boiling water
1 box (4-serving size) sugar-free lemon-flavored gelatin
1 cup unsweetened pineapple juice
1½ cups graham cracker crumbs
½ cup sugar

¼ cup shredded coconut
¼ cup chopped pecans
3 tablespoons butter, melted
1 package (8 oz) fat-free cream cheese
1 container (8 oz) fat-free sour cream
1 can (8 oz) crushed pineapple, undrained

1. In large bowl, pour boiling water on gelatin; stir until gelatin is dissolved. Stir in pineapple juice. Refrigerate about 30 minutes or until mixture is syrupy and just beginning to thicken.

2. Meanwhile, in 13x9-inch (3-quart) glass baking dish, mix graham cracker crumbs, ¼ cup of the sugar, the coconut, pecans and melted butter. Reserve ½ cup crumb mixture for topping. Press remaining mixture in bottom of dish.

3. In medium bowl, beat cream cheese, sour cream and remaining ¼ cup sugar with electric mixer on medium speed until smooth; set aside.

4. Beat gelatin mixture with electric mixer on low speed until foamy; beat on high speed until light and fluffy (mixture will look like beaten egg whites). Beat in cream cheese mixture just until mixed. Gently stir in pineapple (with liquid). Pour into crust-lined dish; smooth top. Sprinkle reserved ½ cup crumb mixture over top. Refrigerate about 4 hours or until set. Cut into 6 rows by 3 rows.

1 Serving: Calories 120 (Calories from Fat 40); Total Fat 4.5g (Saturated Fat 2g; Trans Fat 0g); Cholesterol 10mg; Sodium 180mg; Total Carbohydrate 18g (Dietary Fiber 0g); Protein 3g **% Daily Value:** Vitamin A 4%; Vitamin C 0%; Calcium 8%; Iron 2% **Exchanges:** 1 Starch, 1 Fat **Carbohydrate Choices:** 1

Health Smart This is a light, refreshing treat, reminiscent of the refrigerator desserts of the 1970s. The pecans lend a nutty, crunchy flavor and texture, as well as a boost of good fats and protein.

raspberry yogurt celebration dessert

140 Calories

Prep Time: 15 Minutes   **Start to Finish:** 15 Minutes   **Makes:** 8 servings   (photo on page C16)

1 bag (10 oz) frozen raspberries (without syrup), thawed
2 cups frozen (thawed) fat-free whipped topping

2 containers (6 oz each) red raspberry fat-free yogurt
1 package (5 oz) meringue cookies, crumbled
   Fresh mint leaves, if desired

1. Place raspberries in blender. Cover; blend on high speed until smooth.

2. In large bowl, mix whipped topping and yogurt. Fold in crumbled cookies and half of the raspberry puree. Spoon into 1 large chilled serving bowl or 8 individual chilled bowls; drizzle with remaining raspberry puree. Garnish with mint.

1 Serving: Calories 140 (Calories from Fat 0); Total Fat 0.5g (Saturated Fat 0g; Trans Fat 0g); Cholesterol 0mg; Sodium 40mg; Total Carbohydrate 30g (Dietary Fiber 2g); Protein 2g **% Daily Value:** Vitamin A 4%; Vitamin C 15%; Calcium 6%; Iron 0% **Exchanges:** ½ Starch, 1½ Other Carbohydrate **Carbohydrate Choices:** 2

lemon meringue pie bowl

Prep Time: 5 Minutes   **Start to Finish:** 5 Minutes   **Makes:** 1 serving

1   container (6 oz) lemon meringue thick and
    creamy low-fat yogurt

2   meringue cookies
1   teaspoon grated lemon peel

1. Spoon yogurt into small dessert bowl.

2. Top with cookies. Sprinkle with lemon peel.

1 Serving: Calories 140 (Calories from Fat 0); Total Fat 0g (Saturated Fat 0g; Trans Fat 0g); Cholesterol 0mg; Sodium 95mg; Total Carbohydrate 30g (Dietary Fiber 0g); Protein 5g **% Daily Value:** Vitamin A 15%; Vitamin C 4%; Calcium 20%; Iron 0% **Exchanges:** 1½ Other Carbohydrate, ½ Skim Milk **Carbohydrate Choices:** 2

incredible apple tart

Prep Time: 30 Minutes   **Start to Finish:** 2 Hours   **Makes:** 16 servings

130 Calories

⅔ cup quick-cooking oats	¼ teaspoon salt
½ cup whole wheat flour	⅓ cup Greek plain yogurt
¼ cup pecans, toasted, ground	¼ cup powdered sugar
1 package (8 oz) ⅓-less-fat cream cheese (Neufchâtel), softened	1 egg white
2 tablespoons butter, softened	¼ cup low-sugar orange marmalade
2 tablespoons packed brown sugar	⅛ teaspoon ground cardamom
1 teaspoon grated orange peel	2 medium red cooking apples, cut crosswise into ⅛-inch slices
¼ teaspoon baking soda	

1. In small bowl, mix oats, flour and ground pecans. In large bowl, beat 4 oz of the cream cheese and the butter with electric mixer on high speed 30 seconds. Add brown sugar, orange peel, baking soda and salt; beat on medium speed until well mixed. Beat in as much of the oat mixture as you can with the mixer. Using wooden spoon, stir in any remaining oat mixture. If necessary, cover and refrigerate dough 30 to 60 minutes or until easy to handle.

2. Heat oven to 375°F. Lightly spray 9-inch tart pan with removable bottom with cooking spray. Pat dough evenly on bottom and up side of pan. Spray double thickness of foil with cooking spray; place foil, sprayed side down, on pastry. Bake 4 minutes. Remove foil. Bake 3 minutes longer. Cool completely on cooling rack.

3. Meanwhile, in medium bowl, beat remaining 4 oz cream cheese, the yogurt, powdered sugar, egg white, 2 tablespoons of the marmalade and the cardamom with electric mixer until smooth. Spread in bottom of partially baked crust. Arrange apple slices in concentric rings on cream cheese mixture, overlapping slices slightly.

4. Cover top of tart with foil. Bake 35 minutes. Uncover; bake 10 to 15 minutes longer or until crust is golden brown and apples are just tender.

5. In small microwavable bowl, place remaining 2 tablespoons marmalade. Cover; microwave on Medium (50%) 10 seconds. Stir; microwave about 10 seconds longer or until melted. Brush over apples. Serve tart slightly warm or cool.

1 Serving: Calories 130 (Calories from Fat 60); Total Fat 6g (Saturated Fat 3g; Trans Fat 0g); Cholesterol 15mg; Sodium 125mg; Total Carbohydrate 15g (Dietary Fiber 1g); Protein 3g **% Daily Value:** Vitamin A 4%; Vitamin C 0%; Calcium 4%; Iron 2% **Exchanges:** 1 Starch, 1 Fat **Carbohydrate Choices:** 1

Try This

If you want to have larger servings, cut this tart into 12 slices for about 170 calories per serving.

pumpkin-ginger bars

Prep Time: 30 Minutes   **Start to Finish:** 2 Hours 30 Minutes   **Makes:** 48 bars

BARS

1½   cups packed brown sugar
1   cup all-purpose flour
1   cup whole wheat flour
¼   cup finely chopped crystallized ginger*
2   teaspoons baking powder
1½   teaspoons ground cinnamon
1   teaspoon baking soda
¼   teaspoon salt
½   cup vegetable oil
½   cup milk

1   teaspoon vanilla
1   can (15 oz) pumpkin (not pumpkin pie mix)
2   eggs

FROSTING

1   package (3 oz) cream cheese, softened
2   tablespoons butter, softened
½   teaspoon vanilla
3   cups powdered sugar
1   to 2 tablespoons milk
     Ground nutmeg, if desired

1. Heat oven to 350°F. Grease 15x10x1-inch pan with shortening or cooking spray; lightly flour. In large bowl, beat all bar ingredients with electric mixer on low speed until moistened. Beat on medium speed 2 minutes. Spread in pan.

2. Bake 20 to 30 minutes or until toothpick inserted in center comes out clean. Cool completely, about 1 hour.

3. In small bowl, beat cream cheese and butter with electric mixer on low speed until blended. Beat in ½ teaspoon vanilla. Gradually beat in powdered sugar, 1 cup at a time, and 1 to 2 tablespoons milk until frosting is smooth and spreadable. Frost cooled bars. Sprinkle with nutmeg. Refrigerate about 30 minutes or until set. Cut into 8 rows by 6 rows. Store in refrigerator.

*Instead of the crystallized ginger, ½ teaspoon ground ginger can be used, but expect a little different texture and flavor.

1 Bar: Calories 120 (Calories from Fat 35); Total Fat 4g (Saturated Fat 1g; Trans Fat 0g); Cholesterol 10mg; Sodium 75mg; Total Carbohydrate 19g (Dietary Fiber 0g); Protein 1g **% Daily Value:** Vitamin A 30%; Vitamin C 0%; Calcium 2%; Iron 4% **Exchanges:** 1 Starch, 1 Fat **Carbohydrate Choices:** 1

cocoa squares

Prep Time: 20 Minutes   **Start to Finish:** 1 Hour 45 Minutes   **Makes:** 24 squares

140 Calories

1 cup all-purpose flour	¾ cup sugar
1 cup whole wheat flour	½ cup canola oil
¼ cup ground flaxseed or wheat germ	⅓ cup fat-free (skim) milk
¼ cup unsweetened baking cocoa	1 cup shredded peeled or unpeeled zucchini
2 teaspoons baking powder	1 medium ripe banana, mashed (½ cup)
½ teaspoon salt	½ cup miniature semisweet chocolate chips
½ cup fat-free egg product	

1. Heat oven to 350°F. Lightly spray 13x9-inch pan with cooking spray.

2. In large bowl, mix flours, flaxseed, cocoa, baking powder and salt. In medium bowl, beat egg product, sugar, oil and milk with whisk. Stir in zucchini and banana. Make well in center of flour mixture; add zucchini mixture all at once and stir just until moistened. Fold in chocolate chips. Pour batter into pan.

3. Bake about 25 minutes or until top springs back when lightly touched. Cool completely, about 1 hour. Cut into 6 rows by 4 rows.

1 Square: Calories 140 (Calories from Fat 60); Total Fat 6g (Saturated Fat 1g; Trans Fat 0g); Cholesterol 0mg; Sodium 100mg; Total Carbohydrate 19g (Dietary Fiber 1g); Protein 2g **% Daily Value:** Vitamin A 0%; Vitamin C 0%; Calcium 4%; Iron 4% **Exchanges:** ½ Starch, 1 Other Carbohydrate, 1 Fat **Carbohydrate Choices:** 1

Try This

These squares are delicious without any topping, but if you want to add frosting, try spreading the contents of one container milk chocolate frosting on cooled squares—you'll add about 75 calories per serving.

70 Calories

glazed lemon bars

Prep Time: 15 Minutes   **Start to Finish:** 1 Hour 50 Minutes   **Makes:** 24 bars

BARS

1	cup Bisquick Heart Smart mix
2	tablespoons powdered sugar
2	tablespoons cold butter
¾	cup granulated sugar
½	cup fat-free egg product, 4 egg whites or 2 eggs

1	tablespoon Bisquick Heart Smart mix
2	teaspoons grated lemon peel
2	tablespoons fresh lemon juice

GLAZE

¾	cup powdered sugar
1	tablespoon plus 1½ teaspoons fresh lemon juice

1. Heat oven to 350°F. In small bowl, mix 1 cup Bisquick and the powdered sugar. Cut in butter, using pastry blender or fork, until mixture looks like fine crumbs. In ungreased 8-inch square pan, press mixture on bottom and ½ inch up sides.

2. Bake about 10 minutes or until light brown. Meanwhile, in small bowl, mix all remaining bar ingredients; pour over baked layer.

3. Bake about 25 minutes longer or until set and golden brown. Meanwhile, in small bowl, stir all glaze ingredients until smooth.

4. While bars are warm, loosen edges from sides of pan. Spread glaze over bars. Cool completely, about 1 hour. Cut into 6 rows by 4 rows.

1 Bar: Calories 70 (Calories from Fat 10); Total Fat 1.5g (Saturated Fat 0.5g; Trans Fat 0g); Cholesterol 0mg; Sodium 60mg; Total Carbohydrate 14g (Dietary Fiber 0g); Protein 1g **% Daily Value:** Vitamin A 0%; Vitamin C 0%; Calcium 2%; Iron 0% **Exchanges:** ½ Starch, ½ Other Carbohydrate **Carbohydrate Choices:** 1

Try This

One fresh lemon will give you 2 to 3 tablespoons of juice. To get the most juice out of a lemon, it should be at room temperature. Some people like to microwave whole lemons in the microwave on High for 20 seconds or so just to warm them.

pick-me-up bars

Prep Time: 20 Minutes   **Start to Finish:** 1 Hour 35 Minutes   **Makes:** 24 bars

3 tablespoons honey	¼ teaspoon baking powder
¼ cup orange juice	¼ cup unsweetened applesauce
2 tablespoons fresh lemon juice	3 tablespoons real maple syrup
1 box (8 oz) pitted whole dates, chopped	2 egg whites
2½ cups whole wheat flour	1 tablespoon canola oil
½ teaspoon baking soda	

1. Heat oven to 350°F. Line 13x9-inch pan with foil, leaving foil overhanging at 2 opposite sides of pan; lightly spray foil with cooking spray.

2. In small bowl, mix honey, orange juice and lemon juice. Stir in dates.

3. In large bowl, mix flour, baking soda and baking powder. In medium bowl, stir applesauce, syrup, egg whites and oil until blended. Add applesauce mixture to flour mixture. Beat with electric mixer on low speed just until combined (mixture will be crumbly). Stir in date mixture. Press evenly in pan with fingers or back of spoon.

4. Bake 12 to 15 minutes or until toothpick inserted in center comes out clean. Cool completely, about 1 hour. Use foil to lift out of pan. Cut into 6 rows by 4 rows.

1 Bar: Calories 100 (Calories from Fat 10); Total Fat 1g (Saturated Fat 0g; Trans Fat 0g); Cholesterol 0mg; Sodium 35mg; Total Carbohydrate 21g (Dietary Fiber 2g); Protein 2g **% Daily Value:** Vitamin A 0%; Vitamin C 0%; Calcium 0%; Iron 4% **Exchanges:** ½ Starch, 1 Other Carbohydrate **Carbohydrate Choices:** 1½

pumpkin drop cookies

Prep Time: 1 Hour   **Start to Finish:** 1 Hour   **Makes:** About 4 dozen cookies

½ cup butter, softened	1 teaspoon baking soda
¾ cup granulated sugar	1 teaspoon salt
¾ cup packed brown sugar	1 teaspoon ground cinnamon
2 eggs	¼ teaspoon ground allspice
1 can (15 oz) pumpkin (not pumpkin pie mix)	¼ teaspoon ground nutmeg
2½ cups all-purpose flour	1 cup raisins
2½ teaspoons baking powder	

1. Heat oven to 375°F. Grease cookie sheets with shortening. In large bowl, mix butter and sugars with spoon. Beat in eggs. Stir in pumpkin. Stir in all remaining ingredients except raisins. Fold in raisins.

2. Drop dough by tablespoonfuls about 2 inches apart onto cookie sheets.

3. Bake 10 to 12 minutes or until set and golden. Cool 1 to 2 minutes; transfer from cookie sheets to cooling racks.

1 Cookie: Calories 80 (Calories from Fat 20); Total Fat 2g (Saturated Fat 1.5g; Trans Fat 0g); Cholesterol 15mg; Sodium 120mg; Total Carbohydrate 15g (Dietary Fiber 0g); Protein 1g **% Daily Value:** Vitamin A 30%; Vitamin C 0%; Calcium 2%; Iron 4% **Exchanges:** ½ Starch, ½ Other Carbohydrate, ½ Fat **Carbohydrate Choices:** 1

healthified fudgy almond cookies

Prep Time: 45 Minutes **Start to Finish:** 1 Hour 15 Minutes **Makes:** 3 dozen cookies

⅓ cup butter, softened	½ teaspoon almond extract
¾ cup packed brown sugar	⅔ cup unsweetened baking cocoa
1 teaspoon instant espresso coffee powder or granules	1½ cups white whole wheat flour
¾ teaspoon baking soda	2 oz white chocolate baking squares (with cocoa butter)
2 egg whites	½ teaspoon shortening
⅓ cup plain low-fat yogurt	36 whole almonds, toasted

1. In large bowl, beat butter with electric mixer on medium speed 30 seconds. Add brown sugar, coffee powder and baking soda; beat until combined, scraping side of bowl occasionally. Add egg whites, yogurt and almond extract; beat until combined. Beat in cocoa. Beat in as much of the flour as you can with the mixer. Using wooden spoon, stir in any remaining flour. If necessary, cover and refrigerate dough 1 to 2 hours or until easy to handle.

2. Heat to 350°F. Shape dough into 1-inch balls. Place balls 2 inches apart on ungreased cookie sheets. Bake 6 to 8 minutes or just until edges are firm. Transfer from cookie sheets to cooling racks; cool.

3. In 1-quart saucepan, heat white chocolate and shortening over low heat, stirring constantly, until melted and smooth. Spoon small amount of melted white chocolate on top of each cookie. Dip each almond halfway into white chocolate mixture; place dipped almond on each cookie. Let stand until set.

1 Cookie: Calories 70 (Calories from Fat 25); Total Fat 3g (Saturated Fat 1.5g; Trans Fat 0g); Cholesterol 5mg; Sodium 45mg; Total Carbohydrate 10g (Dietary Fiber 1g); Protein 2g **% Daily Value:** Vitamin A 2%; Vitamin C 0%; Calcium 2%; Iron 2% **Exchanges:** ½ Starch, ½ Fat **Carbohydrate Choices:** ½

Kitchen Tip When it's your turn to bring treats, tote a tin full of these double chocolate-mocha cookies. Nobody will guess they're made with egg whites, yogurt and whole wheat flour.

40 Calories

dazzling raspberry marshmallows

Prep Time: 1 Hour   **Start to Finish:** 9 Hours   **Makes:** 77 marshmallows

1 tablespoon butter	1 cup corn syrup
⅓ cup powdered sugar	1 box (4-serving size) raspberry-flavored gelatin
2 envelopes unflavored gelatin	
½ cup cold water	¼ teaspoon salt
1½ cups granulated sugar	½ cup water

1. Grease bottom and sides of 11x7-inch (2-quart) glass baking dish with butter; sprinkle with 1 tablespoon of the powdered sugar. In bowl of stand mixer, sprinkle unflavored gelatin on ½ cup cold water to soften; set aside.

2. In 3-quart saucepan, heat granulated sugar, corn syrup, raspberry gelatin, salt and ½ cup water over medium heat, stirring constantly, until sugar and gelatin are dissolved. Heat to boiling; reduce heat to medium-low. Cook without stirring about 30 minutes to 240°F on candy thermometer or until small amount of mixture dropped into cup of very cold water forms a ball that holds its shape but is pliable; remove from heat. (While mixture is cooking, watch so it doesn't boil over; reduce heat to low if necessary.)

3. Slowly pour syrup into softened gelatin while beating on low speed. Increase speed to medium-high; beat 8 to 10 minutes or until mixture is light pink and has almost tripled in volume. Pour into dish; spread and smooth top with rubber spatula. Let stand uncovered at least 8 hours or overnight.

4. Sprinkle large cutting board with about 1 tablespoon powdered sugar. Place remaining powdered sugar in small bowl. Loosen sides of marshmallow mixture from dish and gently lift in one piece onto cutting board. Spray sharp knife with cooking spray. Cut marshmallows into 1-inch squares (11 rows by 7 rows). Dip bottoms and sides of marshmallows into bowl of powdered sugar. Store tightly covered at room temperature up to 2 weeks.

1 Marshmallow: Calories 40 (Calories from Fat 0); Total Fat 0g (Saturated Fat 0g; Trans Fat 0g); Cholesterol 0mg; Sodium 20mg; Total Carbohydrate 9g (Dietary Fiber 0g); Protein 0g **% Daily Value:** Vitamin A 0%; Vitamin C 0%; Calcium 0%; Iron 0% **Exchanges:** ½ Other Carbohydrate **Carbohydrate Choices:** ½

Kitchen Tip These marshmallows are perfect for bake-sale treats—place them in specialty paper baking cups and seal in a plastic bag tied with brightly colored ribbon. Or make the marshmallows a few days ahead for a child's birthday party or springtime brunch.

dulce de leche fillo cups

40 Calories

Prep Time: 15 Minutes   **Start to Finish:** 15 Minutes   **Makes:** 15 servings

2 oz ⅓-less-fat cream cheese (Neufchâtel), softened
2 tablespoons dulce de leche (caramel) syrup
1 tablespoon reduced-fat sour cream

1 package (1.9 oz) frozen mini fillo shells (15 shells)
⅓ cup sliced fresh strawberries
2 tablespoons diced mango

1. In small bowl, beat cream cheese with electric mixer on low speed until creamy. Beat in syrup and sour cream until blended.

2. Spoon cream cheese mixture into each fillo shell. Top with strawberries and mango.

1 Serving: Calories 40 (Calories from Fat 20); Total Fat 2g (Saturated Fat 0.5g; Trans Fat 0g); Cholesterol 0mg; Sodium 35mg; Total Carbohydrate 4g (Dietary Fiber 0g); Protein 0g **% Daily Value:** Vitamin A 0%; Vitamin C 2%; Calcium 0%; Iron 0% **Exchanges:** ½ Other Carbohydrate, ½ Fat **Carbohydrate Choices:** 0

120
Calories

mango-lime mini cupcake bites

Prep Time: 30 Minutes   **Start to Finish:** 1 Hour 10 Minutes   **Makes:** 24 mini cupcake bites

CUPCAKES
1	cup all-purpose flour
1	teaspoon baking powder
⅛	teaspoon salt
¼	cup unsalted butter, softened
⅓	cup granulated sugar
2	eggs
⅓	cup milk

1	teaspoon grated lime peel
½	cup finely chopped mango

FROSTING
¼	cup unsalted butter, softened
2	cups powdered sugar
½	teaspoon grated lime peel
2	tablespoons fresh lime juice

1. Heat oven to 350°F. Place mini paper baking cup in each of 24 mini muffin cups; spray paper cups with cooking spray. In small bowl, mix flour, baking powder and salt; set aside.

2. In medium bowl, beat ¼ cup butter and the granulated sugar with electric mixer on medium speed 1 minute. Add eggs, one at a time, beating on low speed after each addition. Alternately add flour mixture, about one-third at a time, and ⅓ cup milk, about half at a time, beating just until blended. Beat in 1 teaspoon lime peel. Stir in mango.

3. Fill each muffin cup with about 1 tablespoon plus 1 teaspoon batter or until about two-thirds full.

4. Bake 12 minutes or until toothpick inserted in center comes out clean. Cool 10 minutes; transfer from pans to cooling racks. Cool completely, about 15 minutes.

5. In medium bowl, beat all frosting ingredients with electric mixer on medium speed until smooth. Spoon frosting into decorating bag fitted with star tip; pipe frosting on each cupcake.

1 Mini Cupcake Bite: Calories 120 (Calories from Fat 40); Total Fat 4.5g (Saturated Fat 2.5g; Trans Fat 0g); Cholesterol 30mg; Sodium 40mg; Total Carbohydrate 18g (Dietary Fiber 0g); Protein 1g **% Daily Value:** Vitamin A 4%; Vitamin C 0%; Calcium 2%; Iron 0% **Exchanges:** 1 Other Carbohydrate, 1 Fat **Carbohydrate Choices:** 1

Try This

You can replace the lime with lemon in this recipe, but do not omit the citrus entirely, as it balances the sweetness of the mango.

lemon dessert shots

110 Calories

Prep Time: 30 Minutes   **Start to Finish:** 1 Hour   **Makes:** 12 servings

2   oz ⅓-less-fat cream cheese (Neufchâtel), softened

½   cup marshmallow crème (from 7-oz jar)

1   container (6 oz) fat-free Greek honey vanilla yogurt

½   cup lemon curd (from 10-oz jar)

36   fresh raspberries

10   gingersnap cookies, crushed

½   cup frozen (thawed) reduced-fat whipped topping

1. In medium bowl, beat cream cheese and marshmallow crème with electric mixer on low speed until smooth. Beat in yogurt until blended. Spoon mixture into 1-quart resealable food-storage plastic bag; seal bag. Spoon lemon curd into 1-pint resealable food-storage plastic bag; seal bag. Cut ⅛-inch opening diagonally across bottom corner of each bag.

2. In bottom of each of 12 (2-oz) shot glasses, place 1 raspberry. Pipe about 2 teaspoons yogurt mixture over raspberry in each glass. Pipe ¼-inch ring of lemon curd around edge of glass; sprinkle with about 1 teaspoon crushed cookies. Repeat layers.

3. Garnish each dessert shot with dollop of about 2 teaspoons whipped topping and 1 raspberry. Place in 9-inch square pan. Refrigerate 30 minutes or until chilled but no longer than 3 hours.

1 Serving: Calories 110 (Calories from Fat 25); Total Fat 3g (Saturated Fat 1.5g; Trans Fat 0g); Cholesterol 15mg; Sodium 70mg; Total Carbohydrate 18g (Dietary Fiber 0g); Protein 2g **% Daily Value:** Vitamin A 2%; Vitamin C 2%; Calcium 4%; Iron 0% **Exchanges:** ½ Starch, ½ Other Carbohydrate, ½ Fat **Carbohydrate Choices:** 1

Kitchen Tip Shot glasses often have some kind of writing on them. For a prettier presentation, purchase plain plastic or glass shot glasses at your local party store or online.

tequila sunrise jelly shots

Prep Time: 30 Minutes   **Start to Finish:** 4 Hours   **Makes:** 12 servings

2 envelopes unflavored gelatin	¼ cup sugar
¾ cup pulp-free orange juice	¼ cup water
6 tablespoons silver or gold tequila	Orange slices or grated orange peel
½ cup 100% pomegranate juice	

1. Lightly spray 12 (2-oz) shot glasses with cooking spray; gently wipe any excess with paper towel. In 1-quart saucepan, sprinkle 1 envelope gelatin on orange juice to soften. Heat over low heat, stirring constantly, until gelatin is completely dissolved; remove from heat. Stir in tequila. Divide mixture evenly among shot glasses (about 2 tablespoons per glass). Place in 9-inch square pan. Refrigerate 30 minutes or until almost set.

2. Meanwhile, in same saucepan, stir together pomegranate juice, sugar and water. Sprinkle remaining 1 envelope gelatin on juice to soften. Heat over low heat, stirring constantly, until gelatin is completely dissolved; remove from heat.

3. Remove shot glasses from refrigerator (orange layer should appear mostly set). Pour pomegranate mixture evenly over top of orange layer (about 4 teaspoons per glass). Refrigerate at least 3 hours or until completely chilled and firm.

4. Just before serving, dip table knife in hot water; slide knife along inside edge of shot glass to loosen. Shake jelly shot out of glass onto plate; repeat with remaining jelly shots. Or serve as is with a spoon. Garnish each jelly shot with orange slice.

1 Serving: Calories 60 (Calories from Fat 0); Total Fat 0g (Saturated Fat 0g; Trans Fat 0g); Cholesterol 0mg; Sodium 0mg; Total Carbohydrate 9g (Dietary Fiber 0g); Protein 1g **% Daily Value:** Vitamin A 0%; Vitamin C 25%; Calcium 0%; Iron 0% **Carbohydrate Choices:** ½

Kitchen Tip Be sure to pay attention to the 30-minute chilling time for the orange juice layer before adding the steaming pomegranate layer. The timing helps to give the 2-layer appearance and also ensures your dessert shots will release from the glasses in 1 piece, rather than in 2 separate layers.

cherry-raspberry
ice cream

Prep Time: 45 Minutes   **Start to Finish:** 4 Hours 45 Minutes   **Makes:** 18 servings (½ cup each)

¾   cup sugar
1   envelope unflavored gelatin
4   cups whole milk
4   eggs, beaten
1   lb fresh dark sweet cherries, pitted and halved, or 1½ bags (10 oz each) frozen sweet cherries

2½   cups fresh raspberries or 1 bag (10 oz) frozen raspberries
¼   cup frozen (thawed) orange juice concentrate

1. In large saucepan, mix sugar and gelatin. Stir in milk. Cook and stir over medium heat just until mixture starts to boil. Remove from heat. Stir about 1 cup of the hot mixture into beaten eggs; return all to saucepan. Cook 2 to 3 minutes, stirring constantly, until mixture coats the back of a metal spoon. Do not boil. Remove from heat.

2. Stir in cherries, raspberries and orange juice concentrate. Cover; refrigerate 4 to 24 hours or until set.

3. Transfer mixture to 4- or 5-quart ice cream freezer; freeze according to manufacturer's directions. Serve immediately or, if desired, ripen in freezer for 4 hours.

1 Serving: Calories 120 (Calories from Fat 30); Total Fat 3g (Saturated Fat 1.5g; Trans Fat 0g); Cholesterol 45mg; Sodium 40mg; Total Carbohydrate 19g (Dietary Fiber 1g); Protein 4g **% Daily Value:** Vitamin A 4%; Vitamin C 10%; Calcium 10%; Iron 2% **Exchanges:** 1 Starch, ½ Other Carbohydrate, ½ Fat **Carbohydrate Choices:** 1

cantaloupe granita

Prep Time: 15 Minutes **Start to Finish:** 3 Hours 15 Minutes **Makes:** 10 servings (½ cup each) (photo on page C16)

2	cups cubed cantaloupe or honeydew melon	3	tablespoons honey
2	cups soy milk or milk	¾	teaspoon ground ginger

1. In blender or food processor, place all ingredients. Cover; blend on high speed about 30 seconds or until smooth. Pour into 8- or 9-inch square (2-quart) glass baking dish.

2. Cover; freeze 30 minutes. When ice crystals begin to form at edges of dish, stir mixture with fork. Freeze 2 hours 30 minutes to 3 hours longer, stirring every 30 minutes, until firm. Scoop into chilled dessert cups or bowls to serve.

1 Serving: Calories 50 (Calories from Fat 5); Total Fat 0.5g (Saturated Fat 0g; Trans Fat 0g); Cholesterol 0mg; Sodium 35mg; Total Carbohydrate 10g (Dietary Fiber 0g); Protein 2g **% Daily Value:** Vitamin A 25%; Vitamin C 10%; Calcium 6%; Iron 0% **Exchanges:** 1 Other Carbohydrate **Carbohydrate Choices:** ½

Try This

For a frosty, slushy drink, make the recipe as directed, spoon into 10 glasses and gently stir ¼ cup sparkling mineral water or ginger ale into each glass. Be sure to use ripe melon for the best flavor.

peachy pops

Prep Time: 10 Minutes **Start to Finish:** 2 Hours 10 Minutes **Makes:** 10 pops

1½ cups vanilla soy milk
2 cups cut-up frozen peaches
⅓ to ½ cup honey, to taste

10 paper cups (3-oz size)
10 craft sticks (flat wooden sticks with round ends)

1. In blender, place soy milk, peaches and honey. Cover; blend on high speed about 1 minute or until smooth and frothy.

2. Place paper cups in 13x9-inch pan; pour mixture into paper cups. Place in freezer 20 to 30 minutes or until partially frozen.

3. Stir each cup with craft stick; leave stick in center of each cup. Freeze until firm, about 1 hour 30 minutes longer.

1 Pop: Calories 70 (Calories from Fat 5); Total Fat 0.5g (Saturated Fat 0g; Trans Fat 0g); Cholesterol 0mg; Sodium 25mg; Total Carbohydrate 16g (Dietary Fiber 1g); Protein 1g **% Daily Value:** Vitamin A 6%; Vitamin C 40%; Calcium 4%; Iron 4% **Exchanges:** ½ Starch, ½ Other Carbohydrate **Carbohydrate Choices:** 1

Kitchen Tip We like the added flavor of the vanilla soymilk in these fun pops, but you could use regular soymilk instead—just add about ½ teaspoon vanilla with the soymilk mixture.

watermelon granita

Prep Time: 25 Minutes   **Start to Finish:** 4 Hours 25 Minutes   **Makes:** 10 servings (1 cup each)

3	tablespoons lime juice (2 to 3 limes)	½	cup sugar
1	cup water	6	cups 1-inch cubes seeded watermelon

1. In 1-quart saucepan, mix lime juice, water and sugar. Cook over low heat about 5 minutes, stirring occasionally, until sugar is dissolved. Cool slightly, about 5 minutes.

2. In blender or food processor, place watermelon. Cover; blend on high speed about 2 minutes or until smooth. Add lime juice mixture; blend until well mixed. Pour into ungreased 13 x 9-inch (3-quart) glass baking dish. Cover; freeze 1 hour.

3. Scrape with fork to distribute ice crystals evenly. Freeze at least 3 hours longer, scraping every 30 minutes, until mixture is consistency of fine ice crystals. Scoop into chilled dessert cups to serve.

1 Serving: Calories 70 (Calories from Fat 0); Total Fat 0g (Saturated Fat 0g; Trans Fat 0g); Cholesterol 0mg; Sodium 0mg; Total Carbohydrate 17g (Dietary Fiber 0g); Protein 0g **% Daily Value:** Vitamin A 10%; Vitamin C 15%; Calcium 0%; Iron 0% **Exchanges:** ½ Fruit, ½ Other Carbohydrate **Carbohydrate Choices:** 1

Kitchen Tip A granita is an Italian ice dessert made of a combination of water, sugar and liquid flavoring. The texture will be grainier than a sorbet—very similar to a slush.

Try This

For a fun presentation, serve the granita in unbreakable stemmed beverage glasses.

grilled pineapple slices with ginger cream

120 Calories

Prep Time: 30 Minutes **Start to Finish:** 30 Minutes **Makes:** 6 servings

GINGER CREAM
½   cup plain fat-free yogurt or fat-free sour cream
1   tablespoon packed brown sugar
1   tablespoon chopped crystallized ginger

PINEAPPLE
1   medium pineapple (3 lb)
1   tablespoon butter, melted
6   maraschino cherries

1. Heat gas or charcoal grill. In small bowl, mix all ginger cream ingredients. Cover and refrigerate until serving.

2. Cut ½-inch slice off top and bottom of pineapple. Cut off rind. Cut pineapple crosswise into 6 slices; remove "eyes" from slices. Drizzle both sides of pineapple slices with butter.

3. Place pineapple slices on grill. Cover grill; cook over medium heat 10 to 15 minutes, turning once, until hot and light brown. To serve, top pineapple with ginger cream; garnish with cherries.

1 Serving: Calories 120 (Calories from Fat 20); Total Fat 2g (Saturated Fat 0g, Trans Fat 0.5g); Cholesterol 0mg; Sodium 55mg; Total Carbohydrate 24g (Dietary Fiber 2g); Protein 1g **% Daily Value:** Vitamin A 4%; Vitamin C 35%; Calcium 4%; Iron 2% **Exchanges:** 1 Fruit, ½ Other Carbohydrate, ½ Fat **Carbohydrate Choices:** 1½

Health Smart Fruits, such as the pineapple in this recipe, offer a host of nutrients including vitamin C to accompany their sweet flavor.

metric conversion guide

Volume

U.S. UNITS	CANADIAN METRIC	AUSTRALIAN METRIC
¼ teaspoon	1 mL	1 ml
½ teaspoon	2 mL	2 ml
1 teaspoon	5 mL	5 ml
1 tablespoon	15 mL	20 ml
¼ cup	50 mL	60 ml
⅓ cup	75 mL	80 ml
½ cup	125 mL	125 ml
⅔ cup	150 mL	170 ml
¾ cup	175 mL	190 ml
1 cup	250 mL	250 ml
1 quart	1 liter	1 liter
1½ quarts	1.5 liters	1.5 liters
2 quarts	2 liters	2 liters
2½ quarts	2.5 liters	2.5 liters
3 quarts	3 liters	3 liters
4 quarts	4 liters	4 liters

Weight

U.S. UNITS	CANADIAN METRIC	AUSTRALIAN METRIC
1 ounce	30 grams	30 grams
2 ounces	55 grams	60 grams
3 ounces	85 grams	90 grams
4 ounces (¼ pound)	115 grams	125 grams
8 ounces (½ pound)	225 grams	225 grams
16 ounces (1 pound)	455 grams	500 grams
1 pound	455 grams	0.5 kilogram

Measurements

INCHES	CENTIMETERS
1	2.5
2	5.0
3	7.5
4	10.0
5	12.5
6	15.0
7	17.5
8	20.5
9	23.0
10	25.5
11	28.0
12	30.5
13	33.0

Temperatures

FAHRENHEIT	CELSIUS
32°	0°
212°	100°
250°	120°
275°	140°
300°	150°
325°	160°
375°	190°
400°	200°
425°	220°
450°	230°
475°	240°
500°	260°

Note: The recipes in this cookbook have not been developed or tested using metric measures. When converting recipes to metric, some variations in quality may be noted.

index

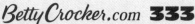

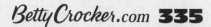

recipe testing and calculating nutrition information

Recipe Testing:

✛ Large eggs and 2% milk were used unless otherwise indicated.

✛ Fat-free, low-fat, low-sodium or lite products were not used unless indicated.

✛ No nonstick cookware and bakeware were used unless otherwise indicated. No dark-colored, black or insulated bakeware was used.

✛ When a pan is specified, a metal pan was used; a baking dish or pie plate means ovenproof glass was used.

✛ An electric hand mixer was used for mixing only when mixer speeds are specified.

Calculating Nutrition:

✛ The first ingredient was used wherever a choice is given, such as ⅓ cup sour cream or plain yogurt.

✛ The first amount was used wherever a range is given, such as 3- to 3½-pound whole chicken.

✛ The first serving number was used wherever a range is given, such as 4 to 6 servings.

✛ "If desired" ingredients were not included.

✛ Only the amount of a marinade or frying oil that is absorbed was included.

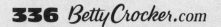